CEOE OSAT
Field 07
English
Teacher Certification Exam

By: Sharon Wynne, M.S
Southern Connecticut State University

"And, while there's no reason yet to panic, I think it's only prudent that we make preparations to panic."

XAMonline, INC.
Boston

Copyright © 2007 XAMonline, Inc.
All rights reserved. No part of the material protected by this copyright notice may be reproduced or utilized in any form or by any means, electronic or mechanical, including photocopying, recording or by any information storage and retrievable system, without written permission from the copyright holder.

To obtain permission(s) to use the material from this work for any purpose including workshops or seminars, please submit a written request to:

XAMonline, Inc.
21 Orient Ave.
Melrose, MA 02176
Toll Free 1-800-509-4128
Email: info@xamonline.com
Web www.xamonline.com
Fax: 1-781-662-9268

Library of Congress Cataloging-in-Publication Data

Wynne, Sharon A.
    OSAT English Field 07: Teacher Certification / Sharon A. Wynne. -2nd ed.
    ISBN 978-1-58197-777-6
    1. OSAT English Field 07.   2. Study Guides.   3. CEOE
    4. Teachers' Certification & Licensure.   5. Careers

Disclaimer:
The opinions expressed in this publication are the sole works of XAMonline and were created independently from the National Education Association, Educational Testing Service, or any state department of education, National Evaluation Systems or other testing affiliates.

Between the time of publication and printing, state-specific standards as well as testing formats and website information may change. Such changes are not addressed in part or in whole within this product. Sample test questions are developed by XAMonline and reflect similar content as on real tests; however, they are not former tests. XAMonline assembles content that aligns with state standards but makes no claims nor guarantees that teacher candidates will achieve a passing score. Numerical scores are determined by testing companies such as NES or ETS and then are compared with individual state standards. A passing score varies from state to state.

Printed in the United States of America

CEOE: OSAT English Field 07
ISBN: 978-1-58197-777-6

TEACHER CERTIFICATION STUDY GUIDE

Requirements for Certification in English for Oklahoma

All individuals seeking an Oklahoma credential in English must pass the Oklahoma General Education Test (OGET) as well as the appropriate Oklahoma Professional Teaching Examination (OPTE) and the English Field 07 exam.

About the OSAT English Field 07 Exam

The OSAT is criterion referenced, meaning that the exam measures a Candidate's knowledge and skills based on an established standard rather than on comparison to other test-takers' performances.

There are four domains covered in the exam:

- **Listening and Speaking**
- **Writing**
- **Reading**
- **Language and Literature**

85% Multiple-choice questions—No penalty for guessing.
15% Constructed response (essays)—Scored based on four characteristics:

- **Purpose**: extent to which the response achieves the purpose of the assignment
- **Subject Matter Knowledge**: accuracy and appropriateness in the application of subject-matter knowledge
- **Support**: quality and relevance of supporting details
- **Rationale**: soundness of argument and degree of understanding of the subject matter

TEACHER CERTIFICATION STUDY GUIDE

Table of Contents

DOMAIN I. LISTENING AND SPEAKING

COMPETENCY 1.0 UNDERSTAND LISTENING AND SPEAKING FOR INFORMATION AND UNDERSTANDING 1

- Skill 1.1 Analyze techniques of organizing information for formal presentations 1
- Skill 1.2 Analyze factors affecting a listener's ability to understand spoken language in different contexts 2
- Skill 1.3 Distinguish among styles of language appropriate to various purposes, content, audiences, and occasions 3
- Skill 1.4 Evaluate visual materials for use in an oral presentation 4

COMPETENCY 2.0 UNDERSTAND LISTENING AND SPEAKING FOR LITERARY RESPONSE AND EXPRESSION, PERSONAL APPRECIATION, AND ENTERTAINMENT 5

- Skill 2.1 Judge the effectiveness or appropriateness of given details or examples for making a presentation or a performance more interesting or appealing 5
- Skill 2.2 Recognize the different roles of voice and intonation patterns in oral presentations of stories, poetry, and drama 7

COMPETENCY 3.0 UNDERSTAND LISTENING AND SPEAKING FOR CRITICAL ANALYSIS, EVALUATION, AND PERSUASION 9

- Skill 3.1 Evaluate strategies of organization and delivery in relation to given content, audience, purpose, and occasion 9
- Skill 3.2 Analyze fallacies in logic 10
- Skill 3.3 Analyze the role of critical-thinking skills in effective listening and speaking 10
- Skill 3.4 Recognize the role of body language, gestures, and visual aids in communicating a point of view 11

ENGLISH HIGH SCHOOL

TEACHER CERTIFICATION STUDY GUIDE

COMPETENCY 4.0 UNDERSTAND LISTENING AND SPEAKING FOR SOCIAL INTERACTION IN A VARIETY OF FORMAL AND INFORMAL SITUATIONS 12

Skill 4.1 Analyze elements of effective listening and speaking in conversation 12

Skill 4.2 Analyze techniques of effective listening and speaking in small- and large-group situations 12

TEACHER CERTIFICATION STUDY GUIDE

| DOMAIN II. | WRITING |

COMPETENCY 5.0 UNDERSTAND WRITING FOR INFORMATION AND UNDERSTANDING 14

Skill 5.1   Evaluate alternative thesis statements or organizational patterns for a formal essay or a research paper on a given topic 14

Skill 5.2   Evaluate information from various sources for use in a research project 15

Skill 5.3   Evaluate the appropriateness of language and formats for various products of expository writing 15

Skill 5.4   Revise drafts to improve their effectiveness 16

COMPETENCY 6.0 UNDERSTAND WRITING FOR PERSONAL EXPRESSION AND SOCIAL INTERACTION 20

Skill 6.1   Demonstrate awareness of connotation and figurative meaning in selecting language for a given expressive purpose 20

Skill 6.2   Judge alternative introductory or concluding sentences for a personal essay on a given theme 21

Skill 6.3   Analyze problems relating to the effectiveness of narrative or descriptive materials and identify appropriate revisions 23

Skill 6.4   Apply strategies for composing personal notes and letters 25

COMPETENCY 7.0 UNDERSTAND WRITING FOR CRITICAL ANALYSIS, EVALUATION, AND PERSUASION 26

Skill 7.1   Analyze the organization of an editorial or argumentative essay on a given topic 26

Skill 7.2   Distinguish reasons, examples, or details that support a given argument or opinion 27

Skill 7.3   Use transitions and commentary to enhance the clarity of a line of argument 28

Skill 7.4   Analyze fallacies in logic in a piece of persuasive writing 29

ENGLISH HIGH SCHOOL

TEACHER CERTIFICATION STUDY GUIDE

COMPETENCY 8.0 UNDERSTAND PROCESSES FOR GENERATING AND DEVELOPING WRITTEN TEXTS 30

Skill 8.1 Apply strategies for generating ideas before writing 30

Skill 8.2 Evaluate the appropriateness of given details for supporting the development of a main point 31

Skill 8.3 Eliminate distracting details interfering with the development of a main point 31

Skill 8.4 Solve problems related to text organization 31

COMPETENCY 9.0 EDIT WRITTEN TEXTS TO ACHIEVE CLARITY AND ECONOMY OF EXPRESSION AND CONFORMITY TO CONVENTIONS OF STANDARD ENGLISH USAGE 33

Skill 9.1 Revise sentences to eliminate wordiness, ambiguity, and redundancy 33

Skill 9.2 Revise sentences and passages to subordinate ideas, maintain parallel form, and connect related ideas 35

Skill 9.3 Revise misplaced or dangling modifiers 36

Skill 9.4 Revise nonstandard capitalization and punctuation 35

ENGLISH HIGH SCHOOL

DOMAIN III. READING

COMPETENCY 10.0 UNDERSTAND READING FOR INFORMATION AND UNDERSTANDING 42

- Skill 10.1 Identify and distinguish between general statements and specific details 42
- Skill 10.2 Draw conclusions from a given passage 43
- Skill 10.3 Infer information from a given passage 44
- Skill 10.4 Summarize a given passage 44

COMPETENCY 11.0 UNDERSTAND READING FOR LITERARY RESPONSE AND PERSONAL ENJOYMENT 45

- Skill 11.1 Analyze an author's use of figurative language to convey sensory impressions or emotional effects 45
- Skill 11.2 Analyze an author's use of language to create irony 47
- Skill 11.3 Interpret the use of rhythm, rhyme, or imagery to evoke a response in the reader 47
- Skill 11.4 Analyze the use of language to portray character, develop plot, or create a mood in a given passage 48

COMPETENCY 12.0 UNDERSTAND READING FOR CRITICAL ANALYSIS AND EVALUATION 50

- Skill 12.1 Distinguish between fact and opinion in a passage 50
- Skill 12.2 Judge the relevance, importance, or sufficiency of facts or examples in a writer's argument 51
- Skill 12.3 Assess the credibility or objectivity of various sources of information 52
- Skill 12.4 Determine how the author uses tone and style to present a particular point of view 53

TEACHER CERTIFICATION STUDY GUIDE

COMPETENCY 13.0	UNDERSTAND THE USE OF METACOGNITIVE TECHNIQUES IN READING COMPREHENSION 55
Skill 13.1	Analyze the purposes and characteristics of reading techniques and strategies 55
Skill 13.2	Analyze thinking strategies related to reading comprehension 56
Skill 13.3	Apply strategies to determine the denotative and connotative meanings of words in given contexts 57

DOMAIN IV. LANGUAGE AND LITERATURE

A. Language

COMPETENCY 14.0	UNDERSTAND THE HISTORICAL, SOCIAL, CULTURAL, AND TECHNOLOGICAL INFLUENCES SHAPING THE ENGLISH LANGUAGE 59
Skill 14.1	Analyze the significance of historical events that have influenced the development of the English language 59
Skill 14.2	Relate English derivatives and borrowings, including slang terms, to their origins in other languages 61
Skill 14.3	Analyze regional and social variations in language in the United States 62

COMPETENCY 15.0	UNDERSTAND FUNDAMENTAL CONCEPTS RELATING TO THE STRUCTURE, ACQUISITION, USE, AND ANALYSIS OF LANGUAGE 64
Skill 15.1	Distinguish structural features of languages 64
Skill 15.2	Apply principles of language acquisition and use 82

TEACHER CERTIFICATION STUDY GUIDE

B. Fundamentals of Literature

COMPETENCY 16.0 UNDERSTAND THE CHARACTERISTIC FEATURES OF VARIOUS GENRES OF FICTION AND DRAMA 86

Skill 16.1 Analyze elements of fiction in passage context 86

Skill 16.2 Compare the characteristics of types of fictional narratives 92

Skill 16.3 Relate types of drama to their characteristics 94

Skill 16.4 Analyze elements of drama and film 94

COMPETENCY 17.0 UNDERSTAND THE CHARACTERISTIC FEATURES OF VARIOUS GENRES OF NONFICTION 100

Skill 17.1 Compare and contrast characteristics of types of nonfiction 100

Skill 17.2 Apply criteria for evaluating nonfiction works of various genres 101

COMPETENCY 18.0 UNDERSTAND THE CHARACTERISTIC FEATURES OF VARIOUS FORMS OF POETRY 102

Skill 18.1 Analyze the formal characteristics and distinctive content of narrative poetry 102

Skill 18.2 Relate various types of lyric poetry to their formal characteristics 103

Skill 18.3 Analyze elements of poetry in context 105

COMPETENCY 19.0 UNDERSTAND THE HISTORICAL, SOCIAL, AND CULTURAL ASPECTS OF LITERATURE, INCLUDING THE WAYS IN WHICH LITERARY WORKS AND MOVEMENTS BOTH REFLECT AND SHAPE CULTURE AND HISTORY 108

Skill 19.1 Apply knowledge of the characteristics and significance of mythology and folk literature 108

Skill 19.2 Analyze the expression of cultural values and ideas through literature 110

Skill 19.3 Analyze the role of given authors and works in influencing public opinion about and understanding of social issues 112

C. History of Literature

COMPETENCY 20.0 UNDERSTAND SIGNIFICANT THEMES, CHARACTERISTICS, TRENDS, WRITERS, AND WORKS IN AMERICAN LITERATURE FROM THE COLONIAL PERIOD TO THE PRESENT, INCLUDING THE LITERARY CONTRIBUTIONS OF WOMEN, MEMBERS OF ETHNIC MINORITIES, AND FIGURES IDENTIFIED WITH PARTICULAR REGIONS 114

Skill 20.1 Analyze the significance of major writers, works, and movements to the development of American literature 114

Skill 20.2 Analyze changes in literary form and style in American literature of the colonial, nineteenth-century, modern, and contemporary periods 121

Skill 20.3 Analyze in passage context major thematic concerns and stylistic and formal characteristics associated with significant American prose writers and dramatists and poets 123

Skill 20.4 Relate given passages to social institutions, historical events, and cultural movements that influenced the development of American literature 129

COMPETENCY 21.0 UNDERSTAND MAJOR THEMES, CHARACTERISTICS, TRENDS, WRITERS, AND WORKS IN BRITISH AND IRISH LITERATURE 132

Skill 21.1 Analyze the significance of writers, works, and movements to the development of British and Irish literature from their origins to the present 132

Skill 21.2 Analyze in passage context significant themes and genres in British literature from the Anglo-Saxon period, the Middle Ages, and the Renaissance 132

Skill 21.3 Analyze in passage context significant themes and characteristics of major British and Irish literary works of the Enlightenment, the romantic and Victorian periods, and the twentieth century 133

Skill 21.4 Relate given passages to major historical events and cultural movements that influenced the development of British literature 136

COMPETENCY 22.0		UNDERSTAND THE LITERATURES OF ASIA, AFRICA, CONTINENTAL EUROPE, LATIN AMERICA, AND THE CARIBBEAN; INCLUDING MAJOR THEMES, CHARACTERISTICS, TRENDS, WRITERS, AND WORKS 145
	Skill 22.1	Distinguish major literary forms, works, writers, and characteristics of literature from ancient civilizations 145
	Skill 22.2	Recognize major literary forms, works, writers, and characteristics of world literature written before the modern period in languages other than English 148
	Skill 22.3	Recognize major forms, works, writers, and characteristics of modern and contemporary literature written in English outside Great Britain and the United States 150
	Skill 22.4	Recognize major forms, writers, works, and characteristics of modern and contemporary world literature in languages other than English 151

Resources 153

Sample Test 159

Answer Key 191

Rationales with Sample Questions 192

TEACHER CERTIFICATION STUDY GUIDE

Great Study and Test-taking Tips!

What to study in order to prepare for the subject assessments is the focus of this study guide, but equally important is *how* you study.

You can increase your chances of truly mastering the information by taking some simple, but effective, steps.

Study Tips:

1. Some foods aid the learning process. Foods such as milk, nuts, seeds, rice, and oats help your study efforts by releasing natural memory enhancers called CCKs (*cholecystokinin*) composed of *tryptophan*, *choline*, and *phenylalanine*. All of these chemicals enhance the neurotransmitters associated with memory. Before studying, try a light, protein-rich meal of eggs, turkey, and fish. All of these foods release the memory-enhancing chemicals. The better the connections, the more you comprehend.

Likewise, before you take a test, stick to a light snack of energy-boosting and relaxing foods. A glass of milk, a piece of fruit, or some peanuts all release various memory-boosting chemicals and help you to relax and focus on the subject at hand.

2. Learn to take great notes. A by-product of our modern culture is that we have grown accustomed to getting our information in short doses (i.e. TV news sound bites or USA-Today-style newspaper articles.)

Consequently, we've subconsciously trained ourselves to assimilate information better in neat little packages. If your notes are scrawled all over the paper, it fragments the flow of the information. Strive for clarity. Newspapers use a standard format to achieve clarity. Your notes can be much clearer through use of proper formatting. A very effective format is called the *"Cornell Method."*

> Take a sheet of loose-leaf lined notebook paper and draw a line all the way down the paper about 1-2" from the left-hand edge.
>
> Draw another line across the width of the paper about 1-2" up from the bottom. Repeat this process on the reverse side of the page.

Look at the highly effective result. You have ample room for notes, a left hand margin for special emphasis items or inserting supplementary data from the textbook, a large area at the bottom for a brief summary, and a little rectangular space for just about anything you want.

3. Get the concept, then the details. Too often we focus on the details and don't gather an understanding of the concept. However, if you simply memorize only dates, places, or names; you may well miss the whole point of the subject. A key way to understand things is to put them in your own words. If you are working from a textbook, automatically summarize each paragraph in your mind. If you are outlining text, don't simply copy the author's words.

Paraphrase them in your own words. You remember your own thoughts and words much better than someone else's, and subconsciously tend to associate the important details to the core concepts.

4. Ask Why? Pull apart written material paragraph by paragraph and don't forget the captions under the illustrations.

Example: If the heading is "Stream Erosion," flip it around to read "Why do streams erode?" Then answer the questions.

If you train your mind to think in a series of questions and answers, not only will you learn more, but you will also feel less test anxiety because you are used to answering questions.

5. Read for reinforcement and future needs. Even if you only have 10 minutes, put your notes or a book in your hand. Your mind is similar to a computer; you have to input data in order to have it processed. *By reading, you are creating the neural connections for future retrieval.* The more times you read something, the more you reinforce the learning of ideas.

Even if you don't fully understand something on the first pass, *your mind stores much of the material for later recall.*

6. Relax to learn, so go into exile. Our bodies respond to an inner clock comprised of biorhythms. Burning the midnight oil works well for some people, but not for everyone.

If possible, set aside a particular place to study that is free of distractions. Shut off the television, cell phone, and pager; and exile your friends and family during your study period.

If you really are bothered by silence, try background music. Light classical music at a low volume has been shown to aid in concentration more than other types of music. Music that evokes pleasant emotions without lyrics is highly suggested. Try just about anything by Mozart. It relaxes you.

7. Use arrows not highlighters. At best, it's difficult to read a page full of yellow, pink, blue, and green streaks.

Try staring at a neon sign for a while, and you'll soon see my point--the horde of colors obscure the message.

A quick note, a brief dash of color, an underline, and an arrow pointing to a particular passage is much clearer than a horde of highlighted words.

8. Budget your study time. Although you shouldn't ignore any of the material, *allocate your available study time in the same ratio that topics are likely to appear on the test.*

TEACHER CERTIFICATION STUDY GUIDE

Testing Tips:

1. Get smart, play dumb. Don't read anything into the question. Don't make an assumption that the test writer is looking for something else than what is asked. Stick to the question as written and don't read extra things into it.

2. Read the question and all the choices *twice* before answering the question. You may miss something by not carefully reading and rereading both the question and the answers.

If you really don't have a clue as to the right answer, leave it blank on the first time through. Go on to the other questions, as they may provide a clue as to how to answer the skipped questions.

If later on, you still can't answer the skipped ones . . . **Guess.**
The only penalty for guessing is that you *might* get it wrong. Only one thing is certain; if you don't put anything down, you will get it wrong!

3. Turn the question into a statement. Look at the way the questions are worded. The syntax of the question usually provides a clue. Does it seem more familiar as a statement rather than as a question? Does it sound strange?

By turning a question into a statement, you may be able to spot if an answer sounds right, and it may also trigger memories of material you have read.

4. Look for hidden clues. It's actually very difficult to compose multiple-foil (choice) questions without giving away part of the answer in the options presented.

In most multiple-choice questions you can often readily eliminate one or two of the potential answers. This leaves you with only two real possibilities, and automatically your odds go to fifty-fifty for very little work.

5. Trust your instincts. For every fact that you have read, you subconsciously retain something of that knowledge. On questions that you aren't really certain about, go with your basic instincts. **Your first impression on how to answer a question is usually correct.**

6. Mark your answers directly on the test booklet. Don't bother trying to fill in the optical scan sheet on the first pass through the test.

7. Watch the clock! You have a set amount of time to answer the questions. Don't get bogged down trying to answer a single question at the expense of 10 questions you can more readily answer.

TEACHER CERTIFICATION STUDY GUIDE

DOMAIN I.	LISTENING AND SPEAKING

COMPETENCY 1.0 UNDERSTAND LISTENING AND SPEAKING FOR INFORMATION AND UNDERSTANDING

Skill 1.1 Analyze techniques of organizing information for formal presentations.

Preparing to speak on a topic should be seen as a process that has stages: **Discovery**, **Organization**, and **Editing**.

Discovery: There are many possible sources for the information that will be used to create an oral presentation. The first step in the discovery process is to settle on a topic or subject. Answer the question, "What is the speech going to be about?" For example, the topic or subject could be immigration. In the discovery stage, one's own knowledge, experience, and beliefs should be the first source; and notes should be taken as the speaker probes this source. The second source can very well be interviews with friends and possibly experts. The third source will be to research what has been written or said publicly on this topic. This stage can get out of hand very quickly, so a plan for the collecting of source information should be well-organized with time limits set for each part.

Organization: At this point, several decisions need to be made. The first is what the *purpose* of the speech is. Does the speaker want to persuade the audience to believe something or to act on something, or does the speaker simply want to present information that the audience might not have? Once that decision is made, a thesis should be developed. What point does the speaker want to make? And what are the points that will support that point? And in what order will those points be arranged? Introductions and conclusions should be written last. The purpose of the introduction is to draw the audience into the topic. The purpose of the conclusion is to polish off the speech, making sure the thesis is clear, reinforcing the thesis, or summarizing the points that have been made.

Editing: This is the most important stage in preparing a speech. Once decisions have been made in the discovery and organization stages, it's good to allow time to let the speech rest for awhile and to go back to it with "fresh eyes." Objectivity is extremely important, and the speaker should be willing to make drastic changes if they are needed. It's difficult to let loose of one's own composition, but good speech-makers are able to do that. On the other hand, this can also get out of hand, and it should be limited. The speaker must recognize that, at some point, the decisions must be made, the die must be cast, and commitment to the speech as it stands must be made if the speaker is to deliver the message with conviction.

Skill 1.2 Analyze factors affecting a listener's ability to understand spoken language in different contexts.

The more information a speaker has about an audience, the more likely he or she is to communicate effectively with it. Several factors figure into the speaker/audience equation: age, ethnic background, educational level, knowledge of the subject, and interest in the subject.

Speaking about computers to senior citizens who have, at best, rudimentary knowledge about the way computers work must take that into account. Perhaps handing out a glossary would be useful for this audience. Speaking to first-graders about computers presents its own challenges. On the other hand, the average high-school student has more experience with computers than most adults, and that should be taken into account. Speaking to a room full of computer-systems engineers requires a rather thorough understanding of the jargon related to the field.

In considering the age of the audience, it's best not to make assumptions. The gathering of senior citizens might include retired systems engineers or people who have made their livings using computers, so research about the audience is important. It might not be wise to assume that high-school students have a certain level of understanding, either.

With an audience that is primarily Hispanic with varying levels of competence in English, the speaker is obligated to adjust the presentation to fit that audience. The same would be true when the audience is composed of people who may have been in the country for a long time but whose families speak their first language at home. Black English presents its own peculiarities, and if the audience is composed primarily of African-Americans whose contacts in the larger community are limited, some efforts need to be made to acquaint oneself with the specific peculiarities of the community those listeners come from.

It's unwise to "speak down" to an audience; they will almost certainly be insulted. On the other hand, speaking to an audience of college graduates will require different skills than speaking to an audience of people who have never attended college.

Finally, has the audience come because of an interest in the topic or because they have been influenced or forced to come to the presentation? If the audience comes with an interest in the subject already, efforts to motivate or draw them into the discussion might not be needed. On the other hand, if the speaker knows the audience does not have a high level of interest in the topic, it would be wise to use devices to motivate them to listen.

Skill 1.3 Distinguish among styles of language appropriate to various purposes, content, audiences, and occasions.

Slang comes about for many reasons: Amelioration is an important one that results often in euphemisms. Examples are "passed away" for dying; "senior citizens" for old people. Some usages have become so embedded in the language that their sources are long-forgotten. For example, "fame" originally meant rumor. Some words that were originally intended as euphemisms, such as "mentally retarded" and "moron" to avoid using "idiot," have themselves become pejorative.

Slang is lower in prestige than Standard English; tends to first appear in the language of groups with low status; is often taboo and unlikely to be used by people of high status; tends to displace conventional terms, either as a shorthand or as a defense against perceptions associated with the conventional term.

Informal and formal language is a distinction made on the basis of the occasion as well as the audience. At a formal occasion, for example, a meeting of executives or of government officials, even conversational exchanges are likely to be more formal. A cocktail party or a golf game are examples where the language is likely to be informal. Formal language uses fewer or no contractions, less slang, longer sentences, and more organization in longer segments.

Speeches delivered to executives, college professors, government officials, etc., is likely to be formal. Speeches made to fellow employees are likely to be informal. Sermons tend to be formal; Bible lessons will tend to be informal.

Jargon is a specialized vocabulary. It may be the vocabulary peculiar to a particular industry such as computers or field such as religion. It may also be the vocabulary of a social group. Black English is a good example. A Hardee's ad has two young men on the streets of Philadelphia discussing the merits of one of their sandwiches, and bylines are required so others may understand what they're saying. A whole vocabulary that has even developed its own dictionaries is the jargon of bloggers. The speaker must be knowledgeable about and sensitive to the jargon peculiar to the particular audience. That may require some research and some vocabulary development on the speaker's part.

Technical language is a form of jargon. It is usually specific to an industry, profession, or field of study. Sensitivity to the language familiar to the particular audience is important.

Regionalisms are those usages that are peculiar to a particular part of the country. A good example is the second person plural pronoun: you. Because the plural is the same as the singular, various parts of the country have developed their own solutions to be sure that they are understood when they are speaking to more than one "you." In the South, "you-all" or "y'all" is common. In the Northeast, one often hears "youse." In some areas of the Middlewest, "you'ns" can be heard.

Vocabulary also varies from region to region. A small stream is a "creek" in some regions but "crick" in some. In Boston, soft drinks are generically called "tonic," but it becomes "soda" in other parts of the northeast. It is "liqueur" in Canada, and "pop" when you get very far west of New York.

Skill 1.4   Evaluate visual materials for use in an oral presentation.

Multimedia refers to a technology for presenting material in both visual and verbal forms. This format is especially effective in the classroom, since it reaches both visual and auditory learners.

Knowing how to select effective teaching software is the first step in efficient multi-media education. First, decide what you need the software for (creating spreadsheets, making diagrams, creating slideshows, etc.) Consult magazines such as *Popular Computing, PC World, MacWorld,* and *Multimedia World* to learn about the newest programs available. Go to a local computer store and ask a customer service representative to help you find the exact equipment you need. If possible, test the programs you are interested in. Check reviews in magazines such as *Consumer Reports, PCWorld, Electronic Learning* or *MultiMedia Schools* to ensure the software's quality.

Software programs useful for producing teaching material
Adobe, Aldus Freehand, CorelDRAW!, DrawPerfect, Claris Works, PC Paintbrush, Harvard Graphics, Visio, Microsoft Word, Microsoft Power Point

Tips for creating visual media
- Limit your graph to just one idea or concept
- Keep the content simple and concise (avoid too many lines, words, or pictures)
- Balance substance and visual appeal
- Make sure the text is large enough for the class to read
- Match the information to the format that will fit it best

COMPETENCY 2.0 UNDERSTAND LISTENING AND SPEAKING FOR LITERARY RESPONSE AND EXPRESSION, PERSONAL APPRECIATION, AND ENTERTAINMENT

Skill 2.1 Judge the effectiveness or appropriateness of given details or examples for making a presentation or a performance more interesting or appealing.

Helping students to discover what types of details or examples will enhance a particular presentation or performance will depend in good part on the assignment/s given. Possibilities for in-class performances are:

- live skits or one-act plays based on original student work
- live skits, plays or recitations based on literary texts assigned for class reading and discussion
- audio or video recordings of either of the above, e.g., a radio play based on Shirley Jackson's story "The Lottery."
- informative reports
- demonstration speeches, e.g., "How to Make a Dirt Cake"
- persuasive speeches
- panel debates on course-related topics

Before assigning presentation or performance work, teachers should familiarize students with several examples of successful speeches, presentations, drama, etc. For instance, if a teacher shows the class a video recording of Martin Luther King's 1963 "I Have a Dream" speech, the teacher should first provide students with written copies of it, then ask them to do the following:

- List all written works and songs mentioned by King.
- List all historical events and persons mentioned by King.
- List all landforms and American place names mentioned by King.
- Make a list of all the metaphors and similes used in the speech.
- Make a list of words, phrases, and ideas repeated in the speech.

Next have the students, singly or in groups, evaluate and analyze all of the above. Typical questions to ask are:

- Why do you think King uses imagery from the natural world—islands, sweltering summer, etc.—to describe abstractions such as freedom, equality, justice, and injustice?
  Do you think that his use of metaphors shows any patterns or conscious intentions? Do you find his imagery effective? Why or why not?
- Why do you think King mentions so many landforms and American place names?
- What is the relationship between the works and songs mentioned in King's speech and his subject?
- What is the effect of King's use of repetition in the speech?
- What words would you use to describe the tone and effect of King's speech?
- How do any of the matters above relate to King's intended audience? Who is his intended audience?
- Do the contents of "I Have a Dream" offer any hints or suggestions about what to put into speeches and/or presentations in general?

A similar set of questions and exercises can apply when evaluating and analyzing a wide variety of well-known speeches, performances, and writings. The content and methods of such an approach are equally relevant and helpful to students as they prepare their own presentations. In addition, numerous speeches are available in both print (online) and video.

Once a presentation or performance has been assigned and the topics chosen, have students prepare by doing the following:

- Conduct research in the library and online to determine what others have done with the same topic and/or similar assignments.
- Consider who the audience is; then determine the appropriate tone, vocabulary, and content to get one's key points across.
- If advocating a particular cause, opinion, and/or course of action, the speaker must determine what type of support will strengthen their case (see below). He or she will also need to take into account any opposing views and determine a strategy to address and counter them.
- Take into consideration matters regarding personal delivery: what to wear, the importance of eye contact with one's audience, body language (gestures, facial expressions), and the need to avoid mumbling, speaking in a monotone, or speaking too fast.

A variety of supporting material is needed to make a successful presentation. Options for a persuasive speech, for instance, include:

- Facts, figures, and statistics
- Quotations from experts or other authoritative sources
- Quotations from literary works or news media
- Personal experience and anecdotes

The above information can be enhanced by presenting it through:

- Photographs, charts, graphs
- Video or audio recordings
- Printed handouts
- Reciting passages from a given work

For other types of speeches or presentations, have students determine what methods, support, and props are appropriate to achieve the effect they desire to have on their audience (see all of the above).

Skill 2.2   Recognize the different roles of voice and intonation patterns in oral presentations of stories, poetry, and drama.

Shifting into a new character calls for an analysis of that character's ways of talking, moving, and relating to others in the world. Everything a student does to portray—both physically and emotionally—a character involves an interpretation of that character's motivations, intentions and passions. Characterization involves the basic decisions students makes regarding the why and how of their characters. Students may justify their decisions based on details they notice in illustration or word, on understanding they have about similar characters in real life, and on their own motivations and intentions.

Basic frame sentence for character analysis:
"Since my character is _____, then he/she would act like _____."

This may result in students employing a goofy, clumsy shuffle when acting in their role or addressing everyone as "baby." The students must evolve from children into actors, and, finally, into specific characters. It is your job to facilitate this transformation.

Child > Actor > Character

To further the immersion in their role, encourage students to call each other by their characters' names. Emphasize the "as if" nature of a play, in which the students treat characters as if they were real, with real emotions and motivations driving them to act the way they do.

Do not give students your own interpretation of a character's personality. Let them create their own interpretation, and follow along with their reading of the character.

Vocal Techniques

Voice is perhaps the most important tool of interpretation in classroom theater. It can portray anger, sadness, jealousy, happiness, fear and excitement. Vocal techniques integrate word choice, emphasis, and attitude; accentuating or deemphasizing them as students see fit. The voice puts life into the words of the play; with intonation, pitch, loudness or softness, and even accent reflecting or obscuring the intent of the speaker.

Just look at the phrase, "It's all right," as an example of the impact of voice and tone. Said with a soothing voice, it implies patience and understanding. Said with a sarcastic, cynical voice, it gives off a dismissive feeling. A host of a party might say the same phrase with suppressed frustration to a guest who has broken a favorite vase. In each case, the vocal choices made either highlight or shadow the inner thoughts of the speaker.

Encourage students to try on different vocal roles. Explain to students that while you must use the words in the script, *how* you say them is up to individual interpretation. A simple explanation is to simply tell them to "read something and then say it in your own way." Have students decide on words they want to stress by highlighting or underlining them in their scripts. Circle words that should be spoken louder and draw a line lightly through words that should be whispered. Allow students to transform vocal inflection to match their vision of their character. They will soon combine their own attitudes and analyses with attitudinal hints the text supplies to create an effective emotional portrayal.

Storytelling Techniques

- It's important to try to have complete silence before you begin so that the students are concentrating and focused on the story and the person reading it. Turn off any background music.
- Make eye contact with everyone. At least you should be able to see all the students from where you are sitting or standing. Move them around if necessary.
- Make sure that there are no distractions behind you – stand in front of a wall, not an interesting bookshelf or window.
- Think about yourself telling a favorite anecdote to your friends. "Did I tell you about the time when I…" How do you tell it? What gestures and effects do you use? At what points are you sure of getting a laugh? What are you doing with your body language and how are you telling the story? Is there a particular pause before the punch-line that works wonders? Apply your style to the story you're telling.

The presentation will be upbeat and not too long. On the other hand, if bad news is being presented, it will probably be the CEO who is making the presentation; and the bad-news announcement will come first followed with details about the news itself and how it came about. It will probably end with a pep talk and encouragement to do better the next time.

Skill 3.2   Analyze fallacies in logic.

A fallacy is, essentially, an error in reasoning. In persuasive speech, logical fallacies are instances of reasoning flaws that make an argument invalid. For example, a premature generalization occurs when you form a general rule based on only one or too few specific cases, ignoring all possible cases. An illustration of this is the statement, "Bob Marley was a Rastafarian singer. Therefore, all Rastafarians sing."

Skill 3.3   Analyze the role of critical thinking skills in effective listening and speaking.

Communication skills are crucial in a collaborative society. In particular, a person can not be a successful communicator without being an active listener. Focus on what others say, rather than planning on what to say next. By listening to everything another person is saying, you may pick up on natural cues that lead effortlessly to the next conversation move.

Facilitating
It is quite acceptable to use standard opening lines to facilitate a conversation. Don't agonize over trying to come up with witty "one-liners;" the main obstacle in initiating conversation is just getting the first statement over with. After that, the real substance begins. A useful technique may be to make a comment or ask a question about a shared situation. This may be anything from the weather, to the food you are eating, to a new policy at work. Use an opener you are comfortable with because, most likely, your partner in conversation will be comfortable with it as well.

Stimulating Higher-Level Critical Thinking Through Inquiry
Many people rely on questions to communicate with others. However, most fall back on simple clarifying questions rather than open-ended inquiries. Try to ask open-ended, deeper-level questions since those tend to have the greatest reward and lead to a greater understanding. In answering those questions, more complex connections are made and more significant realizations are achieved.

COMPETENCY 3.0 UNDERSTAND LISTENING AND SPEAKING FOR CRITICAL ANALYSIS, EVALUATION, AND PERSUASION

Skill 3.1 Evaluate strategies of organization and delivery in relation to given content, audience, purpose, and occasion.

The content in material to be presented orally plays a big role in how it is organized and delivered. For example, a literary analysis or a book report will be organized inductively, laying out the details and then presenting a conclusion which will usually identify the author's purpose, message, and intent. If the analysis is focusing on multiple layers in a story, treatment of those layers will probably follow the preliminary conclusion. On the other hand, keeping in mind that the speaker will want to keep the audience's attention, if the content has to do with difficult-to-follow facts and statistics, slides (or PowerPoint) may be used as a guide to the presentation, and the speaker will intersperse interesting anecdotes, jokes, or humor from time to time so the listeners don't fall asleep.

It's also important to take the consistency of the audience into account when organizing a presentation. If the audience can be counted on to have a high level of interest in what is being presented, little would need to be done in the way of organizing and presenting to hold its interest. On the other hand, if many of those in the audience are there because they have to be, or if the level of interest can be counted on not to be very high, something like a PowerPoint presentation can be very helpful. Also the lead-in and introduction need to be structured not only to be entertaining and interest-grabbing, they should create an interest in the topic. If the audience is senior citizens, it's important to keep the presentation lively and to be careful not to "speak down" to them. Carefully written introductions aimed specifically at this audience will help to attract their interest in the topic.

No speaker should stand up to make a presentation if the purpose has not been carefully determined ahead of time. If the speaker is not focused on the purpose, the audience will quickly lose interest. As to organizing for a particular purpose, some of the decisions to be made are where it will occur in the presentation—beginning, middle, or end—and whether displaying the purpose on a chart, PowerPoint, or banner will enhance the presentation. The purpose might be the lead-in for a presentation if it can be counted on to grab the interest of the listeners, in which case the organization will be deductive. If it seems better to save the purpose until the end, the organization, of course, will be inductive.

The occasion, of course, plays an important role in the development and delivery of a presentation. A celebration speech when the company has achieved an important accomplishment will be organized around congratulating those who were most responsible for the accomplishment and giving some details about how it was achieved and probably something about the competition for the achievement.

Skill 3.4 **Recognize the role of body language, gestures, and visual aids in communicating a point of view.**

Physicality in a classroom calls for the performer to embody the emotion of the words into the motion of the character. This can drastically alter the perception of the character's personality, dilemma or situation.

Take a look at the phrase, "No, I don't mind waiting." Said while leaning back in a chair with a casual wave of the hand, the speaker comes off as easy going and calm. On the other hand, if the speaker is tapping his or her foot and constantly checking his or her watch, the message is very different. Simple gestures from the raising of an eyebrow to jumping in the air indicate the speaker's state of mind, supplementing vocal tone and inflection.

Physical techniques can be especially helpful for students who have trouble getting into their character. For young people who naturally gravitate towards physical activity, getting into the physical quality of a character can lead to the emotional quality as well. Ask students to draw on their own experiences to determine what the most natural physical expression would be. Generally, boys are more physically active than girls. They are willing to fall down, hunch over, jump on top of desks, and dramatically exaggerate their movements to enhance the performance (or often just to be comical).

Posture: Maintain a straight, but not stiff, posture. Instead of shifting weight from hip to hip, point your feet directly at the audience and distribute your weight evenly. Keep shoulders orientated towards the audience. If you have to turn your body to use a visual aid, turn 45 degrees and continue speaking towards the audience.

Movement: Instead of staying glued to one spot or pacing back and forth, stay within four to eight feet of the front row of your audience, and take maybe a step or half-step to the side every once in a while. If you are using a lectern, feel free to move to the front or side of it to engage your audience more. Avoid distancing yourself from the audience; you want them to feel involved and connected.

Gestures: Gestures are a great way to keep a natural atmosphere when speaking publicly. Use them just as you would when speaking to a friend. They shouldn't be exaggerated, but they should be utilized for added emphasis. Avoid keeping your hands in your pockets or locked behind your back, wringing your hands and fidgeting nervously, or keeping your arms crossed.

Eye Contact: Many people are intimidated by using eye contact when speaking to large groups. Interestingly, eye contact usually *helps* speakers overcome speech anxiety by connecting with their attentive audience and easing feelings of isolation. Instead of looking at a spot on the back wall or at your notes, scan the room and make eye contact for one to three seconds per person.

COMPETENCY 4.0 UNDERSTAND LISTENING AND SPEAKING FOR SOCIAL INTERACTION IN A VARIETY OF FORMAL AND INFORMAL SITUATIONS

Skill 4.1 Analyze elements of effective listening and speaking in conversation.

The successful conversationalist is a person who keeps up with what's going on in the world both far and near and ponders the meanings of events and developments. That person also usually reads about the topics that are of the most interest to him, both in printed materials and online. In addition, the effective conversationalist has certain areas that are of particular interest and that have been probed in some depth. An interest in human behavior is usually one of this person's most particular interests. Why do people behave as they do? Why do some succeed and some fail? This person will also be interested in and concerned about social issues--particularly in the immediate community, but also on a wider scale--and will have ideas for solving some of those problems.

With all of this, the most important thing a good conversationalist can do is to *listen*--not just wait until the other person quits speaking so that he or she can take the floor again, but actually listening to learn what the other person has to say and also to learn more about that other person. Following a gathering, the person who will be remembered the longest and with the most regard is the one who was interested enough to listen to other's ideas and opinions.

It's acceptable to be passionate about one's convictions in polite conversation; it is not acceptable to be overbearing or unwilling to hear and consider another's point of view. It's important to keep one's emotions under control in these circumstances even if the other person does not.

Skill 4.2 Analyze techniques of effective listening and speaking in small- and large-group situations.

"Political correctness" is a new concept tossed around frequently in the 21st century. It has always existed, of course. The successful speaker of the 19th century understood and was sensitive to audiences. However, that person was typically a man, of course, and the only audience that was important was a male audience; and, more often than not, the only important audience was a white one.

Many things have changed in discourse since the 19th century just as the society the speaker lives in and addresses has changed, and the speaker who disregards the existing conventions regarding "political correctness" usually finds himself or herself in trouble. Rap music makes a point of ignoring those conventions, particularly with regard to gender, and is often the target of very hostile attacks.

On the other hand, by thumbing their noses at establishment conventions, rap performers often intend to be revolutionary and have developed their own audiences and have become outrageously wealthy by exploiting those newly-developed audiences.

Even so, the successful speaker must understand and be sensitive to what is current in "political correctness." The "n word" is a case in point. There was a time when that term was thrown about at will by politicians and other public speakers, but no more. Nothing could spell the end of a politician's career more certainly than using that term in his campaign or public addresses.

These terms are called "pejorative"—A word or phrase that expresses contempt or disapproval. Such terms as *redneck*, *queer*, or *cripple* may only be considered pejorative if used by a non-member of the group they apply to. For example, the "n word," which became very inflammatory in the 1960s, is now being used sometimes by African-American artists to refer to themselves, especially in their music, with the intention of underscoring their protest of the establishment.

References to gender have became particularly sensitive in the 20th century as a result of the women's rights movement, and the speaker who disregards these sensitivities does so at his or her peril. The generic "he" is no longer acceptable, and this requires a strategy to deal with pronominal references without repetitive he/she or his/her structures. Several ways to approach this: switch to a passive construction that does not require a subject; switch back and forth, using the male pronoun in one reference and the female pronoun in another one, being sure to sprinkle them reasonably evenly; or switch to the plural. The last alternative is the one most often chosen. This requires some care, and the speaker should spend time developing these skills before stepping in front of an audience.

DOMAIN II. WRITING

COMPETENCY 5.0 UNDERSTAND WRITING FOR INFORMATION AND UNDERSTANDING

Skill 5.1 Evaluate alternative thesis statements or organizational patterns for a formal essay or a research paper on a given topic.

In the past teachers have assigned reports, paragraphs, and essays that focused on the teacher as the audience with the purpose of explaining information. However, for students to be meaningfully engaged in their writing, they must write for a variety of reasons. Writing for different audiences and aims allows students to be more involved in their writing. If they write for the same audience and purpose, they will continue to see writing as just another assignment. Listed below are suggestions that give students an opportunity to write in more creative and critical ways.

* Write letters to the editor, to a college, to a friend, to another student that would be sent to the intended audience.
* Write stories that would be read aloud to a group (the class, another group of students, to a group of elementary school students) or published in a literary magazine or class anthology.
* Have students discuss the parallels between the different speech styles we use and writing styles for different readers or audiences.
* Allow students to write a particular piece for different audiences.
* Make sure students consider the following when analyzing the needs of their audience.

    1. Why is the audience reading my writing? Do they expect to be informed, amused or persuaded?
    2. What does my audience already know about my topic?
    3. What does the audience want or need to know? What will interest them?
    4. What type of language suits my readers?

* As part of the prewriting have students identify the audience.
* Expose students to writing that is on the same topic but for different audience, and have them identify the variations in sentence structure and style.
* Remind your students that it is not necessary to identify all the specifics of the audience in the initial stage of the writing process, but that at some point they must make some determinations about audience.

Skill 5.2 Evaluate information from various sources for use in a research project.

The best place to start research is usually at your local library. Not only does it have numerous books, videos, and periodicals to use for references, the librarian is always a valuable resource for information, or where to get that information.

"Those who declared librarians obsolete when the internet rage first appeared are now red faced. We need them more than ever. The internet is full of 'stuff' but its value and readability is often questionable. 'Stuff' doesn't give you a competitive edge, high-quality related information does."
-Patricia Schroeder, President of the Association of American Publishers

The internet is a multi-faceted goldmine of information, but you must be careful to discriminate between reliable and unreliable sources. Stick to sites that are associated with an academic institution, whether it be a college, a university, or a scholarly organization.

Keep **content** and **context** in mind when researching. Don't be so wrapped up in how you are going to apply your resource to your project that you miss the author's entire purpose or message. Remember that there are multiple ways to get the information you need. Read an encyclopedia article about your topic to get a general overview, and then focus in from there. Note important names of people, time periods, and geographic areas associated with your subject. Make a list of key words and their synonyms to use while searching for information. And finally, don't forget about articles in magazines, newspapers, and personal interviews with experts related to your field of interest!

Skill 5.3 Evaluate the appropriateness of language and formats for various products of expository writing.

Gone are the days when students engage in skill practice with grammar worksheets. Grammar needs to be taught in the context of the students' own work. Listed below is a series of classroom practices that encourage meaningful, context-based grammar instruction combined with occasional mini-lessons and other language strategies that can be used on a daily basis.

* Connect grammar with the student's own writing while emphasizing grammar as a significant aspect of effective writing.

* Emphasize the importance of editing and proofreading as an essential part of classroom activities.

* Provide students with an opportunity to practice editing and proofreading cooperatively.

* Give instruction in the form of 15-20 minute mini-lessons.

* Emphasize the sound of punctuation by connecting it to pitch, stress, and pause.

* Involve students in all facets of language learning including reading, writing, listening, speaking and thinking. Good use of language comes from exploring all forms of it on a regular basis.

There are a number of approaches that involve grammar instruction in the context of the writing.

> 1. Sentence Combining - try to use the student's own writing as much as possible. The theory behind combining ideas and the correct punctuation should be emphasized.
>
> 2. Sentence and paragraph modeling - provide students with the opportunity to practice imitating the style and syntax of professional writers.
>
> 3. Sentence transforming - give students an opportunity to change sentences from one form to another, i.e. from passive to active, inverting the sentence order, change forms of the words used.
>
> 4. Daily Language Practice - introduce or clarify common errors using daily language activities. Use actual student examples whenever possible. Correct and discuss the problems with grammar and usage.

Skill 5.4   Revise drafts to improve their effectiveness.

When assessing and responding to student writing, there are several guidelines to remember.

Responding to non-graded writing (formative).

1. Avoid using a red pen. Whenever possible use a #2 pencil.
2. Explain the criteria that will be used for assessment in advance.
3. Read the writing once while asking the question, "Is the student's response appropriate for the assignment?"
4. Reread and make note at the end whether the student met the objective of the writing task.
5. Responses should be supportive and employ encouraging language.

6. Resist writing on or over the student's writing.
7. Highlight the ideas you wish to emphasize, question, or verify.
8. Encourage your students to take risks.

Responding to and evaluating graded writing (summative).

1. Ask students to submit prewriting and rough-draft materials including all revisions with their final draft.
2. For the first reading, use a holistic method, examining the work as a whole.
3. When reading the draft for the second time, assess it using the standards previously established.
4. Responses to the writing should be written in the margin and should use supportive language.
5. Make sure you address the process as well as the product. It is important that students value the learning process as well as the final product.
6. After scanning the piece a third time, write final comments at the end of the draft.

The most recent research reinforces what teachers have always known—that cooperative learning is a powerful strategy in the classroom. Cooperative or collaborative learning is working together as we have always tried to do, but with a new understanding borrowed from the areas of communication and psychology about how groups work together. Grouping can be a very effective way to work, but it can also be very ineffective. So, the question becomes how to maximize the productivity of groups. While you are experimenting, keep the following ideas in mind:

1. Cooperative learning allows teachers to move away from the center of the room and rely less on lecturing.

2. Cooperative learning gives students the opportunity to verbalize their ideas.

3. Cooperative learning gives students more ownership of what they learn and therefore motivates them more.

Listed below are the group skills that you will want to emphasize when working in groups. Also, you will find three strategies that work. It is important to provide peer-evaluation guidelines.

Guidelines for the writer

- Make a list of questions or concerns for your peers.

- Maintain an open attitude. It is important to use the evaluator's comments rather than being defensive. Keep in mind that the readers are only trying to help you.

Guidelines for the peer-evaluator

- Begin by pointing out the strengths first. Then, identify the areas that need to be improved.

- Provide encouragement and suggest things the writer can do to improve the piece of writing.

- Focus on content and organization. Avoid commenting on errors of punctuation or mechanics. These problems can be fixed during the editing stage.

- Be sensitive to the writer's feelings and give the peer-response your best effort.

When creating peer-response groups, keep in mind the following ideas.

1. Make sure each group is balanced with students of varying ability. Peer-response groups will not work effectively if all the strong writers are in one or two groups. Spread out the talents of the class evenly among the groups. It is usually better for the teacher to assign the groups because this method not only prevents hurt feelings, it also allows the teacher to balance the groups with varying academic abilities and skill levels to ensure maximum benefit for all students.

2. Allow the groups to work together for more than one session. It takes time to create a group that will work effectively together and for peers to become comfortable working together.

3. Don't expect groups to produce significant results initially. Remember evaluating and revising are the most demanding stages of writing.

When responding to student writing, there are a variety of approaches you can use depending on the focus and purpose of the assignment. You may want to vary the approaches.

- Analytical Evaluation identifies the qualities of a successful piece of writing and attributes point values for each aspect. The student's grade is determined by the point total. Students often like this type of evaluation since it is concrete and highlights specific strengths and weaknesses. One drawback for this type of evaluation is that it places a greater emphasis on the part rather than the whole.

- Holistic Scoring assesses a piece of writing as a whole. Usually a paper is read quickly through once to get a general impression. The writing is graded according to the impression of the whole work rather than the sum of its parts. Often holistic scoring uses a rubric that establishes the overall criteria for a certain score to evaluate each paper.

- A Performance System identifies established criteria, and as long as the student meets the acceptable level of activity, the points are awarded. This particular approach is useful for activities like journal writing.

- Portfolio Grading allows the students to select the pieces of work to be graded. Often this technique is used with writing workshops. Students often like this method because they have control over the evaluation process. Also, since teachers do not have to grade everything, it lessens their workload.

When the time comes to assign grades, keep a few things in mind.

1. Each piece of writing should have clearly established criteria.

2. Involve students in the process of defining the criteria. Students are more apt to understand criteria they have helped develop.

3. Give students numerous experiences with formative evaluation (evaluation as the student is writing the piece). Give students points for the work they have done throughout the process.

4. During the summative evaluation phase (final evaluation), students play an active role. Provide them with a form to identify the best parts of the writing and the things they would work on given more time.

5. Focus on content, fluency and freshness of ideas with young writers. Correctness and punctuation will follow as they gain control of the language.

COMPETENCY 6.0 UNDERSTAND WRITING FOR PERSONAL EXPRESSION AND SOCIAL INTERACTION

Skill 6.1 **Demonstrate awareness of connotation and figurative meaning in selecting language for a given expressive purpose.**

Before assigning any other written work, familiarize students with definitions, examples, and detailed explanations of the following:

- connotation/connote
- denotation/denote
- figurative language/figurative meaning
- literal language/literal meaning
- symbol/symbolism/symbolize
- metaphor/mixed metaphor
- simile
- analogy/false analogy
- oxymoron
- cliché

With students working individually and/or in groups, ask them to evaluate and analyze, in writing, the connotations (as to social setting, the speaker, etc.), literal meanings, and contrasts in groups of topically related expressions, such as the following:

- Dinner is served, madam.
- Hey, let's hit the feedbag!

- Sigmund is a zombie.
- Poor Sigmund works so hard and looks so tired.

- Cassandra is an eloquent speaker.
- Pollyanna has a silver tongue.

Assign individual homework requiring students to incorporate literal and figurative language in an essay or story about a person, event, activity, or idea. Explain the necessity of unified imagery in a written work, the perils of clichés and mixed metaphors, and the need to avoid overwriting (see also **Skill 6.3**). If students are having trouble generating figurative language, suggest that they consider the following as potential sources of metaphors, similes, analogies, etc.:

- work
- play
- food
- sleep
- time
- love
- animals
- plants
- learning

Teachers may also wish to assign students the task of presenting and explaining to the class an example of figurative language from a favorite poem, song, or prose excerpt.

Lastly, since all language appeals to at least one of the senses, encourage students to look to sight, smell, hearing, touch, and taste as apt starting points for creating vivid written language, whether figurative or literal.

Skill 6.2 Judge alternative introductory or concluding sentences for a personal essay on a given theme.

Introductory Sentences

In order to gain favorable reader interest and attention, an essay's introduction should quickly and clearly give readers key information about the essay's theme. If a writer is in doubt about what this information is, she or he can follow the guideline commonly used by journalists when introducing a subject: answer the questions Who? What? Where? When? How? and Why? as they pertain to one's theme. For example, consider the following introductory sentences.

- High school and college are very different.
- I find that high school and college are very different.
- During my first semester at Oklahoma State, I discovered that high school and college are very different.
- During my first semester at Oklahoma State, I discovered that campus life is freer and academic standards are tougher than at high school.

The first sentence answers only the thematic "what" question; the second only the "what" and "who." The third sentence adds answers to the "when" and "where" questions but, unlike the fourth sentence, remains vague as to just *how* college differs from high school. Ask students to evaluate the above sentences or similar examples for clarity and comprehensiveness.

Using the journalists' guidelines mentioned above, have students practice writing introductory sentences and paragraphs about a variety of personal essay subjects. After they have done this, provide them with some sample sentences in need of revision. For example:

- High school and college are very different. I discovered this during my first semester at Oklahoma State. I discovered that Oklahoma State's social life and academic life are very different than at high school.
- Sarah and Jeanne are sisters. They are identical twins. Both of them are on the high school volleyball team.

Emphasize the need to make multiple short sentences like those above into longer sentences. Doing so will avoid choppy, repetitive writing. Have students do the same with their own sentences wherever necessary.

Offer the following examples as common pitfalls to avoid when introducing an essay topic. Avoid distracting opening statements such as:

- "After carefully considering for a long time which topic to choose, I selected…" The reader doesn't need to know how much care or time goes into choosing a topic.
- "I chose this topic because it interests me very much." Readers will assume that writers are interested in their chosen topics.
- "This topic was very difficult for me but I decided to write about…" By itself, such a statement can seem like a kind of special pleading. Generally it is preferable to introduce a topic factually; any difficulties (complexity, controversy, etc.) can be addressed at the end of the introduction and/or in the body of the essay.

A final note: An essay's introductory paragraph/s should provide both a comprehensive account of what the topic is and what the writer is going to say about it. If the body or conclusion of an essay introduces perspectives and/or thematic material not covered in the introduction, readers may become confused. Have students check their writings for this before handing them in.

Concluding Sentences

Successful conclusions/concluding sentences accomplish several things:

- They provide a clear and concise summary of the essay's topic.
- They provide a decisive summary of the writer's view/s on the topic.

Ask students to evaluate and discuss the following concluding sentences (or similar examples).

- *Romeo and Juliet* is a lousy play.
- Well, I guess that *Romeo and Juliet* is a pretty good play.
- *Romeo and Juliet* shows us the lengths to which some people will go to oppose true love. Shakespeare shows his readers how hate is stronger than love.
- I was saddened by the play's tragic ending but was also deeply inspired by the emotional power of Romeo and Juliet's commitment to each other.

The first example is merely a sweeping dismissal. The second is indecisive. The third example is better than the first two but relies on vague expressions e.g., "some people," and "true love"; its conclusion is also rather simplistic. The final sentence is more specific in vocabulary, context, and point of view.

Have students work individually, in pairs, or in groups (or in a combination of all three) to write conclusions based on class reading assignments. This work should emphasize that one can "start" an essay with a conclusion, then work "backward" from there by giving support—through reasoning, quotations, data, character analyses, personal experiences or current events—for it. Teachers should also emphasize that conclusions will need to be altered or abandoned if support for them is lacking or contradicted by other factual evidence, perspectives, etc.

Skill 6.3 Analyze problems relating to the effectiveness of narrative or descriptive materials and identify appropriate revisions.

Some people say that God is in the details; others say that the devil is in the details. Either way, the message is the same with regards to vivid, informative writing: details are the key. Before assigning other written work, ask students to evaluate and analyze sentences such as the following for clarity and comprehensiveness.

- While walking I saw an accident.
- While walking to the store I saw a car accident.
- While walking to the drugstore last night, I saw a bad, three-car accident in front of the gas station.

Each of these sentences report on the same event but only the last one meets the informative standard—the "journalistic guidelines"—explained in **Skill 6.2**. This sentence provides information that answers the who, what, where, and when aspects of the writer's chosen subject. Review the significance of this with students, then assign homework/class work accordingly.

Students also need to be aware of the pitfalls of providing too much information, especially redundant, marginal or irrelevant information, as in the following examples or ones like them. Have students point out, in writing, whatever is wrong with each example. Then have them revise each one.

- Last night 30 cm of cold white snow fell from the clouds in the sky above us.
- Before you swallow your food down into your stomach, you should chew it with your teeth.
- The great novelist hand-wrote his masterpiece novel on paper.

Students must also be made aware of how to "manage topic and time" in their writings. For example, in a 400-word essay assignment a topic such as "my year as a foreign exchange student in Germany" cannot likely be done justice: the time frame is too long and the topic too broad for 400 words. Instead, encourage students to focus on smaller, more manageable topics. For example: "one big difference between German and American life," "a memorable day in my German neighborhood," etc. Less can be more. Emphasize this prior to assigning any written work.

Encourage students to write about what they know: the people in their lives, their personal experiences, opinions, their hobbies and interests, favorite literary works or music, sports, the future, etc. Assign written work accordingly.

Students who show an aptitude or interest for longer, even book-length, writing should be encouraged to take on larger topics and time frames, perhaps as extra credit assignments.

Emphasize to students the importance of avoiding certain words and expressions that either overstate a case or leave no room for exceptions to it. Avoid readily falsifiable statements such as:

- "No-one thinks the way you do."
- "That's the way it's always been."
- "Everyone has always loved this song."

Have students revise all of the above into readily defensible statements. Teachers may also wish to provide students with a list of words to be especially careful with, lest a statement become an overstatement:

- always, never, forever, every time, any time
- no-one, nobody, none, all, every, everyone, everybody
- anywhere, everywhere, nowhere
- without exception, without a doubt

Skill 6.4 Apply strategies for composing personal notes and letters.

When writing personal notes or letters, the writer needs to keep the following key matters in mind:

- Once the topic is determined, the writer must determine the appropriate tone to introduce and express it. Is humor appropriate? Seriousness? Bluntness or subtlety? Does the situation call for formal or informal language? The answers to these questions will depend, in good part, on the writer's relationship to the reader. Plan appropriately regarding situation and audience.
- Does the writer's introduction clearly explain the topic/situation to a reader who doesn't know or feel everything that the reader knows or feels? Don't assume that the writer and reader are "on the same page." Make a checklist to make sure that all key information is clearly and concisely expressed.
- If a note or letter involves a request, what type of response/result does the writer desire? Devise a strategy or strategies for achieving a desired outcome.
- If a note or letter involves a complaint about the reader, the writer will need to decide whether to ask for particular amends or to let the reader decide what, if anything, to do. If no amends are requested, the writer may wish to suggest ideas that would help to avoid similar conflicts in the future. Asking the reader for his or her opinions is also a possibility.
- If a timely response to any note or letter is needed, the writer must mention this.

Give students in-class opportunities to write a variety of personal notes and letters, whether involving "real life" or hypothetical situations. Invitations, thank-you notes, complaints, requests for favors, or personal updates are a few of the options available. Have students experiment with a variety of tones and strategies on a particular piece of personal correspondence, e.g., write a complaint letter in a blunt tone, then write the same complaint in a humorous tone; compare and contrast the drafts. Structure in-class activities to allow for peer feedback.

COMPETENCY 7.0 UNDERSTAND WRITING FOR CRITICAL ANALYSIS, EVALUATION, AND PERSUASION

Skill 7.1 Analyze the organization of an editorial or argumentative essay on a given topic.

Logical Argument

A logical argument consists of three stages.

First of all, the propositions which are necessary for the argument to continue are stated. These are called the premises of the argument. They are the evidence or reasons for accepting the argument and its conclusions.

Premises (or assertions) are often indicated by phrases such as "because", "since", "obviously" and so on. (The phrase "obviously" is often viewed with suspicion, as it can be used to intimidate others into accepting suspicious premises. If something doesn't seem obvious to you, don't be afraid to question it. You can always say "Oh, yes, you're right, it is obvious" when you've heard the explanation.)

Next, the premises are used to derive further propositions by a process known as inference. In inference, one proposition is arrived at on the basis of one or more other propositions already accepted. There are various forms of valid inference.

The propositions arrived at by inference may then be used in further inference. Inference is often denoted by phrases such as "implies that" or "therefore".

Finally, we arrive at the conclusion of the argument -- the proposition which is affirmed on the basis of the premises and inference. Conclusions are often indicated by phrases such as "therefore", "it follows that", "we conclude" and so on. The conclusion is often stated as the final stage of inference.

Classical Argument

In its simplest form, the classical argument has five main parts:

The **introduction**, which warms up the audience, establishes goodwill and rapport with the readers, and announces the general theme or thesis of the argument.

The **narration**, which summarizes relevant background material, provides any information the audience needs to know about the environment and circumstances that produce the argument, and set up the stakes–what's at risk in this question.

The **confirmation**, which lays out in a logical order (usually strongest to weakest or most obvious to most subtle) the claims that support the thesis, providing evidence for each claim.

The **refutation and concession**, which looks at opposing viewpoints to the writer's claims, anticipating objections from the audience, and allowing as much of the opposing viewpoints as possible without weakening the thesis.

The **summation**, which provides a strong conclusion, amplifying the force of the argument, and showing the readers that this solution is the best at meeting the circumstances.

Skill 7.2 Distinguish reasons, examples, or details that support a given argument or opinion.

Once a thesis is put forth, there are various ways to support it. The most obvious one is reasons. Usually a reason will answer the question why. Another technique is to give examples. A third is to give details.

The presentation of a prosecutor in a court trial is a good example of an argument that uses all of these.

The **thesis** of the prosecutor may be: John O'Hara stole construction materials from a house being built at 223 Hudson Ave. by the Jones Construction Company. As a **reason**, he might cite the following: He is building his own home on Green Street and needs materials and tools. This will answer the question why. He might give **examples**: 20 bags of concrete disappeared the night before Mr. O'Hara poured the basement for his house on Green Street. The electronic nail-setter disappeared from the building site on Hudson Ave. the day before Mr. O'Hara began to erect the frame of his house on Green Street. He might fill in the **details**: Mr. O'Hara's truck was observed by a witness on Hudson Ave. in the vicinity of the Jones Construction Company site the night the concrete disappeared. Mr. O'Hara's truck was observed again on that street by a witness the night the nail-setter disappeared.

Another example of a trial might be: **Thesis**, Adam Andrews murdered Joan Rogers in cold blood on the night of December 20. **Reason #1**: She was about to reveal their affair to his wife. **Reason #2**: Andrews' wife would inherit half of his sizeable estate in case of a divorce since there is no prenuptial agreement. **Example #1**: Rogers has demonstrated that he is capable of violence in an incident with a partner in his firm. **Example #2**: Rogers has had previous affairs where he was accused of violence. **Detail #1**: Andrews' wife once called the police and signed a warrant. **Detail #2**: A previous lover sought police protection from Andrews.

An **opinion** is a thesis and requires support. It can also use reasons, examples, and details.

For example:

Opinion: Our borders must be protected.

Reason #1: Terrorists can get into the country undetected. **Example #1**: An Iranian national was able to cross the Mexican border and live in this country for years before being detected. **Detail**: The Iranian national came up through Central America to Mexico then followed the route that Mexican illegal immigrants regularly took. **Example #2**: a group of Middle Eastern terrorists were arrested in Oregon after they had crossed the Canadian border. **Detail**: There was no screening at that border.

Reason #2: Illegal aliens are an enormous drain on resources such as health care. **Example**: The states of California and Texas bear enormous burdens for health care and education for illegal immigrants. **Detail**: Legal citizens are often denied care in those states because resources are stretched so thin.

Skill 7.3 Use transitions and commentary to enhance the clarity of a line of argument.

A mark of maturity in writing is the effective use of transitional devices at all levels. For example, a topic sentence can be used to establish continuity, especially if it is positioned at the beginning of a paragraph. The most common use would be to refer to what has preceded, repeat it, or summarize it; and then go on to introduce a new topic. An essay by W. H. Hudson uses this device: "Although the potato was very much to me in those early years, it grew to be more when I heard its history." It summarizes what has preceded, makes a comment on the author's interest, and introduces a new topic: the history of the potato.

Another example of a transitional sentence could be, "Not all matters end so happily." This refers to the previous information and prepares for the next paragraph, which will be about matters that do not end happily. This transitional sentence is a little more forthright: "The increase in drug use in our community leads us to another general question."

Another fairly simple and straightforward transitional device is the use of numbers or their approximation: "First, I want to talk about the dangers of immigration; second, I will discuss the enormity of the problem; third, I will propose a reasonable solution."

An entire paragraph may be transitional in purpose and form. In "Darwiniana," Thomas Huxley used a transitional paragraph:

So much, then, by way of proof that the method of establishing laws in science is exactly the same as that pursued in common life. Let us now turn to another matter (though really it is but another phase of the same question), and that is, the method by which, from the relations of certain phenomena, we prove that some stand in the position of causes toward the others.

The most common transitional device is a single word. Some examples: *and, furthermore, next, moreover, in addition, again, also, likewise, similarly, finally, second*, etc. There are many.

In marking student papers, a teacher can encourage a student to think in terms of moving coherently from one idea to the next by making transitions between the two. If the shift from one thought to another is too abrupt, the student can be asked to provide a transitional paragraph. Lists of possible transitions can be put on a handout and students can be encouraged to have the list at hand when composing essays. These are good tools for nudging students to more mature writing styles.

Skill 7.4   Analyze fallacies in logic in a piece of persuasive writing.

See Skill 3.2.

COMPETENCY 8.0 UNDERSTAND PROCESSES FOR GENERATING AND DEVELOPING WRITTEN TEXTS

Skill 8.1 Apply strategies for generating ideas before writing.

Remind students that as they prewrite they need to consider their audience. Prewriting strategies assist students in a variety of ways. Listed below are the most common prewriting strategies students can use to explore, plan, and write on a topic. It is important to remember when teaching these strategies that not all prewriting must eventually produce a finished piece of writing. In fact, in the initial lesson of teaching prewriting strategies, it might be more effective to have students practice prewriting strategies without the pressure of having to write a finished product.

* Keep an idea book so that they can jot down ideas that come to mind.

* Write in a daily journal.

* Write down whatever comes to mind; this is called free writing. Students do not stop to make corrections or interrupt the flow of ideas. A variation of this technique is focused free writing - writing on a specific topic - to prepare for an essay.

* Make a list of all ideas connected with their topic; this is called brainstorming. Make sure students know that this technique works best when they let their minds work freely. After completing the list, students should analyze the list to see if a pattern or way to group the ideas.

* Ask the questions Who? What? When? Where? When? and How? Help the writer approach a topic from several perspectives.

* Create a visual map on paper to gather ideas. Cluster circles and lines to show connections between ideas. Students should try to identify the relationship that exists between their ideas. If they cannot see the relationships; have them pair up, exchange papers, and have their partners look for some related ideas.

* Observe details of sight, hearing, taste, touch, and taste.

* Visualize by making mental images of something and write down the details in a list

After they have practiced with each of these prewriting strategies, ask them to pick out the ones they prefer, and ask them to discuss how they might use the techniques to help them with future writing assignments. It is important to remember that they can use more than one prewriting strategy at a time. Also they may find that different writing situations may suggest certain techniques.

Skill 8.2 Evaluate the appropriateness of given details for supporting the development of a main point.

See Skill 7.2.

Skill 8.3 Eliminate distracting details that interfere with the development of a main point.

Paragraphs are clusters of information that support an author's main points or advance a story's action. They should be clearly focused, well developed, organized, coherent, and neither too long nor too short for easy reading.

Techniques to Maintain Focus:

- **Focus on a main point.** The point should be clear to readers, and all sentences in the paragraph should relate to it.
- **Start the paragraph with a topic sentence.** This should be a general, one-sentence summary of the paragraph's main point, relating both back towards the thesis and toward the content of the paragraph. (A topic sentence is sometimes unnecessary if the paragraph continues a developing idea clearly introduced in a preceding paragraph or if the paragraph appears in a narrative of events where generalizations might interrupt the flow of the story.)
- **Stick to the point.** Eliminate sentences that do not support the topic sentence.
- **Be flexible.** If there is not enough evidence to support the claim your topic sentence is making, do not fall into the trap of wandering or introducing new ideas within the paragraph. Either find more evidence, or adjust the topic sentence to collaborate with the evidence that is available.

Skill 8.4 Solve problems related to text organization.

Writing is a recursive process. As students engage in the various stages of writing, they develop and improve not only their writing skills, but their thinking skills as well. The stages of the writing process are as follows:

PREWRITING

Students gather ideas before writing. Prewriting may include clustering, listing, brainstorming, mapping, free writing, and charting. Providing many ways for a student to develop ideas on a topic will increase his/her chances for success.

WRITING

Students compose the first draft.

REVISING

Students examine their work and make changes in sentences, wording, details and ideas. Revise comes from the Latin word *revidere*, meaning, "to see again."

EDITING

Students proofread the draft for punctuation and mechanical errors.

PUBLISHING

Students may have their work displayed on a bulletin board, read aloud in class, or printed in a literary magazine or school anthology.

It is important to realize that these steps are recursive; as a student engages in each aspect of the writing process, he or she may begin with prewriting, write, revise, write, revise, edit, and publish. They do not engage in this process in a lockstep manner; it is more circular.

TEACHING THE COMPOSING PROCESS

Prewriting Activities

1. Class discussion of the topic.
2. Map out ideas, questions, graphic organizers on the chalkboard.
3. Break into small groups to discuss different ways of approaching the topic and develop an organizational plan and create a thesis statement.
4. Research the topic if necessary.

Drafting/Revising

1. Students write first draft in class or at home.
2. Students engage in peer response and class discussion.
3. Using checklists or a rubric, students critique each other's writing and make suggestions for revising the writing.
4. Students revise the writing.

Editing and Proofreading

1. Students, working in pairs, analyze sentences for variety.
2. Students work in groups to read papers for punctuation and mechanics.
3. Students perform final edit.

TEACHER CERTIFICATION STUDY GUIDE

COMPETENCY 9.0 EDIT WRITTEN TEXTS TO ACHIEVE CLARITY AND ECONOMY OF EXPRESSION AND CONFORMITY TO CONVENTIONS OF STANDARD ENGLISH USAGE

Skill 9.1 Revise sentences to eliminate wordiness, ambiguity, and redundancy.

Enhancing Interest:

- Start out with an attention-grabbing introduction. This sets an engaging tone for the entire piece and will be more likely to pull the reader in.
- Use dynamic vocabulary and varied sentence beginnings. Keep the reader on their toes. If they can predict what you are going to say next, switch it up.
- Avoid using clichés (as cold as ice, the best thing since sliced bread, nip it in the bud). These are easy shortcuts, but they are not interesting, memorable, or convincing.

Ensuring Understanding:

- Avoid using the words, "clearly," "obviously," and "undoubtedly." Often, things that are clear or obvious to the author are not as apparent to the reader. Instead of using these words, make your point so strongly that it is clear on its own.
- Use the word that best fits the meaning you intend for, even if they are longer or a little less common. Try to find a balance, a go with a familiar yet precise word.
- When in doubt, explain further.

Skill 9.2 Revise sentences and passages to subordinate ideas, maintain parallel form, and connect related ideas.

Students need to be trained to become effective at proofreading, revising and editing strategies. Begin by training them using both desk-side and scheduled conferences. Listed below are some strategies to use to guide students through the final stages of the writing process.

* Provide some guide sheets or forms for students to use during peer responses.

* Allow students to work in pairs and limit the agenda.

* Model the use of the guide sheet or form for the entire class.

* Give students a time limit.

* Have the students read their partners' papers and ask at least three who, what, when, why, how questions. The students answer the questions and use them as a place to begin discussing the piece.

Provide students with a series of questions that will assist them in revising their writing.

1. Do the details give a clear picture? Add details that appeal to more than just the sense of sight.

2. How effectively are the details organized? Reorder the details if it is needed.

3. Are the thoughts and feelings of the writer included? Add personal thoughts and feelings about the subject.

As you discuss revision, you begin with discussing the definition of revise. Also, state that all writing must be revised to improve it. After students have revised their writing, it is time for the final editing and proofreading. There are a few key points to remember when helping students learn to edit and proofread their work.

* It is crucial that students are not taught grammar in isolation, but in context of the writing process.

* At this point in the writing process, a mini-lesson that focuses on some of the problems your students are having would be appropriate.

* Ask students to read their writing and check for specific errors like using a subordinate clause as a sentence.

* Provide students with a proofreading checklist to guide them as they edit their work.

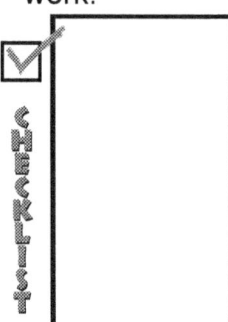

Skill 9.3   Revise misplaced or dangling modifiers.

Misplaced and Dangling Modifiers

Particular phrases that are not placed near the one word they modify often result in misplaced modifiers. Particular phrases that do not relate to the subject being modified result in dangling modifiers.

Error: Weighing the options carefully, a decision was made regarding the punishment of the convicted murderer.

Problem: Who is weighing the options? No one capable of weighing is named in the sentence; thus, the participle phrase weighing the options carefully dangles. This problem can be corrected by adding a subject of the sentence capable of doing the action.

Correction: Weighing the options carefully, the judge made a decision regarding the punishment of the convicted murderer.

Error: Returning to my favorite watering hole, brought back many fond memories.

Problem: The person who returned is never indicated, and the participle phrase dangles. This problem can be corrected by creating a dependent clause from the modifying phrase.

Correction: When I returned to my favorite watering hole, many fond memories came back to me.

Error: One damaged house stood only to remind townspeople of the hurricane.

Problem: The placement of the misplaced modifier only suggests that the sole reason the house remained was to serve as a reminder. The faulty modifier creates ambiguity.

Correction: Only one damaged house stood, reminding townspeople of the hurricane.

Skill 9.4 Revise nonstandard capitalization and punctuation.

Capitalization

Capitalize all proper names of persons (including specific organizations or agencies of government); places (countries, states, cities, parks, and specific geographical areas); and things (political parties, structures, historical and cultural terms, and calendar and time designations); and religious terms (any deity, revered person or group, sacred writings).

Percy Bysshe Shelley, Argentina, Mount Rainier National Park, Grand Canyon, League of Nations, the Sears Tower, Birmingham, Lyric Theater, Americans, Midwesterners, Democrats, Renaissance, Boy Scouts of America, Easter, God, Bible, Dead Sea Scrolls, Koran

Capitalize proper adjectives and titles used with proper names.

California gold rush, President John Adams, French fries, Homeric epic, Romanesque architecture, Senator John Glenn

Note: Some words that represent titles and offices are not capitalized unless used with a proper name.

Capitalized	Not Capitalized
Congressman McKay	the congressman from Florida
Commander Alger	commander of the Pacific Fleet
Queen Elizabeth	the queen of England

Capitalize all main words in titles of works of literature, art, and music. (See "Using Italics" in the Punctuation section.)

The candidate should be cognizant of proper rules and conventions of punctuation, capitalization, and spelling. Competency exams will generally test the ability to apply the more advanced skills; thus, a limited number of more frustrating rules is presented here. Rules should be applied according to the American style of English, i.e. spelling *theater* instead of *theatre* and placing terminal marks of punctuation almost exclusively within other marks of punctuation.

Punctuation

Using terminal punctuation in relation to quotation marks

In a quoted statement that is either declarative or imperative, place the period inside the closing quotation marks.

"The airplane crashed on the runway during takeoff."

If the quotation is followed by other words in the sentence, place a comma inside the closing quotations marks and a period at the end of the sentence.

"The airplane crashed on the runway during takeoff," said the announcer.

In most instances in which a quoted title or expression occurs at the end of a sentence, the period is placed before either the single or double quotation marks.

"The middle school readers were unprepared to understand Bryant's poem 'Thanatopsis.'"

Early book-length adventure stories like *Don Quixote* and *The Three Musketeers* were known as "picaresque novels."

There is an instance in which the final quotation mark would precede the period - if the content of the sentence were about a speech or quote so that the understanding of the meaning would be confused by the placement of the period.

The first thing out of his mouth was "Hi, I'm home."
but
The first line of his speech began "I arrived home to an empty house".

In sentences that are interrogatory or exclamatory, the question mark or exclamation point should be positioned outside the closing quotation marks if the quote itself is a statement or command or cited title.

Who decided to lead us in the recitation of the "Pledge of Allegiance"?

Why was Tillie shaking as she began her recitation, "Once upon a midnight dreary..."?

I was embarrassed when Mrs. White said, "Your slip is showing"!

In sentences that are declarative but the quotation is a question or an exclamation, place the question mark or exclamation point inside the quotation marks.

ENGLISH HIGH SCHOOL

The hall monitor yelled, "Fire! Fire!"

"Fire! Fire!" yelled the hall monitor.

Cory shrieked, "Is there a mouse in the room?" (In this instance, the question supersedes the exclamation.)

Using periods with parentheses or brackets

Place the period inside the parentheses or brackets if they enclose a complete sentence, independent of the other sentences around it.

Stephen Crane was a confirmed alcohol and drug addict. (He admitted as much to other journalists in Cuba.)

If the parenthetical expression is a statement inserted within another statement, the period in the enclosure is omitted.

Mark Twain used the character Indian Joe (He also appeared in *The Adventures of Tom Sawyer*) as a foil for Jim in *The Adventures of Huckleberry Finn*.

When enclosed matter comes at the end of a sentence requiring quotation marks, place the period outside the parentheses or brackets.

"The secretary of state consulted with the ambassador [Albright]."

Using commas

Separate two or more coordinate adjectives modifying the same word; and three or more nouns, phrases, or clauses in a list.

Maggie's hair was dull, dirty, and lice-ridden.

Dickens portrayed the Artful Dodger as skillful pickpocket, loyal follower of Fagin, and defendant of Oliver Twist.

Ellen daydreamed about getting out of the rain, taking a shower, and eating a hot dinner.

In Elizabethan England, Ben Johnson wrote comedy, Christopher Marlowe wrote tragedies, and William Shakespeare composed both.

Use commas to separate antithetical or complimentary expressions from the rest of the sentence.

The veterinarian, not his assistant, would perform the delicate surgery.

The more he knew about her, the less he wished he had known.

Randy hopes to, and probably will, get an appointment to the Naval Academy.

His thorough, though esoteric, scientific research could not easily be understood by high school students.

Using double quotation marks with other punctuation

Quotations - whether words, phrases, or clauses - should be punctuated according to the rules of the grammatical function they serve in the sentence.

The works of Shakespeare, "the Bard of Avon," have been contested as originating with other authors.

"You'll get my money," the old man warned, "when 'Hell freezes over'."

Sheila cited the passage that began "Four score and seven years ago...." (Note the ellipsis followed by an enclosed period.)

"Old Ironsides" inspired the preservation of the U.S.S. Constitution.
Use quotation marks to enclose the titles of shorter works: songs, short poems, short stories, essays, and chapters of books. (See "Using Italics" for punctuating longer titles.)

"The Tell-Tale Heart"   "Casey at the Bat"   "America the Beautiful"

Using semicolons

Use semicolons to separate independent clauses when the second clause is introduced by a transitional adverb. (These clauses may also be written as separate sentences, preferably by placing the adverb within the second sentence.)

The Elizabethans modified the rhyme scheme of the sonnet; thus, it was called the English sonnet.
or
The Elizabethans modified the rhyme scheme of the sonnet. It thus was called the English sonnet.

Use semicolons to separate items in a series that are long and complex or have internal punctuation.

The Italian Renaissance produced masters in the fine arts: Dante Alighieri, author of the *Divine Comedy;* Leonardo da Vinci, painter of *The Last Supper;* and Donatello, sculptor of the *Quattro Coronati*, the four saints.

The leading scorers in the WNBA were Haizhaw Zheng, averaging 23.9 points per game; Lisa Leslie, 22; and Cynthia Cooper, 19.5.

Using colons

Place a colon at the beginning of a list of items. (Note its use in the sentence about Renaissance Italians on the previous page.)

The teacher directed us to compare Faulkner's three symbolic novels: *Absalom, Absalom; As I Lay Dying;* and *Light in August.*

Do **not** use a colon if the list is preceded by a verb.

Three of Faulkner's symbolic novels are *Absalom, Absalom; As I Lay Dying;* and *Light in August.*

Using dashes

Place dashes to denote sudden breaks in thought.

Some periods in literature - the Romantic Age, for example - spanned different time periods in different countries.

Use dashes instead of commas if commas are already used elsewhere in the sentence for amplification or explanation.

The Fireside Poets included three Brahmans - James Russell Lowell, Henry David Wadsworth, Oliver Wendell Holmes - and John Greenleaf Whittier.

Use italics to punctuate the titles of long works of literature, names of periodical publications, musical scores, works of art and motion pictures, television, and radio programs. (When unable to write in italics, students should be instructed to underline in their own writing where italics would be appropriate.)

The Idylls of the King	*Hiawatha*	*The Sound and the Fury*
Mary Poppins	*Newsweek*	*The Nutcracker Suite*

DOMAIN III. READING

COMPETENCY 10.0 UNDERSTAND READING FOR INFORMATION AND UNDERSTANDING

Skill 10.1 Identify and apply distinctions between general statements and specific details.

From general to specific is a continuum. In other words, a term or phrase may be more specific than another term or more general than another one. For example, car is about the middle of the continuum; however, if I mention John Smith's car, it has become more specific. The most specific is a unique item: John Smith's 2007 Lexus, serial #000000000. Cars is a general term that can be narrowed and narrowed and narrowed to suit whatever purposes the writer has for the term. For instance, it would be possible to make a statement about all the cars in the United States, which has been narrowed somewhat from cars. It is, however, a very general term. A thesis statement is typically a generality: All the cars in the United States run on gasoline. Then specifics would be needed to prove that generalization.

In developing a line of reasoning, the choice will be either inductive--going from the specific to the general, or deductive--going from the general to the specific. Inductive reasoning might be as follows: "I tasted a green apple from my grandfather's yard when I was five years old, and it was sour. I also tasted a green apple that my friend brought to school in his lunchbox when I was eight years old, and it was sour. I was in Browns' roadside market and bought some green Granny Smith apples last week, and they were sour." This is a series of specifics. From those specifics, I might draw a conclusion—a generalization—all apples are sour, and I would have reasoned inductively to arrive at that generalization.

The same simplistic argument developed deductively would begin with the generalization: all apples are sour. Then specifics would be offered to support that generalization: the sour green apple I tasted in my grandfather's orchard, the sour green apple in my friend's lunchbox, the Granny Smith apples from the market.

When reasoning is this simple and straightforward, it's easy to follow, but it's also easy to see fallacies. For example, this person hasn't tasted all the green apples in the world; and, in fact, some green apples are not sour. However, it's rarely that easy to see the generalizations and the specifics. In determining whether a point has been proven, it's necessary to do that.

Sometimes generalizations are cited on the assumption that they are commonly accepted and do not need to be supported. An example: all men die sooner or later. Examples wouldn't be needed because that is commonly accepted.

Now, some people might require that "die" be defined, but even the definition of "die" is assumed in this generalization.

Some current generalizations that may assume common acceptance: Providing healthcare for all citizens is the responsibility of the government. All true patriots will support any war the government declares.

Flaws in argument, either intended or unintended, frequently have to do with generalizations and specifics. Are the specifics sufficient to prove the truth of the generality? Does a particular specific actually apply to this generalization? Many times it will depend on definitions. The question can always be asked whether the writer (or speaker) has established the generalization.

Skill 10.2   Draw conclusions from a given passage.

A common fallacy in reasoning is the *post hoc ergo propter hoc* ("after this, therefore because of this"), or the false-cause fallacy. These occur in cause/effect reasoning, either from cause to effect or effect to cause. They happen when an inadequate cause is offered for a particular effect; when the possibility of more than one cause is ignored; and when a connection between a particular cause and a particular effect is not made.

An example of a *post hoc*: Our sales shot up thirty-five percent after we ran that television campaign; therefore the campaign caused the increase in sales. It might have been a cause, of course, but more evidence is needed to prove it.

An example of an inadequate cause for a particular effect: An Iraqi truck driver reported that Saddam Hussein had nuclear weapons; therefore, Saddam Hussein is a threat to world security. More causes are needed to prove the conclusion.

An example of ignoring the possibility of more than one possible cause: John Brown was caught out in a thunderstorm, and his clothes were wet before he was rescued; therefore, he developed influenza the next day because he got wet. Being chilled may have played a role in the illness, but Brown would have had to contract the influenza virus before he would come down with it whether or not he had gotten wet.

An example of failing to make a connection between a particular cause and an effect assigned to it. Anna fell into a putrid pond on Saturday; on Monday she came down with polio; therefore, the polio was caused by the pond. This, of course, is not acceptable unless the polio virus is found in a sample of water from the pond. A connection must be proven.

Skill 10.3   Infer information from a given passage.

See Skill 10.2.

Skill 10.4   Summarize a given passage.

Paraphrasing is the art of rewording text. The goal is to maintain the original purpose of the statement while translating it into your own words. Your newly generated sentence can be longer or shorter than the original. Concentrate on the meaning, not on the words. Do not change concept words, special terms, or proper names. There are numerous ways to effectively paraphrase:

- Change the key words' form or part of speech. Example: "American news **coverage** is frequently **biased** in favor of Western views," becomes "When American journalists **cover** events, they often display a Western **bias**."
- Use synonyms of "relationship words." Look for a relationship word such as **contrast, cause,** or **effect** and replace it with a word that conveys a similar meaning, thus creating a different structure for your sentence. Example: "**Unlike** many cats, Purrdy can sit on command," becomes "Most cats are not able to be trained, **but** Purrdy can sit on command."
- Use synonyms of phrases and words. Example: "The Beatnik writers were relatively unknown at **the start of the decade**," becomes "**Around the early 1950s**, the Beatnik writers were still relatively unknown."
- Change passive voice to active voice or move phrases and modifiers. Example: "Not to be outdone by the third graders, the fourth grade class added a musical medley to their Christmas performance," becomes "The fourth grade class added a musical medley to their Christmas performance to avoid being shown up by the third graders."
- Use reversals or negatives that do not change the meaning of the sentence. Example: "That burger chain is only found in California," becomes "That burger chain is not found on the East Coast."

COMPETENCY 11.0 UNDERSTAND READING FOR LITERARY RESPONSE AND PERSONAL ENJOYMENT

Skill 11.1 Analyze an author's use of figurative language to convey sensory impressions or emotional effects.

Figurative language is also called figures of speech. If all figures of speech that have ever been identified were listed, it would be a very long list. However, for purposes of analyzing poetry, a few are sufficient.

1. Simile: Indirect comparison between two things. "My love is like a red-red rose."
2. Metaphor: Direct comparison between two things. The use of a word or phrase denoting one kind of object or action in place of another to suggest a comparison between them. While poets use them extensively, they are also integral to everyday speech. For example, chairs are said to have "legs" and "arms" although we know that it's humans and other animals that have these appendages.
3. Parallelism: The arrangement of ideas in phrases, sentences, and paragraphs that balance one element with another of equal importance and similar wording. An example from Francis Bacon's *Of Studies:* "Reading maketh a full man, conference a ready man, and writing an exact man."
4. Personification: Human characteristics are attributed to an inanimate object, an abstract quality, or animal. Examples: John Bunyan wrote characters named Death, Knowledge, Giant Despair, Sloth, and Piety in his *Pilgrim's Progress.* The metaphor of an arm of a chair is a form of personification.
5. Euphemism: The substitution of an agreeable or inoffensive term for one that might offend or suggest something unpleasant. Many euphemisms are used to refer to death to avoid using the real word such as "passed away," "crossed over," or nowadays "passed."
6. Hyperbole: Deliberate exaggeration for effect or comic effect. An example from Shakespeare's *The Merchant of Venice*:
    > Why, if two gods should play some heavenly match
    > And on the wager lay two earthly women,
    > And Portia one, there must be something else
    > Pawned with the other, for the poor rude world
    > Hath not her fellow.

7. Climax: A number of phrases or sentences are arranged in ascending order of rhetorical forcefulness. Example from Melville's *Moby Dick*:

   All that most maddens and torments; all that stirs up the lees of things; all truth with malice in it; all that cracks the sinews and cakes the brain; all the subtle demonisms of life and thought; all evil, to crazy Ahab, were visibly personified and made practically assailable in Moby Dick.

8. Bathos: A ludicrous attempt to portray pathos—that is, to evoke pity, sympathy, or sorrow. It may result from inappropriately dignifying the commonplace, elevated language to describe something trivial, or greatly exaggerated pathos.

9. Oxymoron: A contradiction in terms deliberately employed for effect. It is usually seen in a qualifying adjective whose meaning is contrary to that of the noun it modifies such as wise folly.

10. Alliteration: The repetition of consonant sounds in two or more neighboring words or syllables. In its simplest form, it reinforces one or two consonant sounds. Example: Shakespeare's Sonnet #12:
    When I do **c**ount the **c**lock that **t**ells the **t**ime.
    Some poets have used more complex patterns of alliteration by creating consonants both at the beginning of words and at the beginning of stressed syllables within words. Example: Shelley's "Stanzas Written in Dejection Near Naples:"
    *The **C**ity's voi**c**e it**s**elf is **s**oft like **S**olitude's*

11. Onomatopoeia: The naming of a thing or action by a vocal imitation of the sound associated with it such as buzz or hiss or the use of words whose sound suggests the sense. A good example: from "The Brook" by Tennyson:

    I chatter over stony ways,
    In little sharps and trebles,
    I bubble into eddying bays,
    I babble on the pebbles.

Poets use figures of speech to sharpen the effect and meaning of their poems and to help readers see things in ways they have never seen them before. Marianne Moore observed that a fir tree has "an emerald turkey-foot at the top." Her poem makes us aware of something we probably had never noticed before. The sudden recognition of the likeness yields pleasure in the reading. Figurative language allows for the statement of truths that more literal language cannot. Skillfully used, a figure of speech will help the reader see more clearly and to focus upon particulars. Figures of speech add many dimensions of richness to our reading and understanding of a poem; they also allow many opportunities for worthwhile analysis. The approach to take in analyzing a poem on the basis of its figures of speech is to ask the question: What does it do for the poem? Does it underscore meaning? Does it intensify understanding? Does it increase the intensity of our response?

Skill 11.2 **Analyze an author's use of language to create irony.**

Irony means expressing something other than and particularly opposite the literal meaning, such as words of praise when blame is intended. In poetry, it is often used as a sophisticated or resigned awareness of contrast between what is and what ought to be and expresses a controlled pathos without sentimentality. It is a form of indirection that avoids overt praise or censure. An early example: the Greek comic character Eiron, a clever underdog who by his wit repeatedly triumphs over the boastful character Alazon.

Skill 11.3 **Interpret the use of rhythm, rhyme, or imagery to evoke a response in the reader.**

- **Rhythm:** Writing can be compared to dancing, in that it is a balance between words and flow. Rhythm refers to the harmony between the words chosen and the smoothness, rapidity, or disjointedness of the way those words are written. Sentences that are too long may disrupt the rhythm of a piece. Reading text out loud is an easy way to impart understanding of literary rhythm.
- **Rhyme:** Writing with rhyme can be especially effective on reader response. Think about the success Dr. Seuss had with his rhyming style. Rhyme is tricky though; used ineffectively or unnecessarily, it can break up the entire rhythm of the piece or fog the reader's understanding of it. Rhyme should be used when it is purely beneficial to the format of the piece. Make sure it is not forcing you to use more words than needed and that each verse is moving the story forward.
- **Diction:** Diction is simply the right word in the right spot for the right purpose. The hallmark of a great writer is precise, unusual, and memorable diction.
- **Imagery:** Imagery involves engaging one or more of your five senses in your writing. An author might use imagery to give the reader a greater, more real picture of the scene they are trying to depict. Imagery may conjure up a past experience that the reader had (the smell of the ocean, the feeling of their childhood blanket) thereby enriching their mental picture of the scene.

Skill 11.4   Analyze the use of language to portray character, develop plot, or create a mood in a given passage.

It's no accident that **plot** is sometimes called action. If the plot does not *move*, the story quickly dies. Therefore, the successful writer of stories uses a wide variety of active verbs in creative and unusual ways. If readers are kept on their toes by the movement of the story, the experience of reading it will be pleasurable. Readers will probably want to read more of this author's work. Careful, unique, and unusual choices of active verbs will bring about that effect. William Faulkner is a good example of a successful writer whose stories are lively and memorable because of his use of unusual active verbs. In analyzing the development of plot, it's wise to look at the verbs. However, the development of believable conflicts is also vital. If there is no conflict, there is no story. What devices does a writer use to develop the conflicts, and are they real and believable?

Character is portrayed in many ways: description of physical characteristics, dialogue, interior monologue, the thoughts of the character, the attitudes of other characters toward this one, etc. Descriptive language depends on the ability to recreate a sensory experience for the reader.

If the description of the character's appearance is a visual one, then the reader must be able to *see* the character. What's the shape of the nose? What color are the eyes? How tall or how short is this character? Thin or chubby? How does the character move? How does the character walk? Terms must be chosen that will create a picture for the reader. It's not enough to say the eyes are blue, for example. What blue? Often the color of eyes is compared to something else to enhance the readers' ability to visualize the character. A good test of characterization is the level of emotional involvement of the reader in the character. If the reader is to become involved, the description must provide an actual experience—seeing, smelling, hearing, tasting, or feeling.

Dialogue will reflect characteristics. Is it clipped? Is it highly dialectic? Does a character use a lot of colloquialisms? The ability to portray the speech of a character can make or break a story. The kind of person the character is in the mind of the reader is dependent on impressions created by description and dialogue. How do other characters feel about this one as revealed by their treatment of the character, their discussions of the character with each other, or their overt descriptions of the character. For example, "John, of course, can't be trusted with another person's possessions." In analyzing a story, it's useful to discuss the devices used to produce character.

Setting may be visual, temporal, psychological, or social. Descriptive words are often used here also. In Edgar Allan Poe's description of the house in "The Fall of the House of Usher" as the protagonist/narrator approaches it, the air of dread and gloom that pervades the story is caught in the setting and sets the stage for the story. A setting may also be symbolic, as it is in Poe's story, where the house is a symbol of the family that lives in it. As the house disintegrates, so does the family.

The language used in all of these aspects of a story—plot, character, and setting—work together to create the **mood** of a story. Poe's first sentence establishes the mood of the story: "During the whole of a dull, dark, and soundless day in the autumn of the year, when the clouds hung oppressively low in the heavens, I had been passing alone, on horseback, through a singularly dreary tract of country; and at length found myself, as the shades of the evening drew on, within view of the melancholy House of Usher."

COMPETENCY 12.0 UNDERSTAND READING FOR CRITICAL ANALYSIS AND EVALUATION

Skill 12.1 Distinguish between fact and opinion in a passage.

Facts are statements that are verifiable. Opinions are statements that must be supported in order to be accepted. Facts are used to support opinions. For example, "Jane is a bad girl" is an opinion. However, "Jane hit her sister with a baseball bat" is a *fact* upon which the opinion is based.

Judgments are opinions—decisions or declarations based on observation or reasoning that express approval or disapproval. Facts report what has happened or exists and come from observation, measurement, or calculation. Facts can be tested and verified whereas opinions and judgments cannot. They can only be supported with facts.

Most statements cannot be so clearly distinguished. "I believe that Jane is a bad girl" is a fact. The speaker knows what he or she believes. However, it obviously includes a judgment that could be disputed by another person who might believe otherwise. Judgments are not usually so firm. They are, rather, plausible opinions that provoke thought or lead to factual development.

Conclusions are drawn as a result of a line of reasoning. Inductive reasoning begins with particulars and reasons to a generality. For example: "When I was a child, I bit into a green apple from my grandfather's orchard, and it was sour" (specific fact #1). "I once bought green apples from a roadside vendor, and when I bit into one, it was sour" (specific fact #2). "My grocery store had a sale on green Granny Smith apples last week, and I bought several only to find that they were sour when I bit into one" (specific fact #3). Conclusion: All green apples are sour. While this is an example of inductive reasoning, it is also an example of the weakness of such reasoning. The speaker has not tasted all the green apples in the world, and there very well may be some apples that are green that are not sour.

Deductive reasoning begins with the generalization: "Green apples are sour" and supports that generalization with the specifics.

An inference is drawn from an inductive line of reasoning. The most famous one is "all men are mortal," which is drawn from the observation that everyone a person knows has died or will die and that everyone else concurs in that judgment. It is assumed to be true and for that reason can be used as proof of another conclusion: "Socrates is a man; therefore, he will die."

Sometimes the inference is assumed to be proven when it is not reliably true in all cases, such as "aging brings physical and mental infirmity." Reasoning from that *inference*, many companies will not hire anyone above a certain age.

Actually, being old does not necessarily imply physical and/or mental impairment. There are many instances where elderly people have made important contributions that require exceptional ability.

Skill 12.2 Judge the relevance, importance, or sufficiency of facts or examples in a writer's argument.

An argument is a generalization that is proven or supported with facts. If the facts are not accurate, the generalization remains unproven. Using inaccurate "facts" to support an argument is called a *fallacy* in reasoning.

Some factors to consider in judging whether the facts used to support an argument are accurate are as follow:

1. Are the facts current or are they out of date? For example, if the proposition "birth defects in babies born to drug-using mothers are increasing," then the data must include the latest that is available.
2. Another important factor to consider in judging the accuracy of a fact is its source. Where were the data obtained, and are those sources reliable?
3. The calculations on which the facts are based may be unreliable. It's a good idea to run one's own calculations before using a piece of derived information.

Even facts that are true and have a sharp impact on the argument may not be relevant to the case at hand.

1. Health statistics from an entire state may have no relevance, or little relevance, to a particular county or zip code. Statistics from an entire country cannot be used to prove very much about a particular state or county.
2. An analogy can be useful in making a point, but the comparison must match up in all characteristics or it will not be relevant. Analogy should be used very carefully. It is often just as likely to destroy an argument as it is to strengthen it.

The importance or significance of a fact may not be sufficient to strengthen an argument. For example, of the millions of immigrants in the U.S., using a single family to support a solution to the immigration problem will not make much difference overall even though those single-example arguments are often used to support one approach or another. They may achieve a positive reaction, but they will not prove that one solution is better than another. If enough cases were cited from a variety of geographical locations, the information might be significant.

How much is enough? Generally speaking, three strong supporting facts are sufficient to establish the thesis of an argument. For example:

Conclusion: All green apples are sour.

- When I was a child, I bit into a green apple from my grandfather's orchard, and it was sour.
- I once bought green apples from a roadside vendor, and when I bit into one, it was sour.
- My grocery store had a sale on green Granny Smith apples last week, and I bought several only to find that they were sour when I bit into one.

The fallacy in the above argument is that the sample was insufficient. A more exhaustive search of literature, etc., will probably turn up some green apples that are not sour.

Sometimes more than three arguments are too many. On the other hand, it's not unusual to hear public speakers, particularly politicians, who will cite a long litany of facts to support their positions.

Skill 12.3   Assess the credibility or objectivity of various sources of information.

When evaluating sources, first go through this checklist to make sure the source is even worth reading:

- Title (How relevant is it to your topic?)
- Date (How current is the source?)
- Organization (What institution is this source coming from?)
- Length (How in depth does it go?)

Check for signs of bias:

- Does the author or publisher have political ties or religious views that could affect their objectivity?
- Is the author or publisher associated with any special-interest groups that might only see one side of an issue, such as Greenpeace or the National Rifle Association?
- How fairly does the author treat opposing views?
- Does the language of the piece show signs of bias?

Keep an open mind while reading, and don't let opposing viewpoints prevent you from absorbing the text. Remember that you are not judging the author's work, you are examining its assumptions, assessing its evidence and weighing its conclusions.

Skill 12.4 Determine how the author uses tone and style to present a particular point of view.

A piece of writing is an integrated whole. It's not enough to just look at the various parts; the total entity must be examined. It should be considered in two ways:
As an emotional expression of the author
As an artistic embodiment of a meaning or set of meanings.

This is what is sometimes called "**tone**" in literary criticism.

It's important to remember that the writer is a human being with his or her own individual bents, prejudices, and emotions. A writer is telling the readers about the world as he or she sees it and will give voice to certain phases of his or her own personality. By reading a writer's works, we can know the personal qualities and emotions of the writer embodied in the work itself. However, it's important to remember that not all the writer's characteristics will be revealed in a single work.

People change and may have very different attitudes at different times in their lives. Sometimes, a writer will be influenced by a desire to have a piece of work accepted or to appear to be current or by the interests and desires of the readers that he or she hopes to attract. It can destroy a work or make it less than it might be. Sometimes the best works are not commercial successes in the generation when they were written, but are discovered at a later time and by another generation.

There are three places to look for tone:
Choice of form: tragedy or comedy; melodrama or farce; parody or sober lyric.
Choice of materials: characters that have human qualities that are attractive; others that are repugnant. What an author shows in a setting will often indicate what his/her interests are.
The writer's interpretation: it may be explicit—telling us how he/she feels.
The writer's implicit interpretations: the author's feelings for a character come through in the description. For example, the use of "smirked" instead of "laughed"; "minced," "stalked," "marched," instead of walked.

The reader is asked to join the writer in the feelings expressed about the world and the things that happen in it. The tone of a piece of writing is important in a critical review of it.

Style, in literature, means a distinctive manner of expression and applies to all levels of language, beginning at the phonemic level—word choices, alliteration, assonance, etc.; the syntactic level—length of sentences, choice of structure and phraseology, patterns, etc.; and extends even beyond the sentence to paragraphs and chapters. What is distinctive about this writer's use of these elements?

In Steinbeck's *Grapes of Wrath*, for instance, the style is quite simple in the narrative sections and the dialogue is in dialect. Because the emphasis is on the story—the narrative—his style is straightforward, for the most part. He just tells the story.

However, there are chapters where he varies his style. He uses symbols and combines them with description that is realistic. He sometimes shifts to a crisp, repetitive pattern to underscore the beeping and speeding of cars. By contrast, some of those chapters are lyrical, almost poetic.

These shifts in style reflect the attitude of the author toward the subject matter. He intends to make a statement, and he uses a variety of styles to strengthen the point.

COMPETENCY 13.0 UNDERSTAND THE USE OF METACOGNITIVE TECHNIQUES IN READING COMPREHENSION

Skill 13.1 Analyze the purposes and characteristics of reading techniques and strategies.

The question to be asked first when approaching a reading task is what is my objective? What do I want to achieve from this reading? How will I use the information I gain from this reading? Do I only need to grasp the gist of the piece? Do I need to know the line of reasoning—not only the thesis but the subpoints? Will I be reporting important and significant details orally or in a written document?

A written document can be expected to have a thesis—either expressed or derived. To discover the thesis, the reader needs to ask what point the writer intended to make? The writing can also be expected to be organized in some logical way and to have subpoints that support or establish that the thesis is valid. It is also reasonable to expect that there will be details or examples that will support the subpoints. Knowing this, the reader can make a decision about reading techniques required for the purpose that has already been established.

If the reader only needs to know the gist of a written document, speed-reading skimming techniques may be sufficient by using the forefinger, moving the eyes down the page, picking up the important statements in each paragraph and deducing mentally that this piece is about such-and-such. If the reader needs to a little better grasp of how the writer achieved his/her purpose in the document, a quick and cursory glance—a skimming—of each paragraph will yield what the subpoints are, the topic sentences of the paragraphs, and how the thesis is developed, yielding a greater understanding of the author's purpose and method of development.

In-depth reading requires the scrutiny of each phrase and sentence with care, looking for the thesis first of all and then the topic sentences in the paragraphs that provide the development of the thesis, also looking for connections such as transitional devices that provide clues to the direction the reasoning is taking.

Sometimes rereading is necessary in order to make use of a piece of writing for an oral or written report upon a document. If this is the purpose of reading it, the first reading should provide a map for the rereading or second reading. The second time through should follow this map, and those points that are going to be used in a report or analysis will be focused upon on more carefully. Some new understandings may occur in this rereading, and it may become apparent that the "map" that was derived from the first reading will need to be adjusted. If this rereading is for the purpose of writing an analysis or using material for a report, either highlighting or note-taking is advisable.

Skill 13.2 Analyze thinking strategies related to reading comprehension.

Reading literature involves a reciprocal interaction between the reader and the text.

Types of responses

Emotional

Readers can identify with the characters and situations so as to project themselves into the story. Readers feel a sense of satisfaction by associating aspects of their own lives with the people, places, and events in the literature. Emotional responses are observed in readers' verbal and non-verbal reactions - laughter, comments on its effects, and retelling or dramatizing the action.

Interpretive

Interpretive responses result in inferences about character development, setting, or plot; analysis of style elements - metaphor, simile, allusion, rhythm, tone; outcomes derivable from information provided in the narrative; and assessment of the author's intent. Interpretive responses are made verbally or in writing.

Critical

Critical responses involve making value judgments about the quality of a piece of literature. Reactions to the effectiveness of the writer's style and language use are observed through discussion and written reactions.

Evaluative

Some reading response-theory researchers also add a response that considers the readers considerations of such factors as how well the piece of literature represents its genre, how well it reflects the social/ethical mores of society, and how well the author has approached the subject for freshness and slant.

Middle school readers will exhibit both emotional and interpretive responses. Naturally, making interpretive responses depends on the degree of knowledge students have of literary elements. Children's being able to say why a particular book was boring or why a particular poem made them sad evidences critical reactions on a fundamental level. Adolescents in ninth and tenth grades should begin to make critical responses by addressing the specific language and genre characteristics of literature.

Evaluative responses are harder to detect and are rarely made by any but a few advanced high school students. However, if teachers know what to listen for, they can recognize evaluative responses and incorporate them into discussions.

For example, "I don't understand why that character is doing that," is an interpretive response to character motivation. However, "What good is that action?" is an evaluative response that should be explored in terms of "What good should it do and why isn't that positive action happening?"

An emotional response would be "I almost broke into a sweat when he was describing the heat in the burning house." An interpretive response says, "The author used descriptive adjectives to bring his setting to life." "The author's use of descriptive language contributes to the success of the narrative and maintains reader interest through the whole story" is a critical response. Wonder why the author allowed the grandmother in the story to die in the fire is an evaluative response.

Levels of response

The levels of reader response will depend largely on readers' level of social, psychological, and intellectual development. Most middle school students have progressed beyond merely involving themselves in the story to be able to retell the events in some logical sequence or to describe the feeling that the story evoked. They are aware to some degree that the feeling evoked was the result of a careful manipulation of good elements of fiction writing. They may not explain that awareness as successfully as high school students, but they are beginning to grasp the concepts and not just the personal reactions. They are beginning to differentiate between responding to the story itself and responding a literary creation.

Skill 13.3 Apply strategies to determine the denotative and connotative meanings of words in given contexts.

To effectively teach language, it is necessary to understand that, as human beings acquire language, they realize that words have <u>denotative</u> and <u>connotative</u> meanings. Generally, denotation points to things and connotation deals with mental suggestions that the words convey. The word *skunk* has a denotative meaning if the speaker can point to the actual animal as he speaks the word and intends the word to identify the animal. *Skunk* has connotative meaning depending upon the tone of delivery, the socially acceptable attitudes about the animal, and the speaker's personal feelings about the animal.

Informative connotations

Informative connotations are definitions agreed upon by the society in which the learner operates. A *skunk* is "a black and white mammal of the weasel family with a pair of perineal glands which secrete a pungent odor." The *Merriam Webster Collegiate Dictionary* adds "...and offensive" odor. Identification of the color, species, and glandular characteristics are informative. The interpretation of the odor as *offensive* is affective.

Affective connotations

Affective connotations are the personal feelings a word arouses. A child who has no personal experience with a skunk and its odor or has had a pet skunk will feel differently about the word *skunk* than a child who has smelled the spray or been conditioned vicariously to associate offensiveness with the animal denoted *skunk*. The very fact that our society views a skunk as an animal to be avoided will affect the child's interpretation of the word. In fact, it is not necessary for one to have actually seen a skunk (that is, have a denotative understanding) to use the word in either connotative expression. For example, one child might call another child a skunk, connoting an unpleasant reaction (affective use) or, seeing another small black and white animal, call it a skunk based on the definition (informative use).

Using connotations

In everyday language, we attach affective meanings to words unconsciously; we exercise more conscious control of informative connotations. In the process of language development, the leaner must come not only to grasp the definitions of words but also to become more conscious of the affective connotations and how his listeners process these connotations. Gaining this conscious control over language makes it possible to use language appropriately in various situations and to evaluate its uses in literature and other forms of communication.

The manipulation of language for a variety of purposes is the goal of language instruction. Advertisers and satirists are especially conscious of the effect word choice has on their audiences. By evoking the proper responses from readers/listeners, we can prompt them to take action.

Choice of the medium through which the message is delivered to the receiver is a significant factor in controlling language. Spoken language relies as much on the gestures, facial expression, and tone of voice of the speaker as on the words he speaks. Slapstick comics can evoke laughter without speaking a word. Young children use body language overtly, and older children more subtly, to convey messages. These refinings of body language are paralleled by an ability to recognize and apply the nuances of spoken language. To work strictly with the written word, the writer must use words to imply the body language.

DOMAIN IV. LANGUAGE AND LITERATURE

A. Language

COMPETENCY 14.0 UNDERSTAND THE HISTORICAL, SOCIAL, CULTURAL, AND TECHNOLOGICAL INFLUENCES SHAPING THE ENGLISH LANGUAGE

Skill 14.1 Analyze the significance of historical events that have influenced the development of the English language.

Language, though an innate human ability, must be learned. Thus, the acquisition and use of language is subject to many influences on the learner. Linguists agree that language is first a vocal system of word symbols that enable a human to communicate his feelings, thoughts, and desires to other human beings. Language was instrumental in the development of all cultures and is influenced by the changes in these societies.

Historical influences

English is an Indo-European language that evolved through several periods. The origin of English dates to the settlement of the British Isles in the fifth and sixth centuries by Germanic tribes called the Angles, Saxons, and Jutes. The original Britons spoke a Celtic tongue while the Angles spoke a Germanic dialect. Modern English derives from the speech of the Anglo-Saxons who imposed not only their language but also their social customs and laws on their new land. From the fifth to the tenth century, Britain's language was the tongue we now refer to as Old English. During the next four centuries, the many French attempts at English conquest introduced many French words to English. However, the grammar and syntax of the language remained Germanic.

Middle English, most evident in the writings of Geoffrey Chaucer, dates loosely from 1066 to 1509. William Caxton brought the printing press to England in 1474 and increased literacy. Old English words required numerous inflections to indicate noun cases and plurals as well as verb conjugations. Middle English continued the use of many inflections and pronunciations that treated these inflections as separately pronounced syllables. English in 1300 would have been written "Olde Anglishe" with the *e*'s at the ends of the words pronounced as our short *a* vowel. Even adjectives had plural inflections: "long dai" became "longe daies" pronounced "long-a day-as." Spelling was phonetic, thus every vowel had multiple pronunciations, a fact that continues to affect the language.

Modern English dates from the introduction of The Great Vowels Shift because it created guidelines for spelling and pronunciation. Before the printing press, books were copied laboriously by hand; the language was subject to the individual interpretation of the scribes. Printers and subsequently lexicographers like Samuel Johnson and America's Noah Webster influenced the guidelines. As reading matter was mass produced, the reading public was forced to adopt the speech and writing habits developed by those who wrote and printed books.

Despite many students' insistence to the contrary, Shakespeare's writings are in Modern English. It is important to stress to students that language, like customs, morals, and other social factors, is constantly subject to change. Immigration, inventions, and cataclysmic events change language as much as any other facet of life affected by these changes. The domination of one race or nation over others can change a language significantly. Beginning with the colonization of the New World, English and Spanish became dominant languages in the Western hemisphere. American English today is somewhat different in pronunciation and sometimes vocabulary from British English. The British call a truck a "lorry;" baby carriages a "pram," short for "perambulator;" and an elevator a "lift." There are very few syntactical differences, and even the tonal qualities that were once so clearly different are converging.

Though Modern English is less complex than Middle English, having lost many unnecessary inflections, it is still considered difficult to learn because of its many exceptions to the rules. It has, however, become the world's dominant language by reason of the great political, military, and social power of England from the fifteenth to the nineteenth century and of America in the twentieth century.

Modern inventions - the telephone, phonograph, radio, television, and motion pictures - have especially affected English pronunciation. Regional dialects, once a hindrance to clear understanding, have fewer distinct characteristics. The speakers from different parts of the United States of America can be identified by their accents, but more and more as educators and media personalities stress uniform pronunciations and proper grammar, the differences are diminishing.

The English language has a more extensive vocabulary than any other language. Ours is a language of synonyms, words borrowed from other languages, and coined words - many of them introduced by the rapid expansion of technology.

It is important for students to understand that language is in constant flux. Emphasis should be placed on learning and using language for specific purposes and audiences. Negative criticism of a student's errors in word choice or sentence structures will inhibit creativity. Positive criticism that suggests ways to enhance communication skills will encourage exploration.

Skill 14.2   Relate English derivatives and borrowings, including slang terms, to their origins in other languages.

Just as countries and families have histories, so do words. Knowing and understanding the origin of a word, where it has been used down through the years, and the history of its meaning as it has changed is an important component of the writing and language teacher's tool kit. Never in the history of the English language, or of any other language for that matter, have the forms and meanings of words changed so rapidly. When America was settled originally, immigration from many countries made it a "melting pot." Immigration accelerated rapidly within the first hundred years, resulting in pockets of language throughout the country. When trains began to make transportation available and affordable, individuals from those various pockets came in contact with each other, shared vocabularies, and attempted to converse. From that time forward, every generation brought the introduction of a technology that made language interchange not only more possible, but also more important.

Radio began the trend to standardize dialects. A Bostonian might not be understood by a native of Louisiana who might not be interested in turning the dial to hear the news, or a drama, or the advertisements of the vendors that had a vested interest in being heard and understood. Soap and soup producers knew a goldmine when they saw it and created a market for radio announcers and actors who spoke without a pronounced dialect. In return, listeners began to hear the English language in a dialect very different from the one they spoke, and, as it settled into their thinking processes, it eventually made its way to their tongues, and spoken English began to lose some of its local peculiarities. It has been a slow process, but most Americans can easily understand other Americans no matter where they come from. They can even converse with a native of Great Britain with little difficulty. The introduction of television carried the evolution further, as did the explosion of electronic communicating devices over the past fifty years.

An excellent example of the changes that have occurred in English is a comparison of Shakespeare's original works with modern translations. Without help, twenty-first-century Americans are unable to read the *Folio*. On the other hand, teachers must constantly be mindful of the vocabularies and etymologies of their students, who are on the receiving end of the escalation brought about by technology and increased global influence and contact.

Skill 14.3 Analyze regional and social variations in language in the United States.

Geographical influences

Dialect differences are basically in pronunciation. Bostoners say "pahty" for "party" and Southerners blend words like "you all" into "y'all." Besides the dialect differences already mentioned, the biggest geographical factors in American English stem from minor word choice variances. Depending on the region where you live, when you order a carbonated, syrupy beverage most generically called a soft drink, you might ask for a "soda" in the South, or a "pop" in the Midwest. If you order a soda in New York, then you will get a scoop of ice cream in your soft drink, while in other areas you would have to ask for a "float."

Social influences

Social influences are mostly those imposed by family, peer groups, and mass media. The economic and educational levels of families determine the properness of language use. Exposure to adults who encourage and assist children to speak well enhances readiness for other areas of learning and contributes to a child's ability to communicate his needs. Historically, children learned language, speech patterns, and grammar from members of their extended family just as they learned the rules of conduct within their family unit and community. In modern times, the mother in a nuclear family became the dominant force in influencing the child's development. With increasing social changes, many children are not receiving the proper guidance in all areas of development, especially language.

Those who are fortunate to be in educational day care programs like Head Start or in certified preschools develop better language skills than those whose care is entrusted to untrained care providers. Once a child enters elementary school, he is also greatly influenced by peer language. This peer influence becomes significant in adolescence as the use of teen jargon gives teenagers a sense of identity within his chosen group(s) and independence from the influence of adults. In some lower socio-economic groups, children use Standard English in school and street language outside the school. Some children of immigrant families become bilingual by necessity if no English is spoken in the home.

Research has shown a strong correlation between socio-economic characteristics and all areas of intellectual development. Traditional paper measurement instruments rely on verbal ability to establish intelligence. Research findings and test scores reflect that children, reared in nuclear families who provide cultural experiences and individual attention, become more language proficient than those who are denied that security and stimulation.

Personal influences

The rate of physical development and identifiable language disabilities also influence language development. Nutritional deficiencies, poor eyesight, and conditions such as stuttering or dyslexia can inhibit a child's ability to master language. Unless diagnosed early they can hamper communication into adulthood. These conditions also stymie the development of self-confidence and, therefore, the willingness to learn or to overcome the handicap. Children should receive proper diagnosis and positive corrective instruction.

In adolescence, the child's choice of role models and his decision about his future determine the growth of identity. Rapid physical and emotional changes and the stress of coping with the pressure of sexual awareness make concentration on any educational pursuits difficult. The easier the transition from childhood to adulthood, the better the competence will be in all learning areas.

Middle school and junior high school teachers are confronted by a student body ranging from fifth graders who are still childish to eighth or ninth graders who, if not in fact at least in their minds, are young adults. Teachers must approach language instruction as a social development tool with more emphasis on vocabulary acquisition, reading improvement, and speaking/writing skills. High school teachers can deal with the more formalized instruction of grammar, usage, and literature for older adolescents whose social development allows them to pay more attention to studies that will improve their chances for a better adult life.

As a tool, language must have relevance to the student's real environment. Many high schools have developed practical English classes for business/ vocational students whose specific needs are determined by their desire to enter the workforce upon graduation. More emphasis is placed upon accuracy of mechanics and understanding verbal and written directions because these are skills desired by employers. Writing résumés, completing forms, reading policy and operations manuals, and generating reports are some of the desired skills. Emphasis is placed on higher level thinking skills, including inferential thinking and literary interpretation, in literature classes for college-bound students.

COMPETENCY 15.0 UNDERSTAND FUNDAMENTAL CONCEPTS RELATING TO THE STRUCTURE, ACQUISITION, USE, AND ANALYSIS OF LANGUAGE

Skill 15.1 Distinguish structural features of languages.

It is assumed that any candidate for a certificate to teach language arts will have a thorough understanding of English grammar.

Test Format

Most teacher tests of professional knowledge of grammar will consist of either multiple-choice questions that require selecting an example of correct sentence structure, grammar, punctuation, capitalization, spelling, or usage from four or five options and/or an essay question that requires application of all grammatical skills. These questions may also require knowledge of traditional and non-traditional approaches to the study of grammar. Familiarity with terms such as prescriptive/ traditional, transformational/ generative, and structural grammars and recognition of their differences in the approaches to learning grammar is to be expected.

Areas of Review

To review rules of grammar in more depth, use any high school/college grammar textbook. (Warriner's books or Strunk and White's *Elements of Style* are highly recommended.)

SYNTAX

Sentence completeness

Avoid fragments and run-on sentences. Recognition of sentence elements necessary to make a complete thought, proper use of independent and dependent clauses (see *Use correct coordination and subordination*), and proper punctuation will correct such errors.

Sentence structure

Recognize simple, compound, complex, and compound-complex sentences. Use dependent (subordinate) and independent clauses correctly to create these sentence structures.

Simple Joyce wrote a letter.
Compound Joyce wrote a letter, and Dot drew a picture.
Complex While Joyce wrote a letter, Dot drew a picture.
Compound/Complex When Mother asked the girls to demonstrate their new-found skills, Joyce wrote a letter, and Dot drew a picture.

Note: Do **not** confuse compound sentence elements with compound sentences.

    Simple sentence with compound subject
        Joyce and Dot wrote letters.
        The girl in row three and the boy next to her were passing notes across the aisle.

    Simple sentence with compound predicate
        Joyce wrote letters and drew pictures.
        The captain of the high school debate team graduated with honors and studied broadcast journalism in college.

    Simple sentence with compound object of preposition
        Coleen graded the students' essays for style and mechanical accuracy.

Parallelism

Recognize parallel structures using phrases (prepositional, gerund, participial, and infinitive) and omissions from sentences that create the lack of parallelism.

Prepositional phrase/single modifier

Incorrect: Coleen ate the ice cream with enthusiasm and hurriedly.
Correct: Coleen ate the ice cream with enthusiasm and in a hurry.
Correct: Coleen ate the ice cream enthusiastically and hurriedly.

Participial phrase/infinitive phrase

Incorrect: After hiking for hours and to sweat profusely, Joe sat down to rest and drinking water.
Correct: After hiking for hours and sweating profusely, Joe sat down to rest and drink water.

Recognition of dangling modifiers

Dangling phrases are attached to sentence parts in such a way they create ambiguity and incorrectness of meaning.

Participial phrase

Incorrect: Hanging from her skirt, Dot tugged at a loose thread.
Correct: Dot tugged at a loose thread hanging from her skirt.

Incorrect: Relaxing in the bathtub, the telephone rang.
Correct: While I was relaxing in the bathtub, the telephone rang.

Infinitive phrase

Incorrect: To improve his behavior, the dean warned Fred.
Correct: The dean warned Fred to improve his behavior.

Prepositional phrase

Incorrect: On the floor, Father saw the dog eating table scraps.
Correct: Father saw the dog eating table scraps on the floor.

Recognition of syntactical redundancy or omission

These errors occur when superfluous words have been added to a sentence or key words have been omitted from a sentence.

Redundancy

Incorrect: Joyce made sure that when her plane arrived that she retrieved all of her luggage.
Correct: Joyce made sure that when her plane arrived she retrieved all of her luggage.

Incorrect: He was a mere skeleton of his former self.
Correct: He was a skeleton of his former self.

Omission

Incorrect: Dot opened her book, recited her textbook, and answered the teacher's subsequent question.
Correct: Dot opened her book, recited from the textbook, and answered the teacher's subsequent question.

Avoidance of double negatives

This error occurs from positioning two negatives that, in fact, cancel each other in meaning.

>Incorrect: Harold couldn't not care less whether he passes this class.
>Correct: Harold couldn't care less whether he passes this class.

>Incorrect: Dot didn't have no double negatives in her paper.
>Correct: Dot didn't have any double negatives in her paper.

Correct use of coordination and subordination

Connect independent clauses with the coordinating conjunctions - *and*, *but*, *or*, *for*, or *nor* - when their content is of equal importance. Use subordinating conjunctions - although, because, before, if, since, though, until, when, whenever, where - and relative pronouns - that, who, whom, which - to introduce clauses that express ideas that are subordinate to main ideas expressed in independent clauses. (See *Sentence Structure* above.)
Be sure to place the conjunctions so that they express the proper relationship between ideas (cause/effect, condition, time, space).

>Incorrect: Because mother scolded me, I was late.
>Correct: Mother scolded me because I was late.

>Incorrect: The sun rose after the fog lifted.
>Correct: The fog lifted after the sun rose.

Notice that placement of the conjunction can completely change the meaning of the sentence. Main emphasis is shifted by the change.

>Although Jenny was pleased, the teacher was disappointed.
>Although the teacher was disappointed, Jenny was pleased.

>The boys who had written the essay won the contest.
>The boys who won the contest had written the essay.

Note: While not syntactically incorrect, the second sentence makes it appear that the boys won the contest for something else before they wrote the essay.

GRAMMAR

Subject-verb agreement

A verb agrees in number with its subject. Making them agree relies on the ability to properly identify the subject.

> One of the boys *was playing* too rough.
> No one in the class, not the teacher nor the students, was listening to the message from the intercom.
> The candidates, including a grandmother and a teenager, are debating some controversial issues.

If two singular subjects are connected by *and* the verb must be plural.

> A *man* and his *dog* were jogging on the beach.

If two singular subjects are connected by *or* or *nor*, a singular verb is required.

> Neither Dot nor Joyce has missed a day of school this year.
> Either Fran or Paul is missing.

If one singular subject and one plural subject are connected by *or* or *nor*, the verb agrees with the subject nearest to the verb.

> Neither the coach nor the players were able to sleep on the bus.

If the subject is a collective noun, its sense of number in the sentence determines the verb: singular if the noun represents a group or unit and plural if the noun represents individuals.

> The House of Representatives has adjourned for the holidays.

> The House of Representatives has failed to reach agreement on the subject of adjournment.

Use of verbs (tense)

Present tense is used to express that which is currently happening or is always true.

> Randy is playing the piano.
>
> Randy plays the piano like a pro.

Past tense is used to express action that occurred in a past time.

> Randy learned to play the piano when he was six years old.

Future tense is used to express action or a condition of future time.

> Randy will probably earn a music scholarship.

Present perfect tense is used to express action or a condition that started in the past and is continued to or completed in the present.

> Randy has practiced piano every day for the last ten years.
>
> Randy has never been bored with practice.

Past perfect tense expresses action or a condition that occurred as a precedent to some other past action or condition.

> Randy had considered playing clarinet before he discovered the piano.

Future perfect tense expresses action that started in the past or the present and will conclude at some time in the future.

> By the time he goes to college, Randy will have been an accomplished pianist for more than half of his life.

Use of verbs (mood)

Indicative mood is used to make unconditional statements; subjunctive mood is used for conditional clauses or wish statements that pose conditions that are untrue. Verbs in subjunctive mood are plural with both singular and plural subjects.

    If I <u>were</u> a bird, I would fly.

    I wish I <u>were</u> as rich as Donald Trump.

Verb conjugation

The conjugation of verbs follow the patterns used in the discussion of tense above. However, the most frequent problems in verb use stem from the improper formation of past and past participial forms.

    Regular verb: believe, believed, (have) believed

    Irregular verbs: run, ran, run; sit, **sat**, **sat**; teach, taught, taught

Other problems stem from the use of verbs that are the same in some tense, but have different forms and different meanings in other tenses.

    I lie on the ground. I lay on the ground yesterday. I have lain down.

    I lay the blanket on the bed. I laid the blanket there yesterday. I have laid the blanket every night.

    The sun rises. The sun rose. The sun has risen.

    He raises the flag. He raised the flag. He had raised the flag.

    I sit on the porch. I sat on the porch. I have sat in the porch swing.

    I set the plate on the table. I set the plate there yesterday. I had set the table before dinner.

Two other verb problems stem from misusing the preposition *of* for the verb auxiliary *have* and misusing the verb *ought* (now rare).

    Incorrect: I should of gone to bed.
    Correct: I should have gone to bed.

    Incorrect: He hadn't ought to get so angry.
    Correct: He ought not to get so angry.

Use of pronouns

A pronoun used as a subject of predicate nominative is in nominative case.

> She was the drum majorette. The lead trombonists were Joe and he. The band director accepted whoever could march in step.

A pronoun used as a direct object, indirect object of object of a preposition is in objective case.

> The teacher praised him. She gave him an A on the test. Her praise of him was appreciated. The students whom she did not praise will work harder next time.

Common pronoun errors occur from misuse of reflexive pronouns:

> Singular: *myself, yourself, herself, himself, itself*
> Plural: *ourselves, yourselves, themselves.*

> Incorrect: Jack cut hisself shaving.
> Correct: Jack cut himself shaving.

> Incorrect: They backed theirselves into a corner.
> Correct: They backed themselves into a corner.

Use of adjectives

An adjective should agree with its antecedent in number.

> Those apples are rotten. This one is ripe. These peaches are hard.

Comparative adjectives end in -er and superlatives in -est, with some exceptions like *worse* and *worst*. Some adjectives that cannot easily make comparative inflections are preceded by *more* and *most*.

> Mrs. Carmichael is the better of the two basketball coaches.

> That is the hastiest excuse you have ever contrived.

> Candy is the most beautiful baby.

Avoid double superlatives.

> Incorrect: This is the most worst headache I ever had.
> Correct: This is the worst headache I ever had.

When comparing one thing to others in a group, exclude the thing under comparison from the rest of the group.

>Incorrect: Joey is larger than any baby I have ever seen. (Since you have seen him, he cannot be larger than himself.)
>Correct: Joey is larger than <u>any other</u> baby I have ever seen.

Include all necessary words to make a comparison clear in meaning.

>I am as tall as my mother. I am as tall as she (is).
>My cats are better behaved than those of my neighbor.

MECHANICS

The candidate should be cognizant of proper rules and conventions of punctuation, capitalization, and spelling. Competency exams will generally test the ability to apply the more advanced skills; thus, a limited number of more frustrating rules is presented here.

Rules should be applied according to the American style of English, i.e. spelling *theater* instead of *theatre* and placing terminal marks of punctuation almost exclusively within other marks of punctuation.

Punctuation

Using terminal punctuation in relation to quotation marks

In a quoted statement that is either declarative or imperative, place the period inside the closing quotation marks.

> "The airplane crashed on the runway during takeoff."

If the quotation is followed by other words in the sentence, place a comma inside the closing quotations marks and a period at the end of the sentence.

> "The airplane crashed on the runway during takeoff," said the announcer.

In most instances in which a quoted title or expression occurs at the end of a sentence, the period is placed before either the single or double quotation marks.

> "The middle school readers were unprepared to understand Bryant's poem 'Thanatopsis.'"
>
> Early book-length adventure stories like *Don Quixote* and *The Three Musketeers* were known as "picaresque novels."

There is an instance in which the final quotation mark would precede the period - if the content of the sentence were about a speech or quote so that the understanding of the meaning would be confused by the placement of the period.

> The first thing out of his mouth was "Hi, I'm home."
> *but*
> The first line of his speech began "I arrived home to an empty house".

In sentences that are interrogatory or exclamatory, the question mark or exclamation point should be positioned outside the closing quotation marks if the quote itself is a statement or command or cited title.

> Who decided to lead us in the recitation of the "Pledge of Allegiance"?
>
> Why was Tillie shaking as she began her recitation, "Once upon a midnight dreary..."?
>
> I was embarrassed when Mrs. White said, "Your slip is showing"!

In sentences that are declarative but the quotation is a question or an exclamation, place the question mark or exclamation point inside the quotation marks.

>The hall monitor yelled, "Fire! Fire!"

>"Fire! Fire!" yelled the hall monitor.

>Cory shrieked, "Is there a mouse in the room?" (In this instance, the question supersedes the exclamation.)

Using periods with parentheses or brackets

Place the period inside the parentheses or brackets if they enclose a complete sentence, independent of the other sentences around it.

>Stephen Crane was a confirmed alcohol and drug addict. (He admitted as much to other journalists in Cuba.)

If the parenthetical expression is a statement inserted within another statement, the period in the enclosure is omitted.

>Mark Twain used the character Indian Joe (He also appeared in *The Adventures of Tom Sawyer*) as a foil for Jim in *The Adventures of Huckleberry Finn*.

When enclosed matter comes at the end of a sentence requiring quotation marks, place the period outside the parentheses or brackets.

>"The secretary of state consulted with the ambassador [Albright]."

Using commas

Separate two or more coordinate adjectives modifying the same word; and three or more nouns, phrases, or clauses in a list.

>Maggie's hair was dull, dirty, and lice-ridden.

>Dickens portrayed the Artful Dodger as skillful pickpocket, loyal follower of Fagin, and defendant of Oliver Twist.

>Ellen daydreamed about getting out of the rain, taking a shower, and eating a hot dinner.

>In Elizabethan England, Ben Johnson wrote comedy, Christopher Marlowe wrote tragedies, and William Shakespeare composed both.

Use commas to separate antithetical or complimentary expressions from the rest of the sentence.

> The veterinarian, not his assistant, would perform the delicate surgery.

> The more he knew about her, the less he wished he had known.

> Randy hopes to, and probably will, get an appointment to the Naval Academy.

> His thorough, though esoteric, scientific research could not easily be understood by high school students.

Using double quotation marks with other punctuation

Quotations - whether words, phrases, or clauses - should be punctuated according to the rules of the grammatical function they serve in the sentence.

> The works of Shakespeare, "the Bard of Avon," have been contested as originating with other authors.

> "You'll get my money," the old man warned, "when 'Hell freezes over'."

> Sheila cited the passage that began "Four score and seven years ago...." (Note the ellipsis followed by an enclosed period.)

> "Old Ironsides" inspired the preservation of the U.S.S. Constitution.

Use quotation marks to enclose the titles of shorter works: songs, short poems, short stories, essays, and chapters of books. (See "Using Italics" for punctuating longer titles.)

> "The Tell-Tale Heart"   "Casey at the Bat"   "America the Beautiful"

Using semicolons

Use semicolons to separate independent clauses when the second clause is introduced by a transitional adverb. (These clauses may also be written as separate sentences, preferably by placing the adverb within the second sentence.)

> The Elizabethans modified the rhyme scheme of the sonnet; thus, it was called the English sonnet.
>
> *or*
>
> The Elizabethans modified the rhyme scheme of the sonnet. It thus was called the English sonnet.

Use semicolons to separate items in a series that are long and complex or have internal punctuation.

> The Italian Renaissance produced masters in the fine arts: Dante Alighieri, author of the *Divine Comedy;* Leonardo da Vinci, painter of *The Last Supper;* and Donatello, sculptor of the *Quattro Coronati*, the four saints.
>
> The leading scorers in the WNBA were Haizhaw Zheng, averaging 23.9 points per game; Lisa Leslie, 22; and Cynthia Cooper, 19.5.

Using colons

Place a colon at the beginning of a list of items. (Note its use in the sentence about Renaissance Italians on this page.)

> The teacher directed us to compare Faulkner's three symbolic novels: *Absalom, Absalom; As I Lay Dying;* and *Light in August*.

Do **not** use a colon if the list is preceded by a verb.

> Three of Faulkner's symbolic novels are *Absalom, Absalom; As I Lay Dying,* and *Light in August*.

Use italics to punctuate the titles of long works of literature, names of periodical publications, musical scores, works of art and motion picture television, and radio programs. (When unable to write in italics, students should be instructed to underline in their own writing where italics would be appropriate.)

The Idylls of the King	*Hiawatha*	*The Sound and the Fury*
Mary Poppins	*Newsweek*	*The Nutcracker Suite*

Capitalization

Capitalize all proper names of persons (including specific organizations or agencies of government); places (countries, states, cities, parks, and specific geographical areas); and things (political parties, structures, historical and cultural terms, and calendar and time designations); and religious terms (any deity, revered person or group, sacred writings).

> Percy Bysshe Shelley, Argentina, Mount Rainier National Park, Grand Canyon, League of Nations, the Sears Tower, Birmingham, Lyric Theater, Americans, Midwesterners, Democrats, Renaissance, Boy Scouts of America, Easter, God, Bible, Dead Sea Scrolls, Koran

Capitalize proper adjectives and titles used with proper names.

California gold rush, President John Adams, French fries, Homeric epic, Romanesque architecture, Senator John Glenn

Note: Some words that represent titles and offices are not capitalized unless used with a proper name.

Capitalized	Not Capitalized
Congressman McKay	the congressman from Florida
Commander Alger	commander of the Pacific Fleet
Queen Elizabeth	the queen of England

Capitalize all main words in titles of works of literature, art, and music. (See "Using Italics" in the Punctuation section.)

Spelling

Concentration in this section will be on spelling plurals and possessives. The multiplicity and complexity of spelling rules based on phonics, letter doubling, and exceptions to rules - not mastered by adulthood - should be replaced by a good dictionary. As spelling mastery is also difficult for adolescents, our recommendation is the same. Learning the use of a dictionary and thesaurus will be a more rewarding use of time.

Most plurals of nouns that end in hard consonants or hard consonant sounds followed by a silent *e* are made by adding *s*. Some words ending in vowels only add *s*.

> fingers, numerals, banks, bugs, riots, homes, gates, radios, bananas

Nouns that end in soft consonant sounds *s, j, x, z, ch,* and *sh*, add *es*. Some nouns ending in *o* add es.

> dresses, waxes, churches, brushes, tomatoes, potatoes

Nouns ending in *y* preceded by a vowel just add *s*.

> boys, alleys

Nouns ending in *y* preceded by a consonant change the *y* to *i* and add *es*.

> babies, corollaries, frugalities, poppies

Some nouns plurals are formed irregularly or remain the same.

> sheep, deer, children, leaves, oxen

Some nouns derived from foreign words, especially Latin, may make their plurals in two different ways - one of them Anglicized. Sometimes, the meanings are the same; other times, the two plurals are used in slightly different contexts. It is always wise to consult the dictionary.

> appendices, appendixes   criterion, criteria
> indexes, indices   crisis, crises

Make the plurals of closed (solid) compound words in the usual way except for words ending in *ful* which make their plurals on the root word.

> timelines, hairpins, cupsful

Make the plurals of open or hyphenated compounds by adding the change in inflection to the word that changes in number.

> fathers-in-law, courts-martial, masters of art, doctors of medicine

Make the plurals of letters, numbers, and abbreviations by adding *s*.

> fives and tens, IBMs, 1990s, *p*s and *q*s (Note that letters are italicized.)

Possessives

Make the possessives of singular nouns by adding an apostrophe followed by the letter *s* (*'s*).

>baby's bottle, father's job, elephant's eye, teacher's desk, sympathizer's protests, week's postponement

Make the possessive of singular nouns ending in *s* by adding either an apostrophe or a (*'s*) depending upon common usage or sound. When making the possessive causes difficulty, use a prepositional phrase instead. Even with the sibilant ending, with a few exceptions, it is advisable to use the (*'s*) construction.

>dress's color, species' characteristics or characteristics of the species, James' hat or James's hat, Delores's shirt

Make the possessive of plural nouns ending in *s* by adding the apostrophe after the *s*.

>horses' coats, jockeys' times, four days' time

Make possessives of plural nouns that do not end in *s* the same as singular nouns by adding *'s*.

>children's shoes, deer's antlers, cattle's horns

Make possessives of compound nouns by adding the inflection at the end of the word or phrase.

>the mayor of Los Angeles' campaign, the mailman's new truck, the mailmen's new trucks, my father-in-law's first wife, the keepsakes' values, several daughters-in-law's husbands

Note: Because a gerund functions as a noun, any noun preceding it and operating as a possessive adjective must reflect the necessary inflection. However, if the "ing" word following the noun is a participle, no inflection is added.

>The general was perturbed by the private's sleeping on duty. (The word *sleeping* is a gerund, the object of the preposition *by*.
>
>but
>
>The general was perturbed to see the private sleeping on duty. (The word *sleeping* is a participle modifying *private*.)

Resources

Basic teaching texts used by teachers at large and found to be most helpful in teaching structure, grammar and composition:

Grades 7-12 - all students

Warriner's *Composition and Grammar: Fourth - First Course*
and *Complete Course*, Orlando, FL: Harcourt, Brace, Jovanovich.

Intermediate to Advanced college-bound students and International-ESOL students

Oshima, Alice and Ann Hogue. *Writing Academic English* (Longman Series) *A Writing and Sentence Structure Handbook*. Reading, MA: Addison-Wesley Publications Co., 1991.

Grades 6-12

Hixon, Mamie W. *The Essentials of English Language*. Piscataway, New Jersey: Research and Education Association, 1995.

English Journal. Urbana, IL: National Council of Teachers of English.

Teachers will find numerous other published local resources in the school library or district resource centers.

Teaching Styles

Teaching styles are an extension of learning styles. Once teachers assess how students learn, they can vary their teaching styles to accommodate student needs. Research in the 1960s and 1970s solidified thinking about learning and teaching that had been evolving since the turn of the century. In the 1980s, several states adopted standards for student performance and began to hold teachers accountable for student progress. Formative and summative evaluation instruments were developed to enable administrators to evaluate teacher performance and to help teachers improve their teaching styles.

Six styles

1. Task-oriented. The teacher prescribes the resources and identifies specific performances, some of which may be individualized.

2. Cooperation-centered. The teacher and students plan the course of study and select resources together.

3. Child-centered. The student plans his own course of study based on his own interests.

4. Subject-oriented. Well-organized content dictates the course of study, with little regard to individual differences.

5. Learning-centered. This style combines both child-centered and subject-oriented approaches. The organized content and specific resources from which the student must select are prescribed.

6. Emotionally exciting. Not centered on any planning method, this style merely categorizes those teachers who instruct with more emotion than structure.

Concerns for the teacher

Within any of these styles, researchers identified specific element - instructional planning, personality traits, educational philosophy, attitudes toward students, teaching environments, methodology, and evaluation techniques - that could be assessed as having an impact on student learning.

As a result, in the last two decades, greater emphasis has been placed on identifying learning and teaching styles and attempting to match learner needs with the appropriate delivery methods. Teachers who have been trained and subscribe to task-oriented and subject-centered instruction are encouraged to abandon the textbook-dependent or lecture approaches to learning in favor of smaller group discussion, independent study and research, and creative student projects. Teachers who have an abundance of enthusiasm, but little organization, have been encouraged to become more learning oriented.

Early in each school year, the teacher needs to assess social, environmental, physical, and perceptual characteristics of each individual and class. This can be done informally through observation or formally with any number of learning style inventories. One inventory asks students to respond *true* or *false* to statements such as "Florescent light bothers my eyes" or "In a group, I always want to be the leader." Another inventory asks students to rank-order descriptive words that are indicators of positive or negative associations related to classroom environment, teacher qualities, student interests and abilities, and social skills.

The drawback of formal inventories is that adolescents aware of the inventory's purpose or youngsters who have been exposed to repeated assessments may intentionally or inadvertently miscue their responses. Many researchers and teachers prefer a hands-on approach to assessment. By trying various styles in the early weeks of a course of study, the teacher can observe the methods that work best.

Using half a class as a control group or altering teaching styles with different classes during the day can result in providing improved instructional strategies and in making better recommendations for study techniques and resources for study.

Skill 15.2   Apply principles of language acquisition and use.

LANGUAGE DEVELOPMENT

Learning approach

Early theories of language development were formulated from learning theory research. The assumption was that language development evolved from learning the rules of language structures and applying them through imitation and reinforcement. This approach also assumed that language, cognitive, and social developments were independent of each other. Thus, children were expected to learn language from patterning after adults who spoke and wrote Standard English. No allowance was made for communication through child jargon, idiomatic expressions, or grammatical and mechanical errors resulting from too strict adherence to the rules of inflection (*childs* instead of *children*) or conjugation (*runned* instead of *ran*). No association was made between physical and operational development and language mastery.

Linguistic approach

Studies spearheaded by Noam Chomsky in the 1950s formulated the theory that language ability is innate and develops through natural human maturation as environmental stimuli trigger acquisition of syntactical structures appropriate to each exposure level. The assumption of a hierarchy of syntax downplayed the significance of semantics. Because of the complexity of syntax and the relative speed with which children acquire language, linguists attributed language development to biological rather than cognitive or social influences.

Cognitive approach

Researchers in the 1970s proposed that language knowledge derives from both syntactic and semantic structures. Drawing on the studies of Piaget and other cognitive learning theorists (see Skill 4.7), supporters of the cognitive approach maintained that children acquire knowledge of linguistic structures after they have acquired the cognitive structures necessary to process language. For example, joining words for specific meaning necessitates sensory motor intelligence. The child must be able to coordinate movement and recognize objects before she can identify words to name the objects or word groups to describe the actions performed with those objects.

Adolescents must have developed the mental abilities for <u>organizing concepts as well as concrete operations</u>, <u>predicting outcomes</u>, and <u>theorizing</u> before they can assimilate and verbalize complex sentence structures, choose vocabulary for particular nuances of meaning, and examine semantic structures for tone and manipulative effect.

Sociocognitive approach

Other theorists in the 1970s proposed that language development results from sociolinguistic competence. Language, cognitive, and social knowledges are interactive elements of total human development. Emphasis on verbal communication as the medium for language expression resulted in the inclusion of speech activities in most language arts curricula.

Unlike previous approaches, the sociocognitive allowed that determining the appropriateness of language in given situations for specific listeners is as important as understanding semantic and syntactic structures. By engaging in conversation, children at all stages of development have opportunities to test their language skills, receive feedback, and make modifications. As a social activity, conversation is as structured by social order as grammar is structured by the rules of syntax. Conversation satisfies the learner's need to be heard and understood and to influence others. Thus, his choices of vocabulary, tone, and content are dictated by his ability to assess the language knowledge of his listeners. He is constantly applying his cognitive skills to using language in a social interaction. If the capacity to acquire language is inborn, without an environment in which to practice language, a child would not pass beyond primitive grunts and gestures.

Of course, the varying degrees of environmental stimuli to which children are exposed at all age levels creates a slower or faster development of language. Some children are prepared to articulate concepts and recognize symbolism by the time they enter fifth grade because they have been exposed to challenging reading and conversations with well-spoken adults at home or in their social groups. Others are still trying to master the sight recognition skills and are not yet ready to combine words in complex patterns.

Concerns for the teacher

Because teachers must, by virtue of tradition and the dictates of the curriculum, teach grammar, usage, and writing as well as reading and later literature; the problem becomes when to teach what to whom. The profusion of approaches to teaching grammar alone is mind-boggling. In the universities, we learn about transformational grammar, stratificational grammar, sectoral grammar, etc.

But in practice, most teachers, supported by presentations in textbooks and by the methods they learned themselves, keep coming back to the same traditional prescriptive approach - read and imitate - or structural approach - learn the parts of speech, the parts of sentence, punctuation rules, sentence patterns. After enough of the terminology and rules are stored in the brain, then we learn to write and speak. For some educators, the best solution is the worst - don't teach grammar at all.

The same problems occur in teaching usage. To what extent can we demand that students communicate in only Standard English? Different schools of thought suggest that a study of dialect and idiom and a recognition of various jargons are vital parts of language development. Social pressures, especially on students in middle and junior high schools, make adolescents resistant to the corrective, remedial approach. In many communities where the immigrant populations are high, new words are entering English from other languages even as words and expressions that were common when we were children have become rare or obsolete.

Regardless of differences of opinion concerning language development, it is safe to say that a language arts teachers will be most effective using the styles and approaches with which they are most comfortable. And, if they subscribe to a student-centered approach, they may find that the students have a lot to teach them and each other. Moffett and Wagner in the Fourth Edition of *Student-centered Language Arts K-12* stress the three I's: individualization, interaction, and integration. Essentially, they are supporting the sociocognitive approach to language development. By providing an opportunity for the students to select their own activities and resources, instruction is individualized. By centering on and teaching each other, students are interactive. Finally, by allowing students to synthesize a variety of knowledge structures, they integrate them. Teachers become facilitators.

Benefits of the sociocognitive approach

This approach has tended to guide the whole-language movement, currently in fashion. Most basal readers utilize an integrated, cross-curricular approach to successful grammar, language, and usage. Reinforcement becomes an intradepartmental responsibility. Language incorporates diction and terminology across the curriculum. Standard usage is encouraged and supported by both the core-classroom textbooks and current software for technology. Teachers need to acquaint themselves with the computer capabilities in their school district and at their individual school sites. Advances in new technologies require teachers to familiarize themselves with programs that would serve their students' needs. Students respond enthusiastically to technology. Several highly effective programs are available in various formats to assist students with initial instruction or remediation.

Grammar texts, such as the Warriner's series, employ various methods to reach individual learning styles. The school library media center should become a focal point for individual exploration.

Professional growth

Attendance as a professional at language arts conferences should be an integral part of teachers' life-long learning strategy. Shared enthusiasms, techniques, assessments, and materials result in energized, focused instructors/facilitators. Technology conferences provide state-of-the-art, hands-on experiences for teachers to take back to students and to the district administrators who have the monies and need direction on how best to spend them to serve the students. We highly encourage teachers to take the time to attend seminars, colloquies, in-services, and conventions. Encourage district in-service supervisors to include offerings that enable faculty members to receive updates from research professionals and to share innovations that are being developed within their own districts.

Also, plan on taking college courses to update teaching skills and methodology to help each student reach his potential. There are various writing and language arts programs specifically created by computer companies. Teachers need to review those available in their district and select those appropriate programs that assist with remediation or with engaging reluctant readers and writers.

B. Fundamentals of Literature

COMPETENCY 16.0 UNDERSTAND THE CHARACTERISTIC FEATURES OF VARIOUS GENRES OF FICTION AND DRAMA

Skill 16.1 Analyze elements of fiction in passage context.

Essential terminology and literary devices germane to literary analysis include alliteration, allusion, antithesis, aphorism, apostrophe, assonance, blank verse, caesura, conceit, connotation, consonance, couplet, denotation, diction, epiphany, exposition, figurative language, free verse, hyperbole, iambic pentameter, inversion, irony, kenning, metaphor, metaphysical poetry, metonymy, motif, onomatopoeia, octava rima, oxymoron, paradox, parallelism personification, quatrain, scansion, simile, soliloquy, Spenserian stanza, synecdoche, terza rima, tone, and wit.

The more basic terms and devices, such as alliteration, allusion, analogy, aside, assonance, atmosphere, climax, consonance, denouement, elegy, foil, foreshadowing, metaphor, simile, setting, symbol, and theme are defined and exemplified in the English 5-9 Study Guide.

Antithesis: Balanced writing about conflicting ideas, usually expressed in sentence form. Some examples are expanding from the center; shedding old habits and searching, but never finding.

Aphorism: A focused, succinct expression about life from a sagacious viewpoint. Writings by Ben Franklin, Sir Francis Bacon, and Alexander Pope contain many aphorisms. "Whatever is begun in anger ends in shame" is an aphorism.

Apostrophe: Literary device of addressing an absent or dead person, an abstract idea, or an inanimate object. Sonneteers, such as Sir Thomas Wyatt, John Keats, and William Wordsworth, address the moon, stars, and the dead Milton. For example, in William Shakespeare's *Julius Caesar*, Mark Antony addresses the corpse of Caesar in the speech that begins: *"O, pardon me, thou bleeding piece of earth, That I am meek and gentle with these butchers! Thou art the ruins of the noblest man That ever lived in the tide of times. Woe to the hand that shed this costly blood!"*

Blank Verse: Poetry written in iambic pentameter, but unrhymed. Works by Shakespeare and Milton are epitomes of blank verse. Milton's Paradise Lost states, *"Illumine, what is low raise and support, That to the height of this great argument I may assert Eternal Providence And justify the ways of God to men."*

Caesura: A pause, usually signaled by punctuation, in a line of poetry. The earliest usage occurs in *Beowulf*, the first English epic dating from the Anglo-Saxon era. *'To err is human, // to forgive, divine'* (Pope).

Conceit: A comparison, usually in verse, between seemingly disparate objects or concepts. John Donne's metaphysical poetry contains many clever conceits. For instance, Donne's "The Flea" (1633) compares a flea bite to the act of love; and in "A Valediction: Forbidding Mourning" (1633) separated lovers are likened to the legs of a compass, the leg drawing the circle eventually returning home to "the fixed foot."

Connotation: The ripple effect surrounding the implications and associations of a given word, distinct from the denotative, or literal meaning. For example, *"Good night, sweet prince, and flights of angels sing thee to thy res"t* refers to a burial.

Consonance: The repeated usage of similar consonant sounds, most often used in poetry. *"Sally sat sifting seashells by the seashore"* is a familiar example.

Couplet: Two rhyming lines of poetry. Shakespeare's sonnets end in heroic couplets written in iambic pentameter. Pope is also a master of the couplet. His *Rape of the Lock* is written entirely in heroic couplets.

Denotation: What a word literally means, as opposed to its connotative meaning. For example, in *"Good night, sweet prince, and flights of angels sing thee to thy **rest**,"* the word 'rest' denotes sleep.

Diction: The right word in the right spot for the right purpose. The hallmark of a great writer is precise, unusual, and memorable diction.

Epiphany: The moment when the proverbial light bulb goes off in one's head and comprehension sets in.

Exposition: Fill-in or background information about characters meant to clarify and add to the narrative; the initial plot element which precedes the buildup of conflict.

Figurative Language: Not meant in a literal sense, but to be interpreted through symbolism. Figurative language is made up of such literary devices as hyperbole, metonymy, synecdoche, and oxymoron. A synecdoche is a figure of speech in which the word for part of something is used to mean the whole; for example, "sail" for "boat," or vice versa.

Free Verse: Poetry that does not have any predictable meter or patterning. Margaret Atwood, E. E. Cummings, and Ted Hughes write in this form.

Hyperbole: Exaggeration for a specific effect. For example, *"I'm so hungry that I could eat a million of these."*

Iambic Pentameter: The two elements in a set five-foot line of poetry. An iamb is two syllables, unaccented and accented, per foot or measure. Pentameter means five feet of these iambs per line, or ten syllables.

Inversion: Atypical sentence order intended to create a given effect or interest. Bacon's and Milton's work use inversion successfully. Emily Dickinson was fond of arranging words outside of their familiar order. For example in "Chartless" she writes *"Yet know I how the heather looks"* and *"Yet certain am I of the spot."* Instead of saying *"Yet I know"* and *"Yet I am certain,"* she reverses the usual order and shifts the emphasis to the more important words.

Irony: An unexpected disparity between what is written or stated and what is really meant or implied by the author. Verbal, situational, and dramatic are the three literary ironies. Verbal irony is when an author says one thing and means something else. Dramatic irony is when an audience perceives something that a character in the literature does not know. Irony of situation is a discrepancy between the expected result and actual results. Shakespeare's plays contain numerous and highly effective use of irony. O. Henry's short stories have ironic endings.

Kenning: Another way to describe a person, place, or thing so as to avoid prosaic repetition. The earliest examples can be found in Anglo-Saxon literature such as *Beowulf* and "The Seafarer." Instead of writing King Hrothgar, the anonymous monk wrote, great Ring-Giver, or Father of his people. A lake becomes the swans' way, and the ocean or sea becomes the great whale's way. In ancient Greek literature, this device was called an "epithet."

Metaphysical Poetry: Verse characterization by ingenious wit, unparalleled imagery, and clever conceits. The greatest metaphysical poet is John Donne. Henry Vaughn and other 17th century British poets contributed to this movement as in *Words*, "I saw eternity the other night, like a great being of pure and endless light."

Metonymy: Use of an object or idea closely identified with another object or idea to represent the second. *"Hit the books"* means *"go study."* Washington, D.C. means the U.S. government and the White House means the U.S. President.

Motif: A key, oft-repeated phrase, name, or idea in a literary work. Dorset/Wessex in Hardy's novels and the moors and the harsh weather in the Bronte sisters' novels are effective use of motifs. Shakespeare's *Romeo and Juliet* represents the ill-fated young lovers' motif.

Onomatopoeia: Word used to evoke the sound in its meaning. The early Batman series used *pow, zap, whop, zonk* and *eek* in an onomatopoetic way.

Octava rima: A specific eight-line stanza of poetry whose rhyme scheme is abababcc. Lord Byron's mock epic, *Don Juan*, is written in this poetic way.

Oxymoron: A contradictory form of speech, such as jumbo shrimp, unkindly kind, or Mellencamp's "It hurts so good."

Paradox: Seemingly untrue statement, which when examined more closely proves to be true. John Donne's sonnet "Death Be Not Proud" postulates that death shall die and humans will triumph over death, at first thought not true, but ultimately explained and proven in this sonnet.

Parallelism: A type of close repetition of clauses or phrases that emphasize key topics or ideas in writing. The psalms in the King James Version of the *Bible* contain many examples.

Personification: Giving human characteristics to inanimate objects or concepts. Great writers, with few exceptions, are masters of this literary device.

Quatrain: A poetic stanza composed of four lines. A Shakespearean or Elizabethan sonnet is made up of three quatrains and ends with a heroic couplet.

Scansion: The two-part analysis of a poetic line. Count the number of syllables per line and determine where the accents fall. Divide the line into metric feet. Name the meter by the type and number of feet. Much is written about scanning poetry. Try not to inundate your students with this jargon; rather allow them to feel the power of the poets' words, ideas, and images instead.

Soliloquy: A highlighted speech, in drama, usually delivered by a major character expounding on the author's philosophy or expressing, at times, universal truths. This is done with the character alone on the stage.

Spenserian Stanza: Invented by Sir Edmund Spenser for usage in *The Fairie Queene*, his epic poem honoring Queen Elizabeth I. Each stanza consists of nine lines, eight in iambic parameter. The ninth line, called an alexandrine, has two extra syllables or one additional foot.

Sprung Rhythm: Invented and used extensively by the poet, Gerard Manley Hopkins. It consists of variable meter, which combines stressed and unstressed syllables fashioned by the author. See "Pied Beauty" or "God's Grandeur."

Stream of Consciousness: A style of writing which reflects the mental processes of the characters expressing, at times, jumbled memories, feelings, and dreams. "Big time players" in this type of expression are James Joyce, Virginia Woolf, and William Faulkner.

Terza Rima: A series of poetic stanzas utilizing the recurrent rhyme scheme of aba, bcb, cdc, ded, and so forth. The second-generation Romantic poets - Keats, Byron, Shelley, and, to a lesser degree, Yeats - used this Italian verse form, especially in their odes. Dante used this stanza in *The Divine Comedy*.

Tone: The discernible attitude inherent in an author's work regarding the subject, readership, or characters. Swift's or Pope's tone is satirical. Boswell's tone toward Johnson is admiring.

Wit: Writing of genius, keenness, and sagacity expressed through clever use of language. Alexander Pope and the Augustans wrote about and were themselves said to possess wit.

In addition to these terms, there are four major time periods of writings. They are neoclassicism, romanticism, realism, and naturalism. Certain authors, among these Chaucer, Shakespeare, Whitman, Dickinson, and Donne, though writing during a particular literary period, are considered to have a style all their own.

Neoclassicism: Patterned after the greatest writings of classical Greece and Rome, this type of writing is characterized by balanced, graceful, well-crafted, refined, elevated style. Major proponents of this style are poet laureates, John Dryden and Alexander Pope. The eras in which they wrote are called the Ages of Dryden and Pope. The self is not exalted and focus is on the group, not the individual, in neoclassic writing.

Romanticism: Writings emphasizing the individual. Emotions and feelings are validated. Nature acts as an inspiration for creativity; it is a balm of the spirit. Romantics hearken back to medieval, chivalric themes and ambiance. They also emphasize supernatural, Gothic themes and settings, which are characterized by gloom and darkness. Imagination is stressed. New types of writings include detective and horror stories (Poe) and autobiographical introspection (Wordsworth and Thoreau). There are two generations in British Literature: First Generation includes William Wordsworth and Samuel Taylor Coleridge whose collaboration, *Lyrical Ballads*, defines romanticism and its exponents. Wordsworth maintained that the scenes and events of everyday life and the speech of ordinary people were the raw material of which poetry could and should be made. Romanticism spread to the United States, where Ralph Waldo Emerson and Henry David Thoreau adopted it in their transcendental romanticism, emphasizing reasoning. Further extensions of this style are found in Edgar Allan Poe's Gothic writings. Second Generation romantics include the ill-fated Englishmen Lord Byron, John Keats, and Percy Bysshe Shelley. Byron and Shelley, who for some most typify the romantic poet (in their personal lives as well as in their work), wrote resoundingly in protest against social and political wrongs and in defense of the struggles for liberty in Italy and Greece. The Second Generation romantics stressed personal introspection and the love of beauty and nature as requisites of inspiration.

Realism: Unlike classical and neoclassical writing, which often deal with aristocracies and nobility or the gods; realistic writers deal with the common man and his socio/economic problems in a non-sentimental way. Muckraking, social injustice, domestic abuse, and inner-city conflicts are examples of writings by writers of realism. Realistic writers include Stephen Crane, Ernest Hemingway, Thomas Hardy, George Bernard Shaw, and Henrik Ibsen.

Naturalism: This is realism pushed to the maximum, writing which exposes the underbelly of society, usually the lower class struggles. This is the world of penury, injustice, abuse, ghetto survival, hungry children, single parenting, and substance abuse. In his series of novels devoted to several generations of one French family, Émile Zola, inspired by his readings in history and medicine, attempted to apply methods of scientific observation to the depiction of pathological human character.

Skill 16.2 Compare the characteristics of types of fictional narratives.

The major literary genres include allegory, ballad, drama, epic, epistle, essay, fable, novel, poem, romance, and the short story.

Allegory: A story in verse or prose with characters representing virtues and vices. There are two meanings, symbolic and literal. John Bunyan's *The Pilgrim's Progress* is the most renowned of this genre.

Ballad: An *in medias res* story told or sung, usually in verse and accompanied by music. Literary devices found in ballads include the refrain, or repeated section, and incremental repetition, or anaphora, for effect. Earliest forms were anonymous folk ballads. Later forms include Coleridge's Romantic masterpiece, "The Rime of the Ancient Mariner."

Drama: Plays – comedy, modern, or tragedy - typically in five acts. Traditionalists and neoclassicists adhere to Aristotle's unities of time, place and action. Plot development is advanced via dialogue. Literary devices include asides, soliloquies and the chorus representing public opinion. Greatest of all dramatists/playwrights is William Shakespeare.
Other dramaturges include Ibsen, Williams, Miller, Shaw, Stoppard, Racine, Moliére, Sophocles, Aeschylus, Euripides, and Aristophanes.

Epic: Long poem usually of book length reflecting values inherent in the generative society. Epic devices include an invocation to a Muse for inspiration, purpose for writing, universal setting, protagonist and antagonist who possess supernatural strength and acumen, and interventions of a God or the gods. Understandably, there are very few epics: Homer's *Iliad* and *Odyssey*, Virgil's *Aeneid*, Milton's *Paradise Lost*, Spenser's *The Fairie Queene*, Barrett Browning's *Aurora Leigh*, and Pope's mock-epic, *The Rape of the Lock*.

Epistle: A letter that is not always originally intended for public distribution, but due to the fame of the sender and/or recipient, becomes public domain. Paul wrote epistles that were later placed in the Bible.

Essay: Typically a limited length prose work focusing on a topic and propounding a definite point of view and authoritative tone. Great essayists include Carlyle, Lamb, DeQuincy, Emerson and Montaigne, who is credited with defining this genre.

Fable: Terse tale offering up a moral or exemplum. Chaucer's "The Nun's Priest's Tale" is a fine example of a *bete fabliau* or beast fable in which animals speak and act characteristically human, illustrating human foibles.

Legend: A traditional narrative or collection of related narratives, popularly regarded as historically factual but actually a mixture of fact and fiction.

Myth: Stories that are more or less universally shared within a culture to explain its history and traditions.

Novel: The longest form of fictional prose containing a variety of characterizations, settings, local color and regionalism. Most have complex plots, expanded description, and attention to detail. Some of the great novelists include Austin, the Brontes, Twain, Tolstoy, Hugo, Hardy, Dickens, Hawthorne, Forster, and Flaubert.

Poem: The only requirement is rhythm. Sub-genres include fixed types of literature such as the sonnet, elegy, ode, pastoral, and villanelle. Unfixed types of literature include blank verse and dramatic monologue.

Romance: A highly imaginative tale set in a fantastical realm dealing with the conflicts between heroes, villains and/or monsters. "The Knight's Tale" from Chaucer's *Canterbury Tales*, *Sir Gawain and the Green Knight* and Keats' "The Eve of St. Agnes" are prime representatives.

Short Story: Typically a terse narrative, with less developmental background about characters. May include description, author's point of view, and tone. Poe emphasized that a successful short story should create one focused impact. Considered to be great short story writers are Hemingway, Faulkner, Twain, Joyce, Shirley Jackson, Flannery O'Connor, de Maupassant, Saki, Edgar Allen Poe, and Pushkin.

Skill 16.3 Relate types of drama to their characteristics.

Comedy: The comedic form of dramatic literature is meant to amuse, and often ends happily. It uses techniques such as satire or parody, and can take many forms, from farce to burlesque. Examples include Dante Alighieri's *The Divine Comedy,* Noel Coward's play *Private Lives,* and some of Geoffrey Chaucer's *Canterbury Tales* and William Shakespeare's plays.

Tragedy: Tragedy is comedy's other half. It is defined as a work of drama written in either prose or poetry, telling the story of a brave, noble hero who, because of some tragic character flaw, brings ruin upon himself. It is characterized by serious, poetic language that evokes pity and fear. In modern times, dramatists have tried to update its image by drawing its main characters from the middle class and showing their nobility through their nature instead of their standing. The classic example of tragedy is Sophocles' *Oedipus Rex*, while Henrik Ibsen and Arthur Miller epitomize modern tragedy.

Drama: In its most general sense, a drama is any work that is designed to be performed by actors onstage. It can also refer to the broad literary genre that includes comedy and tragedy. Contemporary usage, however, denotes drama as a work that treats serious subjects and themes but does not aim for the same grandeur as tragedy. Drama usually deals with characters of a less stately nature than tragedy. A classical example is Sophocles' tragedy *Oedipus Rex,* while Eugene O'Neill's *The Iceman Cometh* represents modern drama.

Dramatic Monologue: A dramatic monologue is a speech given by an actor, usually intended for themselves, but with the intended audience in mind. It reveals key aspects of the character's psyche and sheds insight on the situation at hand. The audience takes the part of the silent listener, passing judgment and giving sympathy at the same time. This form was invented and used predominantly by Victorian poet Robert Browning.

Skill 16.4 Analyze elements of drama and film.

Set: Theater can be performed almost anywhere, and is especially useful, although tricky, in a classroom environment. Make sure there is enough space. Avoid distracting sounds (like air conditioning) or noisy areas (next to the cafeteria). Take measurements both vertically and horizontally so you may be sure of how big to build your scenery. Take storage space into account, as you will have to store scenery that is not being used and should not be visible to the audience. Within a classroom setting, desks can be versatile and useful scenery, able to band together to form a wall, be covered with cloth to form a rabbit's hole, or stacked on top of each other to form a tower. Changing booths and prop tables are sometimes needed as well. You must read a script like a set designer, visualizing the number and kinds of spaces the show will require.

Costume: Anything worn by a performer, including clothes, masks and jewelry, is considered a costume. Makeup and wigs are usually grouped into the same category. It is useful to have a costume designer, who is assisted by a first hand; as well as cutters, stitchers, and drapers. Attention must be paid to the coherency between the set and the costumers. They should use colors that work well together, and are not too similar, but not too different.

Lighting: Lighting discriminates between where the show is happening and where it is not. On a basic level, the audience must be able to see the performers and the scenery clearly. There is a fine line between lighting that is so bright it strains the audience's eyes and lighting that is so dim it puts the audience to sleep. The most attractive lighting angle for actors is forty-five degrees, and the face is best illuminated by a light on either side of the stage. Use back light to separate figures from scenery or foot lights to give the scene an old-time theatrical look.

Sound: This includes the use of microphones (which can be as cheap as ten dollars), sound effects, and the playback of recorded sound. All sound systems are composed of four pieces:
- Source- This is where the sound comes from, whether it is a naturally occurring sound captured by a microphone or a recorded sound coming from a CD player.
- Routing- The sound must be sent to the proper place at the proper volume. This is done by a mixer, does the same thing you do at home when you choose "tape" or "CD" on your stereo, but does it more quietly and with more options. On a mixer, you may play input from several different sources simultaneously, and set different volumes for each sound.
- Amplification- For the sound to be loud enough for a theatrical production, you need an amplifier. This is usually a unit that takes the output from the mixer and pumps it up to a strong enough level for the speakers.
- Output- This is the way the sound gets out of the system so people can hear it. Essentially, speakers.

When using microphones, there are a few guidelines to remember:
- Do not run mics next to power cords, video cables or lighting equipment.
- Do not blow into the mic. It may damage the diaphragm. Instead, tap the mic gently to check if it is turned on.
- When speaking into the mic, put your mouth about a hand's distance away and keep it at a constant distance.
- Do not point the mic at a speaker. This creates feedback which is an unpleasant noise to say the least.

Props: Anything that is carried by an actor, or could be carried by an actor within the context of the play, is considered a prop. Therefore, a picture on the wall is labeled a prop, while a fireplace is deemed scenery. Prop work can be a great job for shy students or those with artistic tendencies. Make a list of all the props the show will need. *Set props* are pre-set on the stage and generally left there. This includes furniture, lamps, rugs, phones, etc. *Personal props*, such as pens, documents and money are carried onstage by actors. *Set dressing* is the lowest priority since it has no affect on the action of the play. Things like paintings on the wall, drapes, and vases are there simply to set the scene.

Buying a prop saves time and labor, but is limited by availability and budget.
Building a prop is usually cheaper then buying, but necessary skill is needed.
Borrowing saves time and money, but is completely dependent on availability.
Pulling a prop from stock is always the best option, but availability is limited.

Conceptualization

The director has two basic duties: (1) to implement a unified vision within the finished production, and (2) to lead others toward its ultimate actualization. To meet these charges, the director must organize the realization of his or her vision. The director must decide upon the interpretation to be given the play, work with the playwright (if possible), designers, and technicians in planning the production, cast and rehearse the actors, and coordinate all elements into the finished production.

To decide upon interpretation, the director must analyze the script to discover the play's structure and meanings. Without understanding, the director cannot make choices. He or she seeks to know what the play is about and to understand each character in terms of both the script and the demands that character places upon the actor. The director must be able to envision the play's atmosphere or mood and know how to actualize in terms of design and theatrical space. And, finally, the director must be able to see the play in terms of both physical and verbal action.

Blocking

Stage blocking is one of the most basic and technical elements of play direction, but should never be taken lightly by the director. Indeed there are a few other elements of a play that are more exciting and glamorous, but blocking provides the backbone and structure needed to make those other elements a reality. Basically, blocking is the choreography of actors' movements throughout the entire play. If a character needs to exit the scene, for example, the actor must be able to move naturally towards the exit. The director's goal is to come up with a plausible means of getting that actor across the stage and through the door, window, transporter beam or whatever. The same holds true for a character delivering a monologue—should they break away from the other actors or deliver the speech in the middle of a crowd? Other considerations when blocking may include entrances of a character, or places for actors to go when their character has no function in the scene.

Here are some things to consider when blocking your actors in a play:

1. Let the script do most of the work for you. As a director, you may have plenty of ideas on changing the setting or the costumes or the dialogue, but leave the basic stage direction as intact as possible. You aren't trying to reinvent the wheel, just making sure your actors know where to stand and when to cross. Most scripts already contain enough staging information to allow you to form a rough idea of blocking. You should know when the characters are supposed to enter and exit, and what obstacles are in their way during their dialogue. Trust the script notes to paint the broadest strokes you will need to do basic blocking.

2. Avoid clutter—keep the audience in mind. A stage should be viewed as a living painting. No artist would dare place all of his painting's elements on one side of the painting. Balance the stage movements so that the audience has a feeling of aesthetics. If a character has no interaction with others in the scene, move them to the opposite side of the stage for balance. If you have furniture on stage, avoid piling every actor on the couch center stage. You might set up more furniture on both sides of the stage to keep your actors from crowding each other. You might also consider building various levels to keep all actors in plain view. Build up different parts of the set, and when one actor moves to a different 'level', move another actor to replace them. If done subtly, the audience should not notice the continuous shift.

3. Allow the actors to improvise and contribute to the blocking process. During the rehearsal process, a director must be a benevolent dictator and democratic leader at the same time. There are some blocking directions that should be seen as final, such as exits, dramatic crosses and entrances. These movements need to be fixed and unchanged, so that lighting directors and other technical people can get a proper fix on actor positions.

But some elements of blocking, such as internal monologues and staged arguments, can be modified through improvisation and actor input. You should listen carefully to your actors' ideas, even if you still veto them. Actors can get a feel for where their characters would want to move during a scene, so their input can be very useful indeed. During a conflict scene, you may feel that the couple would naturally move away from each other to get some emotional distance, whereas the actors involved may feel like moving in closer to increase the tension between them. Both actions seem reasonable, so see which movements improve the scene. Be prepared to adjust your original ideas accordingly—move other actors out of the scene or change the stage layout.

4. Never let the props or set do the acting. If your set has a lot of furniture or levels or props, keep their presence to a minimum. Make sure your actors' movements upstage the furniture, rather than risk the furniture upstaging the actors. Unless the stage directions call for it, do not allow actors to perform entire scenes BEHIND a prop or furniture. Keep the actors visible and clutter-free. If a prop is misplaced or a set piece is in the way of an actor's path, tell your actors to get it out of the way by any means necessary. No one should feel obligated to tip-toe around a piece of misplaced scenery.

Tempo

Interpretation of dialogue must be connected to motivation and detail. During this time, the director is also concerned with pace and seeks a variation of tempo. If the overall pace is too slow, then the action becomes dull and dragging. If the overall pace is too fast, then the audience will not be able to understand what is going on, for they are being hit with too much information to process.

Dramatic Arc

Good drama is built on conflict of some kind — an opposition of forces or desires that must be resolved by the end of the story. The conflict can be internal, involving emotional and psychological pressures, or it can be external, drawing the characters into tumultuous events. These themes are presented to the audience in a narrative arc that looks roughly like this:

Following the Arc

Although any performance may have a series of rising and falling levels of intensity, in general the opening should set in motion the events which will generate an emotional high toward the middle or end of the story. Then, regardless of whether the ending is happy, sad, bittersweet, or despairing, the resolution eases the audience down from those heights and establishes some sense of closure. Reaching the climax too soon undermines the dramatic impact of the remaining portion of the performance, whereas reaching it too late rushes the ending and creates a jarringly abrupt end to events.

COMPETENCY 17.0 UNDERSTAND THE CHARACTERISTIC FEATURES OF VARIOUS GENRES OF NONFICTION.

Skill 17.1 Compare and contrast characteristics of types of nonfiction.

Biography: A form of nonfiction literature, the subject of which is the life of an individual. The earliest biographical writings were probably funeral speeches and inscriptions, usually praising the life and example of the deceased. Early biographies evolved from this and were almost invariably uncritical, even distorted, and always laudatory. Beginning in the 18th century, this form of literature saw major development; an eminent example is James Boswell's *Life of Johnson*, which is very detailed and even records conversations. Eventually, the antithesis of the grossly exaggerated tomes praising an individual, usually a person of circumstance, developed. This form is denunciatory, debunking, and often inflammatory. A famous modern example is Lytton Strachey's *Eminent Victorians* (1918).

Autobiography: A form of biography, but it is written by the subject himself or herself. Autobiographies can range from the very formal to intimate writings made during one's life that were not intended for publication. These include letters, diaries, journals, memoirs, and reminiscences. Autobiography, generally speaking, began in the 15th century; one of the first examples is one written in England by Margery Kempe. There are four kinds of autobiography: thematic, religious, intellectual, and fictionalized. Some "novels" may be thinly disguised autobiography, such as the novels of Thomas Wolfe.

Informational books and articles: Make up much of the reading of modern Americans. Magazines began to be popular in the 19th century in this country, and while many of the contributors to those publications intended to influence the political/social/religious convictions of their readers, many also simply intended to pass on information. A book or article whose purpose is simply to be informative, that is, not to persuade, is called exposition (adjectival form: expository). An example of an expository book is the *MLA Style Manual*.

The writers do not intend to persuade their readers to use the recommended stylistic features in their writing; they are simply making them available in case a reader needs such a guide. Articles in magazines such as *Time* may be persuasive in purpose, such as Joe Klein's regular column, but for the most part they are expository, giving information that television coverage of a news story might not have time to include.

Newspaper accounts of events: Expository in nature, of course, a reporting of a happening. That happening might be a school board meeting, an automobile accident that sent several people to a hospital and accounted for the death of a passenger, or the election of the mayor. They are not intended to be persuasive although the bias of a reporter or of an editor must be factored in. A newspapers' editorial stance is often openly declared, and it may be reflected in such things as news reports. Reporters are expected to be unbiased in their coverage, and most of them will defend their disinterest fiercely, but what a writer *sees* in an event is inevitably shaped to some extent by the writer's beliefs and experiences.

Skill 17.2 Apply criteria for evaluating nonfiction works of various genres.

See Competency 12.0

COMPETENCY 18.0 UNDERSTAND THE CHARACTERISTIC FEATURES OF VARIOUS FORMS OF POETRY.

Skill 18.1 Analyze the formal characteristics and distinctive content of narrative poetry.

The greatest difficulty in analyzing narrative poetry is that it partakes of many genres. It can have all the features of poetry: meter, rhyme, verses, stanzas, etc., but it can have all the features of prose; not only fiction prose, but also nonfiction. It can have a protagonist, characters, conflicts, action, plot, climax, theme, and tone. It can also be a persuasive discourse and have a thesis (stated or implicit) and supporting points. The arrangement of an analysis will depend to a great extent upon the peculiarities of the poem itself.

In an epic, the conflicts take place in the social sphere rather than a personal life, and it will have a historical basis or one that is accepted as historical. The conflict will be between opposed nations or races and will involve diverging views of civilization that are the foundation of the challenge. Often it will involve the pitting of a group that conceives of itself as a higher civilization against a lower civilization; and, more often than not, divine will determines that the higher one will win, exerting its force over the lower, barbarous, and profane enemy. Examples are the conflict of Greece with Troy, the fates of Rome with the Carthaginian and the Italian, the Crusaders with the Saracen, or even of Milton's Omnipotent versus Satan.

In analyzing these works, protagonist and antagonist need to be clearly identified, the conflicts established, and the climax that sets the world right in the mind of the writer clearly expressed.

At the same time, the form of the epic as a poem must be considered. What meter, rhyme scheme, verse form, and stanza form have been chosen to tell this story? Is it consistent? If it varies, where does it vary, and what does the varying do for the poem/story? What about figures of speech? Is there alliteration or onomatopoeia? Etc.

The epic is a major literary form historically although it had begun to fall out of favor by the end of the seventeenth century. There have been notable efforts to produce an American epic, but they always seem to slide over into prose. The short story and the novel began to take over the genre. Even so, some would say that *Moby Dick* is an American epic.

Narrative poetry, totally apart from attempts to write epics, has been very much a part of the output of modern American writers. Many of Emily Dickenson's poems are narrative in form and retain the features that we look for in the finest of American poetry. The first two verses of "A Narrow Fellow in the Grass" illustrate the use of narrative in a poem:

A narrow fellow in the grass
Occasionally rides;
You may have met him—did you not?
His notice sudden is.

The grass divides as with a comb,
A spotted shaft is seen;
And then it closes at your feet
And opens further on. . . .

This is certainly narrative in nature and has many of the aspects of prose narrative. At the same time, it is a poem with rhyme, meter, verses, stanzas, etc. and can be analyzed as such.

Skill 18.2 Relate various types of lyric poetry to their formal characteristics.

The sonnet is a fixed-verse form of Italian origin, which consists of 14 lines that are typically five-foot iambics rhyming according to a prescribed scheme. Popular since its creation in the thirteenth century in Sicily, it spread at first to Tuscany, where it was adopted by Petrarch. The Petrarchan sonnet generally has a two-part theme. The first eight lines, the octave, state a problem, ask a question, or express an emotional tension. The last six lines, the sestet, resolve the problem, answer the question, or relieve the tension. The rhyme scheme of the octave is abbaabba; that of the sestet varies.

Sir Thomas Wyatt and Henry Howard, Earl of Surrey, introduced this form into England in the sixteenth century. It played an important role in the development of Elizabethan lyric poetry, and a distinctive English sonnet developed, which was composed of three quatrains, each with an independent rhyme-scheme, and it ended with a rhymed couplet. A form of the English sonnet created by Edmond Spenser combines the English form and the Italian. The Spenserian sonnet follows the English quatrain and couplet pattern, but resembles the Italian in its rhyme scheme, which is linked: abab bcbc cdcd ee. Many poets wrote sonnet sequences where several sonnets were linked together, usually to tell a story. Considered to be the greatest of all sonnet sequences is one of Shakespeare's, which is addressed to a young man and a "dark lady," and wherein the love story is overshadowed by the underlying reflections on time and art, growth and decay, and fame and fortune.

The sonnet continued to develop, more in topics than in form. When John Donne in the seventeenth century used the form for religious themes, some of which are almost sermons, or on personal reflections ("When I consider how my light is spent"); there were no longer any boundaries on the themes it could take.

That it is a flexible form is demonstrated in the wide range of themes and purposes it has been used for—all the way from more frivolous concerns to statements about time and death. Wordsworth, Keats, and Elizabeth Barrett Browning used the Petrarchan form of the sonnet. A well-known example is Wordsworth's "The World Is Too Much With Us." Rainer Maria Rilke's Sonnette on Orpheus (1922) is a well-known twentieth-century sonnet.

Analysis of a sonnet should focus on the form—does it fit a traditional pattern or does it break from tradition? If so, why did the poet choose to make that break? Does it reflect the purpose of the poem? What is the theme? What is the purpose? Is it narrative? If so, what story does it tell and is there an underlying meaning? Is the sonnet appropriate for the subject matter?

The limerick probably originated in County Limerick, Ireland, in the 18th century. It is a form of short, humorous verse, often nonsensical, and often ribald. Its five lines rhyme aabbaa with three feet in all lines except the third and fourth, which have only two. Rarely presented as serious poetry, this form is popular because almost anyone can write it.

Analysis of a limerick should focus on its form. Does it conform to a traditional pattern or does it break from the tradition? If so, what impact does that have on the meaning? Is the poem serious or frivolous? Is it funny? Does it try to be funny but does not achieve its purpose? Is there a serious meaning underlying the frivolity?

A cinquain is a poem with a five-line stanza. Adelaide Crapsey (1878-1914) called a five-line verse form a cinquain and invented a particular meter for it. Similar to the haiku, there are two syllables in the first and last lines and four, six, and eight in the middle three lines. It has a mostly iambic cadence. Her poem, "November Night," is an example:

> *Listen...*
> *With faint dry sound*
> *Like steps of passing ghosts,*
> *the leaves,* frost-crisp'd, break from the trees
> And fall.

Haiku is a very popular unrhymed form that is limited to seventeen syllables arranged in three lines thus: five, seven, and five syllables. This verse form originated in Japan in the seventeenth century where it is accepted as serious poetry and is Japan's most popular form. Originally, it was to deal with the season, the time of day, and the landscape although as it has come into more common use, the subjects have become less restricted. The imagist poets and other English writers used the form or imitated it. It's a form much used in classrooms to introduce students to the writing of poetry.

Analysis of a cinquain and a haiku poem should focus on form first. Does the haiku poem conform to the seventeen-syllables requirement and are they arranged in a five, seven, and five pattern? For a cinquain, does it have only five lines? Does the poem distill the words so as much meaning as possible can be conveyed? Does it treat a serious subject? Is the theme discernable? Short forms like these seem simple to dash off; however, they are not effective unless the words are chosen and pared so the meaning intended is conveyed. The impact should be forceful; and that often takes more effort, skill, and creativity than longer forms. This should be taken into account in their analysis.

Skill 18.3 Analyze elements of poetry in context.

Imagery can be described as a word or sequence of words that refers to any sensory experience—that is, anything that can be seen, tasted, smelled, heard, or felt on the skin or fingers. While writers of prose may also use these devices, it is most distinctive of poetry. The poet intends to make an experience available to the reader. In order to do that, poets must appeal to one of the senses. The most-often-used one, of course, is the visual sense. Poets will deliberately paint a scene in such a way that readers can see it. However, the purpose is not simply to stir the visceral feeling, but also to stir the emotions. A good example is "The Piercing Chill" by Taniguchi Buson (1715-1783):

> *The piercing chill I feel:*
> *My dead wife's comb, in our bedroom,*
> *Under my heel . . .*

In only a few short words, readers can feel many things: the shock that might come from touching the corpse, a literal sense of death, the contrast between her death and the memories he has of her when she was alive.

Imagery might be defined as speaking of the abstract in concrete terms, a powerful device in the hands of a skillful poet.

A **symbol** is an object or action that can be observed with the senses in addition to its suggesting many other things. The lion is a symbol of courage; the cross a symbol of Christianity; the color green a symbol of envy. These can almost be defined as metaphors because society pretty much agrees on the one-to-one meaning of them. Symbols used in literature are usually of a different sort. They tend to be private and personal; their significance is only evident in the context of the work where they are used. A good example is the huge pair of spectacles on a sign board in Fitzgerald's *The Great Gatsby*. They are interesting as a part of the landscape, but they also symbolize divine myopia. A symbol can certainly have more than one meaning, and the meaning may be as personal as the memories and experiences of the particular reader. In analyzing a poem or a story, it's important to identify symbols and their possible meanings.

Looking for symbols is often challenging, especially for novice poetry readers. However, these suggestions may be useful: First, pick out all the references to concrete objects such as a newspaper, black cats, rainbows, etc. Note any that the poet emphasizes by describing in detail, by repeating, or by placing at the very beginning or ending of a poem. Ask yourself, what is the poem about? What does it add up to? Paraphrase the poem and determine whether or not the meaning depends upon certain concrete objects. Then ponder what the concrete object symbolizes in this particular poem. Look for a character with the name of a prophet who does little but utter prophecy or a trio of women who resemble the Three Fates. A symbol may be a part of a person's body (such as the eye of the murder victim in Poe's story *The Tell-Tale Heart*), a look, a voice, or a mannerism.

Some things that are not symbols include abstractions such as truth, death, and love or well-developed characters who are not at all mysterious.

An **allusion** is very much like a symbol, and the two sometimes tend to run together. An allusion is defined by Merriam Webster's *Encyclopedia of Literature* as "an implied reference to a person, event, thing, or a part of another text." Allusions are based on the assumptions that there is a common body of knowledge shared by poet and reader and that a reference to that body of knowledge will be immediately understood. Allusions to the Bible and to classical mythology are common in literature because in the past most of the reading public was familiar with those works. This is not always the case now, of course. T. S. Eliot's *The Wasteland* requires research and annotation for understanding. He assumed more background on the part of the average reader than actually exists.

However, when Michael Moore on his web page headlines an article on the war in Iraq: "Déjà Fallouja: Ramadi surrounded, thousands of families trapped, no electricity or water, onslaught impending," we probably understand immediately that he is referring first of all to a repeat of the human disaster in New Orleans although the "onslaught" is not a storm but an invasion by American and Iraqi troops.

The use of allusion is a sort of shortcut for poets. They can use an economy of words and count on meaning to come from the reader's own experience.

Poets use figures of speech to sharpen the effect and meaning of their poems and to help readers see things in ways they have never seen them before. Marianne Moore observed that a fir tree has "an emerald turkey-foot at the top." Her poem makes us aware of something we probably had never noticed before. The sudden recognition of the likeness yields pleasure in the reading. Figurative language allows for the statement of truths that more literal language cannot convey. Skillfully used, a figure of speech will help the reader see more clearly and to focus upon particulars. Figures of speech add many dimensions of richness to our reading and understanding of a poem; they also allow many opportunities for worthwhile analysis. The approach to take in analyzing a poem on the basis of its figures of speech is to ask the questions: What does it do for the poem? Does it underscore meaning? Does it intensify understanding? Does it increase the intensity of our response?

COMPETENCY 19.0 UNDERSTAND THE HISTORICAL, SOCIAL, AND CULTURAL ASPECTS OF LITERATURE, INCLUDING THE WAYS IN WHICH LITERARY WORKS AND MOVEMENTS BOTH REFLECT AND SHAPE CULTURE AND HISTORY.

Skill 19.1 Apply knowledge of the characteristics and significance of mythology and folk literature.

Literary allusions are drawn from classic mythology, national folklore, and religious writings that are supposed to have such familiarity to readers that they can recognize the comparison between the subject of the allusion and the person, place, or event in the current reading. Children and adolescents who have knowledge of proverbs, fables, myths, epics, and the *Bible* can understand these allusions and thereby appreciate their reading to a greater degree than those who cannot recognize them.

Fables and folktales

This literary group of stories and legends was originally orally transmitted to the common populace to provide models of exemplary behavior or deeds. In fables, animals talk, feel, and behave like human beings. The fable always has a moral, and the animals illustrate specific people or groups without directly identifying them. For example, in Aesop's *Fables,* the lion is the "King," and the wolf is the cruel, often unfeeling, "noble class." In the fable of "The Lion and the Mouse," the moral is that "Little friends may prove to be great friends." In "The Lion's Share," it is "Might makes right." Many British folktales (*How Robin Became an Outlaw* and *St. George - Slaying of the Dragon*) stress the correlation between power and right.

Classical mythology

Much of the mythology that produces allusions in modern English writings is a product of ancient Greece and Rome because these myths have been more liberally translated. Some Norse myths are also well known. Children are fond of myths because those ancient people were seeking explanations for those elements in their lives that predated scientific knowledge just as children seek explanations for the occurrences in their lives. These stories provide insight into the order and ethics of life as ancient heroes overcome the terrors of the unknown and bring meaning to the thunder and lightning, to the changing of the seasons, to the magical creatures of the forests and seas, and to the myriad of natural phenomena that can frighten mankind. There is often a childlike quality in the emotions of supernatural beings with which children can identify. Many good translations of myths exist for readers of varying abilities, but Edith Hamilton's *Mythology* is the most definitive reading for adolescents.

Fairy tales

Fairy tales are lively fictional stories involving children or animals that come in contact with super-beings via magic. They provide happy solutions to human dilemmas. The fairy tales of many nations are peopled by trolls, elves, dwarfs, and pixies--child-sized beings capable of fantastic accomplishments.

Among the most famous are "Beauty and the Beast," "Cinderella," "Hansel and Gretel," "Snow White and the Seven Dwarfs," "Rumplestiltskin," and "Tom Thumb." In each tale, the protagonist survives prejudice, imprisonment, ridicule, and even death to receive justice in a cruel world.

Older readers encounter a kind of fairy tale world in Shakespeare's *The Tempest* and in his *A Midsummer Night's Dream*, which use pixies and fairies as characters. Adolescent readers today are fascinated by the creations of fantasy realms in the works of Piers Anthony, Ursula LeGuin, and Anne McCaffrey. An extension of interest in the supernatural explains the popularity of science fiction, the genre that allows us to use current knowledge to predict the possible course of the future.

Angels (or sometimes fairy godmothers) play a role in some fairy tales, and Milton in *Paradise Lost* and in *Paradise Regained* also used symbolic angels and devils.

Biblical stories provide many allusions. Parables, moralistic like fables, but having human characters; include the stories of the Good Samaritan and the Prodigal Son. References to the treachery of Cain and the betrayal of Christ by Judas Iscariot are oft-cited examples.

American folk tales

American folktales are divided into two categories.

Imaginary tales, also called tall tales (humorous tales based on non-existent, fictional characters developed through blatant exaggeration)

> John Henry is a two-fisted steel driver who beats out a steam drill in competition.
>
> Rip Van Winkle sleeps for twenty years in the Catskill Mountains and, upon awakening, cannot understand why no one recognizes him.
>
> Paul Bunyan, a giant lumberjack, owns a great blue ox named Babe and has extraordinary physical strength. He is said to have plowed the Mississippi River, and the impression of Babe's hoof prints created the Great Lakes.

Real tales, also called legends (based on real persons who accomplished the feats that are attributed to them even if they are slightly exaggerated)

For more than forty years, Johnny Appleseed (John Chapman) roamed Ohio and Indiana planting apple seeds.

> Daniel Boone - scout, adventurer, and pioneer - blazed the Wilderness Trail and made Kentucky safe for settlers.

> Paul Revere, an colonial patriot, rode through the New England countryside warning of the approach of British troops.

> George Washington cut down a cherry tree, which he could not deny, or did he?

Skill 19.2   Analyze the expression of cultural values and ideas through literature.

Literature is powerful in influencing the thinking of individual readers and all of society. Waves of philosophical ideas have swept over the reading world almost from the time of the invention of the printing press. It's possible to trace the emergence of a particular set of values over centuries. Feminism is a case in point. While the matter of women's rights didn't reach a boiling point until the 1960s, it can be traced through history for many years.

For example, Empress Theodora of Byzantium was a proponent of legislation that would afford greater protections and freedoms to her female subjects, and Christine de Pizan, the first professional female writer, advanced many feminist ideas as early as the 1300s in the face of attempts to restrict female inheritance and guild membership. In 1869, John Stuart Mill published *The Subjection of Women* to demonstrate that "the legal subordination of one sex to the other is wrong…and…one of the chief hindrances to human improvement." Norwegian playwright Henrik Ibsen wrote a highly controversial play, *A Doll's House,* in 1879. It was a scathing criticism of the traditional roles of men and women in Victorian marriages. These and many other works with feminist themes led to changes in the way society viewed women throughout the civilized world. The impact of the literature and the changes in thinking on this issue led to many countries granting the vote to women in the late 1800s and the early years of the 20th century.

Regional literature has played an important role in the themes of popular literature, particularly in American literature. The best-known of the regional American writers is Samuel Langhorne Clemens (better known as Mark Twain) with his stories about the Mississippi River and the state of Missouri. Although his home state was a slave state and considered by many to be part of the South, it declined to join the Confederacy and remained loyal to the Union. He included sympathetic slave characters in many of his stories.

Some regional American writers:

Harriet Beecher Stowe
Sarah Orne Jewett
George Washington Cable
Joel Chandler Harris
Edward Eggleston
James Whitcomb Riley
Bret Harte

Ethnic themes are also very popular in American literature.

Toni Morrison, who writes African-American stories, is considered to be the most important American writer of the last 25 years and won the Nobel Prize for Literature in 1993 for her collected works. Saul Bellow wrote of his own Jewish background and won the Nobel Prize in 1976.

James Michener wrote historical fiction: *Tales of the South Pacific* (for which he won the Pulitzer Prize for Fiction in 1948), *Hawaii*, *The Drifters*, *Centennial*, *The Source*, *The Fires of Spring*, *Chesapeake*, *Caribbean*, *Caravans*, *Alaska*, *Texas*, and *Poland*.

Literature about a particular period has also been very popular with American writers. The Civil War era has been a very successful subject for novels, most notable of which is *Gone With the Wind* by Margaret Mitchell.

Some novels about the American Civil War:

- *The Red Badge of Courage* by Stephen Crane
- *Cold Mountain* by Charles Frazier
- *Love and War* by John Jakes
- *Gods and Generals*; *The Last Full Measure* by Jeffrey Shaara
- *By Valour and Arms* by James Street
- *Fort Pillow* by Harry Turtledove
- *Lincoln* by Gore Vidal

Skill 19.3 Analyze the role of given authors and works in influencing public opinion about and understanding of social issues.

From the time of the invention of the printing press, writers have played important roles in shaping public opinion, not only in their own countries, but also around the world. Worldwide philosophical trends can be traced to the literature that was popular in a particular period of time. America has always been a nation of readers. With the development of theaters and, ultimately, movies and television dramatizing popular novels, the power of the written word has increased.

John Steinbeck's *Grapes of Wrath* focused the attention of Americans on the plight of the common people who suffered more than anyone else during the Great Depression. His revelation that Americans were starving to death in a land of great abundance still resonates with the public. Members of the "establishment" in the farms and towns of California are revealed as callous and greedy. Church members, particularly clergy and leaders, don't come off much better in his revealing story. Steinbeck lived with some of the migrants, so he could write authentically and with first-hand knowledge. Many of the writers who have influenced public opinion write from personal experience.

The feminist movement has virtually been fueled by literature going back several hundred years.

Although the organized movement began with the first women's rights convention at Seneca Falls, New York, in 1948; by 1869, John Stuart Mill had already published *The Subjection of Women* to demonstrate that the legal subordination of one sex to the other is wrong. Virginia Woolf's essay, *A Room of One's Own*, first published in 1929, had a strong influence on how women were beginning to see their roles.

However, in the crusade that was ignited by the Civil Rights movement of the 1960s, Betty Friedan's book, *The Feminine Mystique*, published in 1963, was very popular and influenced many women to become involved, both in changes in their own outlooks and behaviors and in the movement at large. Feminism has been so much a part of the thinking throughout the world that it should always be included in the potential themes one looks for when writing a critique of a literary work.

Uncle Tom's Cabin broke new ground in literature on social injustice and was very powerful in influencing the thinking of American people about slavery. It was the best-selling novel of the 19th century and is credited with helping to fuel the abolitionist cause prior to the American Civil War. Written by Harriet Beecher Stowe and published in 1852, slavery is its central theme.

The Vietnam War inspired many novels although most were written after the war was over. However, the attitudes of Americans about the war have been influenced by these novels, and, for many, they have formed the concept they carry with them about the conflict.

Some examples of novels about the Vietnam War:

- *Apocalypse Now*
- *Full Metal Jacket*
- *Platoon*
- *Good Morning Vietnam*
- *The Deer Hunter*
- *Born on the Fourth of July*
- *Hamburger Hill*

C. History of Literature

COMPETENCY 20.0 UNDERSTAND SIGNIFICANT THEMES, CHARACTERISTICS, TRENDS, WRITERS, AND WORKS IN AMERICAN LITERATURE FROM THE COLONIAL PERIOD TO THE PRESENT, INCLUDING THE LITERARY CONTRIBUTIONS OF WOMEN, MEMBERS OF ETHNIC MINORITIES, AND FIGURES IDENTIFIED WITH PARTICULAR REGIONS.

Skill 20.1 Analyze the significance of major writers, works, and movements to the development of American literature.

The Colonial Period

William Bradford's excerpts from *The Mayflower Compact* relate vividly the hardships of crossing the Atlantic in such a tiny vessel, the misery and suffering of the first winter, the approaches of the American Indians, the decimation of their ranks, and the establishment of the Bay Colony of Massachusetts.

Anne Bradstreet's poetry relates much concerning colonial New England life. From her journals, modern readers learn of the everyday life of the early settlers, the hardships of travel, and the responsibilities of different groups and individuals in the community, Early American literature also reveals the commercial and political adventures of the Cavaliers who came to the New World with King George's blessing.

William Byrd's journal, *A History of the Dividing Line,* concerning his trek into the Dismal Swamp separating the Carolinian territories from Virginia and Maryland, makes quite lively reading. A privileged insider to the English Royal Court, Byrd, like other Southern Cavaliers, was given grants to pursue business ventures.

The Revolutionary Period

There were great orations such as Patrick Henry's *Speech to the Virginia House of Burgesses* -- the "Give me liberty or give me death" speech - and George Washington's *Farewell to the Army of the Potomac.* Less memorable (and thought to ramble by modern readers) are Washington's inaugural addresses.

The *Declaration of Independence*, the brainchild predominantly of Thomas Jefferson

(with some prudent editing by Ben Franklin), is a prime example of neoclassical writing because it is balanced, well crafted, and focused.

Epistles include the exquisitely written, moving correspondence between John Adams and Abigail Adams. The poignancy of their separation (she in Boston, he in Philadelphia) is palpable and real.

The Romantic Period

Nathaniel Hawthorne and Herman Melville are the preeminent early American novelists, writing on subjects definitely regional, specific and American; yet sharing insights about human foibles, fears, loves, doubts, and triumphs. Hawthorne's writings range from children's stories (the Cricket on the Hearth series) to adult fare of dark, brooding short stories ("Dr. Heidegger's Experiment," "The Devil and Tom Walker," and "Rapuccini's Daughter"). His masterpiece, *The Scarlet Letter*, takes on the society of hypocritical Puritan New Englanders, who ostensibly left England to establish religious freedom, but who have became entrenched in judgmental finger wagging. They ostracize Hester and condemn her child, Pearl, as a child of Satan. Great love, sacrifice, loyalty, suffering, and related epiphanies add universality to this tale. *The House of the Seven Gables* also deals with kept secrets, loneliness, societal pariahs, and love ultimately triumphing over horrible wrong. Herman Melville's great opus, *Moby Dick*, follows a crazed Captain Ahab on his Homeric odyssey to conquer the great white whale that has outwitted him and his whaling crews time and again. The whale has even taken Arab's leg and, according to Ahab, wants all of him. Melville recreates in painstaking detail, and with insider knowledge, the harsh life of a whaler out of New Bedford by way of Nantucket. For those who don't want to learn about every guy rope or all parts of the whaler's rigging, Melville offers up the succinct tale of Billy Budd and his Christ-like sacrifice to the black and white maritime laws on the high seas. An accident results in the death of one of the ship's officers, a slug of a fellow, who had taken a dislike to the young, affable, shy Billy. Captain Vere must hang Billy for the death of Claggert, but knows that this is not right. However, an example must be given to the rest of the crew so that discipline can be maintained.

Edgar Allan Poe created a distinctly American version of romanticism with his 16-syllable line in "The Raven," the classical "To Helen," and his Gothic "Annabelle Lee." The horror short story can be said to originate from Poe's pen. "The Tell-Tale Heart," "The Cask of Amontillado," "The Fall of the House of Usher," and "The Masque of the Red Death" are exemplary short stories. The new genre of detective story also emerges with Poe's "Murders in the Rue Morgue."

American Romanticism has its own offshoot in the Transcendentalism of Ralph Waldo Emerson and Henry David Thoreau. One wrote about transcending the complexities of life; the other, who wanted to get to the marrow of life, immersed himself in nature at Walden Pond and wrote an inspiring autobiographical account of his sojourn, aptly titled *On Walden Pond*. He also wrote passionately on his objections to the government's interference with the individual in "On the Duty of Civil Disobedience."

Emerson's elegantly crafted essays and war poetry still validate several important universal truths.

Probably most remembered for his address to Thoreau's Harvard graduating class, "The American Scholar;" he defined the qualities of hard work and intellectual spirit required of Americans in their growing nation.

The Transition between Romanticism and Realism

The Civil War period ushered in the poignant poetry of Walt Whitman and his homages to all who suffered from the ripple effects of war and presidential assassination. His "Come up from the Fields, Father" about a Civil War soldier's death and his family's reaction and "When Lilacs Last in the Courtyard Bloom'd" about the effects of Abraham Lincoln's death on the poet and the nation should be required readings in any American literature course. Further, his *Leaves of Grass* gave America its first poetry truly unique in form, structure, and subject matter.

Emily Dickinson, like Walt Whitman, leaves her literary fingerprints on a vast array of poems, all but three of which were never published in her lifetime. Her themes of introspection and attention to nature's details and wonders are, by any measurement, world-class works. Her posthumous recognition reveals the timeliness of her work. American writing had most certainly arrived!

Mark Twain also left giant footprints with his unique blend of tall tale and fable. "The Celebrated Jumping Frog of Calaveras County" and "The Man who Stole Hadleyburg" are epitomes of short story writing. Move to novel creation, and Twain again rises head and shoulders above others by his bold, still disputed, oft-banned *The Adventures of Huckleberry Finn*, which examines such taboo subjects as a white person's love of a slave, the issue of leaving children with abusive parents, and the outcomes of family feuds. Written partly in dialect and southern vernacular, *The Adventures of Huckleberry Finn* is touted by some as the greatest American novel.

Contemporary American Literature

America Drama

The greatest and most prolific of American playwrights include:

Eugene O'Neill -- *Long Day's Journey into Night*, *Mourning Becomes Electra*, and *Desire Under the Elms*

Arthur Miller -- *The Crucible*, *All My Sons*, and *Death of a Salesman*

Tennessee Williams -- *Cat on a Hot Tin Roof*, *The Glass Menagerie*, and *A Street Car Named Desire*

Edward Albee -- *Who's Afraid of Virginia Woolf?*, *Three Tall Women*, and *A Delicate Balance*

American Fiction

The renowned American novelists of this century include

John Updike -- *Rabbit Run* and *Rabbit Redux*

Sinclair Lewis -- *Babbit* and *Elmer Gantry*

F. Scott Fitzgerald -- *The Great Gatsby* and *Tender is the Night*

Ernest Hemingway -- *A Farewell to Arms* and *For Whom the Bell Tolls*

William Faulkner -- *The Sound and the Fury* and *Absalom, Absalom*

Bernard Malamud -- *The Fixer* and *The Natural*

American Poetry

The poetry of the twentieth century is multifaceted, as represented by Edna St. Vincent Millay, Marianne Moore, Richard Wilbur, Langston Hughes, Maya Angelou, and Rita Lone. Head and shoulders above all others are the many-layered poems of Robert Frost. His New England motifs of snowy evenings, birches, apple picking, stone wall mending, hired hands, and detailed nature studies relate universal truths in exquisite diction, polysyllabic words, and rare allusions to either mythology or the *Bible*.

American Indian Literature

The foundation of American Indian writing is found in story-telling, oratory, autobiographical and historical accounts of tribal village life, reverence for the environment, and the postulation that the earth with all of its beauty was given in trust to be cared for and passed on to future generations.

Early American Indian writings

Barland, Hal. *When The Legends Die*

Barrett, S.M. Editor: *Geronimo: His Own Story - Apache*

Eastman, C. & Eastman E. *Wigwam Evenings: Sioux Folktales Retold*

Riggs, L. *Cherokee Night* - drama

Twentieth Century Writers

Deloria, V. *Custer Died for your Sins* (Sioux)

Dorris, M. *The Broken Cord: A Family's on-going struggle with fetal alcohol syndrome* (Modoc)

Hogan, L. *Mean Spirited* (Chickasaw)

Taylor, C.F. *Native American Myths and Legends*

Afro-American Literature

The three phases of Afro-American Literature can be broken down as follows:

- Oppression, slavery, and the re-construction of the post-Civil War/rural South

- Inner city strife/single parenting, drug abuse, lack of educational opportunities and work advancement etc. that was controlled by biased and disinterested factions of society.

- Post-Civil Rights and the emergence of the Black movement focusing on biographical and autobiographical Black heroes and their contribution to Black and American culture.

Resources:

1. Pre-Civil War

Bethune, Mary McLoed. *Voice of Black Hope*
Fast, Howard. *Freedom Ride*
Haskins, James. *Black Music in America - A History through its People*
Huggins, Nathan Irving. *Black Odyssey*
Lemann, Nicolas. *The Promised Land*
Stowe, Harriet Beecher. *Uncle Tom's Cabin*
Wheatley, Phyllis. *Memoirs and Poems*

2. Post-Civil War and Reconstruction

Armstrong, William. *Sounder*
Bonham, Frank. *Durango Street*
Childress, Alice. *A Hero Ain't Nothin' But a Sandwich*
Gaines, Ernest. *The Autobiography of Miss Jane Pittman*

3. Post Civil War - Present

Angelou, Maya. *I Know Why the Caged Bird Sings*
Baldwin, James. *Go Tell It on the Mountain*
Haley, Alex. *Roots*
Hansberry, Lorraine. *A Raisin in the Sun*
Lee, Harper. *To Kill a Mockingbird*
Hughes, Langston. *I, Too, Sing America*
Wright, Richard. *White Man, Listen!* and *Native Son*

Latino/a Literature

In the field of literature, we have two new expanding areas; Latino/a and feminist writers. These authors write to retain cultural heritage; to share their people's struggle for recognition, independence, and survival; and to express their hopes for the future.

Latino/Latina Writers
De Cervantes, Lora (Chicana). *Starfish*
Cisneros, Sandra (Hispanic). *Red Sweater* and other short story collections
Marquez, Gabriel Garcia (Colombian). *Hundred Years of Solitude*
Nunoz, A. Lopez (Spanish). *Programas Para Dias Especiales*
Neruda, Pablo (Chile). Nobel Prize Winner- Collections of Poetry
Silko, Leslie Marmon (Mexican). *The Time We Climbed Snake Mountain*
Soto, Gary (Mexican). *The Tales of Sunlight*

Feminist / gender concern literature written by women in the United States

Edith Wharton's *Ethan Frome* is a heartbreaking tale of lack of communication, lack of funds, the unrelenting cold of the Massachusetts winter, and a toboggan ride which gnarls Ethan and Mattie so that they resemble the old tree which they smash into. The *Age of Innocence*, in contrast to *Ethan Frome*, is set in the upper echelons of fin-de-siècle New York and explores marriage without stifling social protocols.

Willa Cather's work moves the reader to the prairies of Nebraska and the harsh eking out of existence by the immigrant families who choose to stay there and farm. Her most acclaimed works include *My Antonia* and *Death Comes for the Archbishop*.

Kate Chopin's regionalism and local color takes her readers to the upper-crust Creole society of New Orleans and resort isles off the Louisiana coast. "The Story of an Hour" is lauded as one of the greatest of all short stories. Her feminist liberation novel, *The Awakening*, is still hotly debated.

Eudora Welty's regionalism and dialect shine in her short stories of rural Mississippi, especially in "The Worn Path."

Modern black female writers who explore the world of feminist/gender issues as well as class prohibitions are Alice Walker -- (*The Color Purple*), Zora Neale Hurston (*Their Eyes Were Watching God*), and Toni Morrison (*Beloved*, *Jazz*, and *Song of Solomon*).

Feminists

Alcott, Louisa May. *Little Women*
Friedan, Betty. *The Feminine Mystique: The Second Stage*
Bronte, Charlotte. *Jane Eyre*
Hurston, Zora Neale. *Their Eyes Were Watching God*
Janeway, Elizabeth. *Woman's World, Woman's Place: A Study in Social Mythology*
Chopin, Kate. *The Awakening*
Rich, Adrienne. Arienne Rich's Poetry: *Motherhood As Experience* and *Driving into the Wreck*
Woolf, Virginia. *A Room of One's Own.*

Skill 20.2 Analyze changes in literary form and style in American literature of the colonial, nineteenth-century, modern, and contemporary periods.

American Literature is defined by a number of clearly identifiable periods.

1. **Native American works from various tribes**

These were originally part of a vast oral tradition that spanned most of continental America from as far back as before the 15th century.

- Characteristics of native Indian literature include
  - Reverence for and awe of nature.
  - The interconnectedness of the elements in the life cycle.

- Themes of Indian literature often reflect
  - The hardiness of the native body and soul.
  - Remorse for the destruction of their way of life.
  - The genocide of many tribes by the encroaching settlement and Manifest Destiny policies of the U. S. government.

2. **The Colonial Period in both New England and the South**

Stylistically, early colonists' writings were neo-classical, emphasizing order, balance, clarity, and reason. Schooled in England, their writing and speaking was still decidedly British even as their thinking became entirely American.

Early American literature reveals the lives and experiences of the New England expatriates who left England to find religious freedom.

The Revolutionary Period contains non-fiction genres: essays, pamphlets, speeches, famous documents, and epistles.

Thomas Paine's pamphlet, *Common Sense*, which, though written by a recently transplanted Englishman, spoke to the American patriots' common sense in dealing with the issues in the cause of freedom.

Other contributions are Benjamin Franklin's essays from *Poor Richard's Almanac* and satires such as "How to Reduce a Great Empire to a Small One" and "A Letter to Madame Gout."

3. **The Romantic Period**

Early American folktales, and the emergence of distinctly American writing, not just a stepchild of English forms, constitute the next period.

Washington Irving's characters, Icabod Crane and Rip Van Winkle, create a uniquely American folklore devoid of English influences. The characters are indelibly marked by their environment and the superstitions of the New Englander. The early American writings of James Fenimore Cooper and his Leatherstocking Tales with their stirring accounts of the Mohawk and the French and Indian Wars, the futile British defense of Fort William Henry, and the brutalities of this time frame allow readers a window into their uniquely American world. Natty Bumppo, Chingachgook, Uncas, and Magua are unforgettable characters that reflect the American spirit in thought and action.

The poetry of Fireside Poets - James Russell Lowell, Oliver Wendell Holmes, Henry Wadsworth Longfellow, and John Greenleaf Whittier - was recited by American families and read in the long New England winters. In "The Courtin'," Lowell used Yankee dialect to tell a story. Spellbinding epics by Longfellow (*Hiawatha*, *The Courtship of Miles Standish*, and *Evangeline*) told of adversity, sorrow, and ultimate happiness.
 "Snowbound," by Whittier, relates the story of a captive family isolated by a blizzard, stressing family closeness. Holmes' "The Chambered Nautilus" and his famous line, "Fired the shot heard round the world," put American poetry on a firm footing with other world writers.

4. **The Transition between Romanticism and Realism**

During this period, such legendary figures as Paul Bunyan and Pecos Bill rose from the oral tradition. Anonymous storytellers told tales around campfires of a huge lumberman and his giant blue ox, Babe, whose adventures supplied explanations of natural phenomena like footprints filled with rainwater becoming the Great Lakes or the whirling-dervish speed of Pecos Bill creating the tornadoes of the Southwest. Like ancient peoples finding reasons for the happenings in their lives, these American pioneer storytellers created a mythology appropriate to the vast reaches of the unsettled frontier.

5. The Realistic Period

The late nineteenth century saw a reaction against the tendency of romantic writers to look at the world through rose-colored glasses. Writers like Frank Norris (*The Pit*) and Upton Sinclair (*The Jungle*) used their novels to decry conditions for workers in slaughterhouses and wheat mills. In *The Red Badge of Courage*, Stephen Crane wrote of the daily sufferings of the common soldier in the Civil War. Realistic writers wrote of common, ordinary people and events using detail that would reveal the harsh realities of life. They broached taboos by creating protagonists whose environments often destroyed them. Romantic writers would have only protagonists whose indomitable wills helped them rise above adversity. Crane's *Maggie: A Girl of the Streets* deals with a young woman forced into prostitution to survive. In "The Occurrence at Owl Creek Bridge," Ambrose Bierce relates the unfortunate hanging of a Confederate soldier.

Short stories, like Bret Harte's "The Outcasts of Poker Flat" and Jack London's "To Build a Fire," deal with unfortunate people whose luck in life has run out. Many writers, sub-classified as naturalists, believed that man was subject to a fate over which he had no control.

6. The Modern Era

The twentieth century American writing can be classified into three basic genres:

- Drama
- Fiction
- Poetry

See Skill 20.1 for highlighted authors and works in these genres.

Skill 20.3   Analyze in passage context major thematic concerns and stylistic and formal characteristics associated with significant American prose writers and dramatists and poets.

Herman Melville was born in 1819 and grew up in upper-class New York neighborhoods. His mother was a strict Calvinist Presbyterian and had strong views regarding proper behavior. Herman tended to be a rebellious sort, and to some extent his conflicts regarding his mother's viewpoints were never resolved. When Herman was eleven years old, his father's business failed, and the father died shortly afterward. Herman tried working in business for awhile, but soon decided that he wanted to go to sea.

Working on ships and traveling, he began to write non-fiction pieces about his experiences. In July of 1851, he wrote his most famous work, *Moby Dick*.

Before he died, he wrote poems and another well-known novel, *Billy Budd*, which was not published until 1924. Just as he began to write *Moby Dick*, he became friends with Nathaniel Hawthorne, who happened to be his neighbor. Hawthorne's works and friendship became an important influence on his writing.

In *Moby Dick*, the style is indicative of the reportorial writing of the earlier period; however, it is far more than that. It is seen as a great American epic, even though it is not poetry. It was not successful while its author was alive. Its success came much later.

Some Themes:

- Man in conflict with the natural world
- Religion and God's role in the universe
- Good and evil
- Cause and effect
- Duty
- Conscience

Richard Wright was the grandson of slaves and grew up in a time when the lives of African-Americans tended to be very grim. His response to life lived so close to those who had so recently risen from bondage permeates his writing.

His writing went through many changes, just as his response to the special reality of life as a black person in a white-dominated world went through many changes. In order to understand his work, the date of the writing—the stage he was undergoing at the time—is very important. He was influenced early by Maxim Gorky, whose own life experience had similarities to Wright's. Later, he was heavily influenced by Dostoevsky, and that writer's themes can be identified in the work from his last period.

Survival for many blacks and black communities required conformity to whatever white people demanded, and Wright rejected that. He felt profoundly alienated and wounded. He became a proletarian revolutionary artist in the earliest years of his career. The American Communist Party nabbed him as their most illustrious recruit to the newly-established literary standards of proletarian realism. He rejected the "conspicuous ornamentation" of institutions imposed by segregation, such as the Harlem Renaissance. At the same time, he felt that consciousness must draw its strength from the lore of a great people, his own. He sought, in the early years of the 20th century, to integrate the progressive aspects of the folk culture of the African-Americans into a collective myth that would promote a revolutionary approach to reality.

He left the Communist Party in 1944, largely as a result of his own evolution. *Black Boy*, an autobiographical account of his childhood and young manhood, appeared in 1945.

He settled in Paris as a permanent expatriate shortly after its publication. His first stories—*Uncle Tom's Children*—are a re-conception of negro spirituals and black Christianity in which the hero chooses to risk martyrdom in progressively more elevated stages of class consciousness.

Some themes:

- The environment of the South is too small to nourish human beings, especially African-Americans
- Rejection of black militancy
- Violent, battered childhood and victorious adulthood
- Suffocation of instinct and stifling of potential
- Mature reminiscences of a battered childhood
- Black mother's protective nurture and the trauma of an absent or impotent father
- Each is responsible for everyone and everything (later works)

His technique and style are not as important as the impact his ideas and attitudes have had on American life. He set out to portray African-Americans to white readers in such a way that the myth of the uncomplaining, comic, obsequious black man might be replaced.

Willa Cather grew up on the western plains in Nebraska, and much of her best fiction focuses on the pioneering period in that part of the country. She was born in Virginia in 1873 on her family's farm; but in 1884, the family moved to Nebraska, where other relatives had settled. Much of the lore that is the basis of her stories came from her visits with immigrant farm women around Red Cloud, where the family eventually made their home.

When she was sixteen, she enrolled at the University of Nebraska in Lincoln, where an essay in her English class was favorably accepted, and she began to support herself as a journalist. She moved to Pittsburgh and was working as a writer and editor when she decided that she wanted to teach school. Even so, she continued to develop her writing career. On a trip back to Nebraska, she witnessed a wheat harvest, which triggered her motive for writing about the pioneer period of American history.

Some Themes:

- The American Dream
- Prejudice
- Coming of Age
- Nostalgia

Maxine Hong Kingston's parents were Chinese immigrants who lived in Stockton, California. Her fiction is highly autobiographical, and she weaves Chinese myths and fictionalized history with the aim of exploring the conflicts between cultures faced by Chinese-Americans. Her writing exposes the ordeals of the Chinese immigrants who were exploited by American companies, particularly railroad and agriculture industries. She also explores relationships within the Chinese families, particularly between parents who were born in China and children who were born in America. In a 1980 *New York Times Book Review* interview, she said "What I am doing in this new book [*China Men*] is churning America."

Some Themes:

- Discovery
- The American Dream
- Male/Female Roles
- Metamorphosis
- Enforced Muteness
- Vocal Expression
- Family

Poets:

Walt Whitman's poetry was more often than not inspired by the Civil War. He is America's greatest romantic poet, and many of his poems are related to, and come directly from, the conflict between the northern and southern states. This is not to say that the war was the only influence; he wrote many poems on topics that are not directly related to it. His major work, *Leaves of Grass,* was revised nine times, the last in 1892 shortly before he died. He used sophisticated linguistic devices much ahead of his time. Even though he dealt with a vast, panoramic vision, his style has a personal and immediate effect on the reader.

When he was born in 1819 on Long Island in New York, it was a time of great patriotism for the new nation; however, he experienced the conflict that presented a serious threat to its survival in the war between the states. It's no wonder that the conflict became the subject matter for most of his creative output. His father was a carpenter and then a farmer. Walt was the second-born of eight, the first son. He had six years of public education before he went to work for Brooklyn lawyers and began to educate himself in the library. He began his writing career with newspaper articles and eventually wrote short stories that were published in newspapers. His unconventional techniques were his own creation, and in *Leaves of Grass* he intended to speak for all Americans.

He worked as a volunteer in hospitals to help care for soldiers and was deeply affected by the horrors of war that he saw first-hand.

His poetry was considered to be indecent by some, and he was both praised and vilified during his lifetime. He died in 1892 of tuberculosis.

Some Themes:

- Imagination vs. Scientific Process
- Individualism

Emily Dickinson has been called the "myth of Amherst" because so little is known of her. She was born in 1830, the second child of Edward and Emily Dickinson. Her family was prominent in Massachusetts and played a major role in the founding of Amherst College. Her father's stern, puritanical control of his family played a pivotal role in the poetry that his daughter eventually wrote. Although he was severe and controlling, he saw that his daughters got a good education. Emily attended Amherst Academy and then Mount Holyoke Female Seminary. She obtained a copy of Emerson's poems in 1850 and began to develop her own beliefs regarding religion and the severe God that her father represented.

Only a few of her poems were published during her lifetime, and she was unknown until after her death. After she withdrew from school, she became more and more reclusive; and, after the death of her father in 1874, she never again left her home. She died of Bright's disease in 1886. Her sister, Lavinia, found roughly 2,000 poems on small pieces of paper, which were published in several editions. The first full edition was released in three-volumes in 1955. She has come to be known for her superb use of concrete language and imagery to express and evoke abstract issues. Most people have a favorite Dickinson poem.

Her themes range widely, but following are a few:

- Sanity/insanity
- Doubt
- Death
- Individuality
- Defiance
- Feminism

Gwendolyn Brooks created acute images of African Americans in the cities of America and was the first African American to receive a Pulitzer Prize for Poetry. Born in 1917 to a schoolteacher and a janitor, she grew up in Chicago. She was named poet laureate of Illinois in 1978 and was the first black woman to be an honorary fellow of the Modern Language Association. Her family was close-knit, and she tended to spend her time reading when she was a child. She began writing poems when she was very young. She has also had a successful teaching career at several universities, including City University of New York as a Distinguished Professor. Gwendolyn was writing about the experience of being black long before it became main-stream.

She underwent an evolution in subject matter and thinking about being black as a result of the movement of the sixties championing the validity of African Americans. She died of cancer in 2000. She was eighty-three years old.

Themes:

- Poverty and Racism
- Self-respect
- Heritage
- Community
- Family
- Black Unity
- The Basic Humanness in Everyone
- Black Solidarity
- Pride

Leslie Marmon Silko is a Laguna Indian of mixed ancestry that includes Cherokee, German, English, Mexican, and Pueblo. There were several remarkable women in her life, grandmothers and aunts, who taught her the traditions and stories of the Pueblo. At the same time, her father's role in his tribe also made her aware of the abuses her people had experienced at the hands of the government. The major issue was the land that had been stolen from her people. She believed that she could change things by writing about them.

Some themes:
- Evil
- Reciprocity
- Individual/Community
- Native American Traditions
- Native American Religion
- Mixed Breeds
- Scapegoats
- Racism
- Prejudice

Skill 20.4 **Relate given passages to social institutions, historical events, and cultural movements that influenced the development of American literature.**

Local Color is defined as the presenting of the peculiarities of a particular locality and its inhabitants. This genre began to be seen primarily after the Civil War although there were certainly precursors such as Washington Irving and his depiction of life in the Catskill Mountains of New York.

However, the local colorist movement is generally considered to have begun in 1865, when humor began to permeate the writing of those who were focusing on a particular region of the country. Samuel L. Clemens (Mark Twain) is best-known for his humorous works about the Southwest, such as The Notorious Jumping Frog of Calaveras County. The country had just emerged from its "long night of the soul," a time when death, despair, and disaster had preoccupied the nation for almost five years. It's no wonder that the artists sought to relieve the grief and pain and lift spirits, nor is it surprising that their efforts brought such a strong response. Mark Twain is generally considered to be not only one of America's funniest writers, but one who also wrote great and enduring fiction.

Other examples of local colorists who used many of the same devices are Harriet Beecher Stowe, Bret Harte, George Washington Cable, Joel Chandler Harris, and Sarah Orne Jewett.

Slavery

The best-known of the early writers who used fiction as a political statement about slavery is Harriet Beecher Stowe, author of *Uncle Tom's Cabin*. This was her first novel, and it was published first as a serial in 1851 and then as a book in 1852. It brought an angry reaction from people living in the South. This antislavery book infuriated Southerners. However, Stowe, herself, had been angered by the 1850 Fugitive Slave Law that made it legal to indict those who assisted runaway slaves. It also took away rights not only of the runaways, but also of the free slaves. She intended to generate a protest of the law and slavery. It was the first effort to present the lives of slaves from their standpoint.

The novel is about three slaves, Tom, Eliza, and George, who are together in Kentucky. Eliza and George are married to each other, but have different masters. They successfully escape with their little boy, but Tom does not. Although he has a wife and children, he is sold, ending up finally with the monstrous Simon Legree, where he eventually dies. Stowe cleverly used depictions of motherhood and Christianity to stir her readers. When President Lincoln finally met her, he told her it was her book that started the war.

Many writers used the printed word to protest slavery. Some of them include:

- Frederick Douglas
- William Lloyd Garrison
- Benjamin Lay, a Quaker
- Connecticut theologian Jonathan Edward
- Susan B. Anthony

Civil Rights

Many of the abolitionists were also early crusaders for civil rights.

The 1960s movement focused attention on the plight of the people who had been "freed" by the Civil War and brought about long overdue changes in the opportunities for, and rights of, African Americans. David Halberstam, who had been a reporter in Nashville at the time of the sit-ins by eight young black college students that initiated the revolution, wrote *The Children* (published in 1998 by Random House) for the purpose of reminding Americans of their courage, suffering, and achievements. Congressman John Lewis, Fifth District, Georgia, was one of those eight young men who has gone on to a life of public service. Halberstam records that when older black ministers tried to persuade these young people not to pursue their protest, John Lewis responded: "If not us, then who? If not now, then when?"

Some examples of protest literature:

- James Baldwin, *Blues for Mister Charlie*
- Martin Luther King, *Where Do We Go from Here?*
- Langston Hughes, *Fight for Freedom: The Story of the NAACP*
- Eldridge Cleaver, *Soul on Ice*
- Malcolm X, *The Autobiography of Malcolm X*
- Stokely Carmichael and Charles V. Hamilton, *Black Power*
- Leroi Jones, *Home*

Vietnam

An America that was already divided over the civil rights movement faced even greater divisions over the war in Vietnam. Those who were in favor of the war and who opposed withdrawal saw it as the major front in the war against communism. Those who opposed the war and who favored withdrawal of the troops believed that it would not serve to defeat communism and was a quagmire.

Catch-22, by Joseph Heller, was a popular antiwar novel that became a successful movie of the time. *Authors Take Sides on Vietnam*, edited by Cecil Woolf and John Bagguley, is a collection of essays by 168 well-known authors throughout the world. *Where is Vietnam?* edited by Walter Lowenfels, consists of 92 poems about the war.

Many writers were publishing works for and against the war, but the genre that had the most impact was rock music. Bob Dylan was an example of the musicians of the time. His music represented the hippie aesthetic characterized by brilliant, swirling colors and hallucinogenic imagery that came to be called psychedelic. Some other bands that originated during this time and became well-known for their psychedelic music (primarily about the Vietnam War in the early years) are the Grateful Dead, Jefferson Airplane, Big Brother, and Sly and the Family Stone. In England, the movement attracted the Beatles and the Rolling Stones.

Immigration

This has been a popular topic for literature from the time of the Louisiana Purchase in 1804. The recent *Undaunted Courage*, by Stephen E. Ambrose, is ostensibly the autobiography of Meriwether Lewis, but is actually a recounting of the Lewis and Clark expedition. Presented as a scientific expedition by President Jefferson, the expedition was actually intended to provide maps and information for the opening up of the West. A well-known novel of the settling of the West by immigrants from other countries is *Giants in the Earth,* by Ole Edvart Rolvaag, a descendant of immigrants.

John Steinbeck's *Cannery Row* and *Tortilla Flats* glorify the lives of Mexican migrants in California. Amy Tan's *The Joy Luck Club* deals with the problems faced by Chinese immigrants.

Leon Uris' *Exodus* deals with the social history that led to the founding of the modern state of Israel. It was published in 1958, only a short time after the Holocaust. It also deals with attempts of concentration camp survivors to get to the land that has become the new Israel. In many ways, it is the quintessential work on immigration—causes and effects.

COMPETENCY 21.0 UNDERSTAND MAJOR THEMES, CHARACTERISTICS, TRENDS, WRITERS, AND WORKS IN BRITISH AND IRISH LITERATURE.

Skill 21.1 **Analyze the significance of writers, works, and movements to the development of British and Irish literature from their origins to the present.**

See Skill 16.1

Skill 21.2 **Analyze in passage context significant themes and genres in British literature from the Anglo-Saxon period, the Middle Ages, and the Renaissance.**

Anglo-Saxon

The Anglo-Saxon period spans six centuries, but produced only a smattering of literature. The first British epic is *Beowulf,* anonymously written by Christian monks many years after the events in the narrative supposedly occurred. This Teutonic saga relates three triumphs over monsters by the hero, Beowulf. "The Seafarer," a shorter poem, some history, and some riddles comprise the rest of the Anglo-Saxon canon.

Medieval

The Medieval period introduces Geoffrey Chaucer, the father of English literature, whose *Canterbury Tales* are written in the vernacular, or street language, of England, not in Latin. Thus, the tales are said to be the first work of British literature. Next, Thomas Malory's *Le Morte d'Arthur* calls together the extant tales from Europe as well as England concerning the legendary King Arthur, Merlin, Guenevere, and the Knights of the Round Table. This work is the generative work that gave rise to the many Arthurian legends that stir the chivalric imagination.

Renaissance and Elizabethan

The Renaissance, a most important period synonymous with William Shakespeare, begins with importing the idea of the Petrarchan, or Italian, sonnet into England. Sir Thomas Wyatt and Sir Philip Sydney wrote English versions. Next, Sir Edmund Spenser invented a variation on this Italian sonnet form, aptly called the Spenserian sonnet. His masterpiece is the epic, *The Fairie Queene*, honoring Queen Elizabeth I's reign. He also wrote books on the Red Cross Knight, St. George and the Dragon, and a series of Arthurian adventures. Spencer was dubbed the Poet's Poet. He created a nine-line stanza, eight lines of iambic pentameter with an extra-footed ninth line, an alexandrine. Thus, he invented the Spencerian stanza as well.

William Shakespeare, the Bard of Avon, wrote 154 sonnets, 39 plays, and two long narrative poems. The sonnets are justifiably called the greatest sonnet sequence in all literature. Shakespeare dispensed with the octave/sestet format of the Italian sonnet and invented his three quatrains-one heroic couplet format. His plays are divided into comedies, history plays, and tragedies. Great lines from these plays are more often quoted than from any other author. The Big Four tragedies, *Hamlet*, *Macbeth*, *Othello*, and *King Lear* are acknowledged to be the most brilliant examples of this genre.

Skill 21.3   Analyze in passage context significant themes and characteristics of major British and Irish literary works of the Enlightenment, the romantic and Victorian periods, and the twentieth century.

Seventeenth century

John Milton's devout Puritanism was the wellspring of his creative genius that closes the remarkable productivity of the English Renaissance.

His social commentary in such works as *Aereopagitica*, *Samson Agonistes*, and his elegant sonnets would be enough to solidify his stature as a great writer. It is his masterpiece based in part on the Book of Genesis that places Milton very near the top of the rung of a handful of the most renowned of all writers. *Paradise Lost*, written in balanced, elegant Neoclassic form, truly does justify the ways of God to man. This great allegory about man's journey to the Celestial City (Heaven) was written at the end of the English Renaissance, as was John Bunyan's *The Pilgrim's Progress*, which personifies virtues and vices. This work is, or was for a long time, second only to the *Bible* in numbers of copies printed and sold.

The Jacobean Age gave us the marvelously witty and cleverly constructed conceits of John Donne's metaphysical sonnets, his insightful meditations, and his version of sermons. "Ask not for whom the bell tolls", and "No man is an island unto himself" are famous epigrams from Donne's *Meditations*. His most famous conceit is that which compares lovers to a footed compass traveling seemingly separate directions, but always leaning towards one another and conjoined in "A Valediction Forbidding Mourning."

Eighteenth century

Ben Johnson, author of the wickedly droll play, *Volpone,* and the Cavalier *carpe diem* poets Robert Herrick, Sir John Suckling, and Richard Lovelace also wrote during King James I's reign.

The Restoration and Enlightenment reflect the political turmoil of the regicide of Charles I, the Interregnum Puritan government of Oliver Cromwell, and the restoring of the monarchy to England by the coronation of Charles II, who had been given refuge by the French King Louis. Neoclassicism became the preferred writing style, especially for Alexander Pope. New genres, such as *The Diary of Samuel Pepys*, the novels of Daniel Defoe, the periodical essays and editorials of Joseph Addison and Richard Steele, and Alexander Pope's mock epic, *The Rape of the Lock*, demonstrate the diversity of expression during this time.

Writers who followed were contemporaries of Dr. Samuel Johnson, the lexicographer of *The Dictionary of the English Language*. Fittingly, this Age of Johnson, which encompasses James Boswell's biography of Dr. Johnson, Robert Burns' Scottish dialect and regionalism in his evocative poetry, and the mystical pre-Romantic poetry of William Blake usher in the Romantic Age and its revolution against Neoclassicism.

Romantic period

The Romantic Age encompasses what is known as the First Generation Romantics, William Wordsworth and Samuel Taylor Coleridge, who collaborated on *Lyrical Ballads,* which defines and exemplifies the tenets of this style of writing. The Second Generation includes George Gordon, Lord Byron, Percy Bysshe Shelley, and John Keats. These poets wrote sonnets, odes, epics, and narrative poems, most dealing with homage to nature. Wordsworth's most famous other works are "Intimations on Immortality" and "The Prelude." Byron's satirical epic, *Don Juan*, and his autobiographical *Childe Harold's Pilgrimage* are irreverent, witty, self-deprecating and, in part, cuttingly critical of other writers and critics. Shelley's odes and sonnets are remarkable for sensory imagery. Keats' sonnets, odes, and longer narrative poem, *The Eve of St. Agnes*, are remarkable for their introspection and the tender age of the poet, who died when he was only twenty-five. In fact, all of the Second Generation died before their times. Wordsworth, who lived to be eighty, outlived them all, as well as his friend and collaborator, Coleridge. Others who wrote during the Romantic Age are the Charles Lamb, and Jane Austin. The Bronte sisters, Charlotte and Emily, wrote one novel each, which are noted as two of the finest ever written, *Jane Eyre* and *Wuthering Heights.* Marianne Evans, also known as George Eliot, wrote several important novels: her masterpiece, *Middlemarch*; *Silas Marner*, *Adam Bede*; and *Mill on the Floss.*

Nineteenth century

The Victorian Period is remarkable for the diversity and proliferation of work in three major areas. Poets who are typified as Victorians include Alfred, Lord Tennyson, who wrote *Idylls of the King*, twelve narrative poems about the Arthurian legend; and Robert Browning, who wrote chilling, dramatic monologues, such as "My Last Duchess," as well as long poetic narratives, such as *The Pied Piper of Hamlin*. His wife Elizabeth wrote two major works: the epic feminist poem, *Aurora Leigh*, and her deeply moving and provocative *Sonnets from the Portuguese,* in which she details her deep love for Robert and his startling (to her) reciprocation. Gerard Manley Hopkins, a Catholic priest, wrote poetry with sprung rhythm. (See Glossary of Literary Terms in 2.2). A. E. Housman, Matthew Arnold, and the Pre-Raphaelites, especially the brother and sister duo, Dante Gabriel Rosetti and Christina Rosetti, contributed much to round out the Victorian Era poetic scene. The Pre-Raphaelites, a group of 19th-century English painters, poets, and critics, reacted against Victorian materialism and the neoclassical conventions of academic art by producing earnest, quasi-religious works. Medieval and early Renaissance painters up to the time of the Italian painter Raphael inspired the group. Robert Louis Stevenson, the great Scottish novelist, wrote his adventure/history lessons for young adults. Victorian prose ranges from the incomparable, keenly-woven plot structures of Charles Dickens to the deeply moving Dorset/Wessex novels of Thomas Hardy, in which women are repressed and life is more struggle than euphoria.

Rudyard Kipling wrote about Colonialism in India in works like *Kim* and *The Jungle Book* that create exotic locales and a distinct main point concerning the Raj, the British Colonial government during Queen Victoria's reign. Victorian drama is a product mainly of Oscar Wilde, whose satirical masterpiece, *The Importance of Being Earnest*, farcically details and lampoons Victorian social mores.

Twentieth century

The early twentieth century is represented mainly by the towering achievement of George Bernard Shaw's dramas: *St. Joan, Man and Superman, Major Barbara,* and *Arms and the Man,* to name a few. Novelists are too numerous to list, but Joseph Conrad, E. M. Forster, Virginia Woolf, James Joyce, Nadine Gordimer, Graham Greene, George Orwell, and D. H. Lawrence comprise some of the century's very best.

Twentieth century poets of renown and merit include W. H. Auden, Robert Graves, T. S. Eliot, Edith Sitwell, Stephen Spender, Dylan Thomas, Philip Larkin, Ted Hughes, Sylvia Plath, and Hugh MacDarmid. This list is by no means complete.

Skill 21.4 Relate given passages to major historical events and cultural movements that influenced the development of British literature.

The reign of Elizabeth I ushered in a Renaissance that led to the end of the Medieval Age. It was a very fertile literary period. The exploration of the New World expanded the vision of all levels of the social order from royalty to peasant, and the rejection of Catholicism by many in favor of a Christianity of their own opened up whole new vistas to thought and daily life. The manufacture of cloth had increased, driving many people from the countryside into the cities, and the population of London exploded, creating a metropolitan business center. Printing had been brought to England by William Caxton in the 1470s, and literacy increased from 30% in the 15th century to over 60% by 1530. These seem dramatic changes (and they were), but they were occurring gradually.

The Italian renaissance had a great influence on the Renaissance in England, and early in the 16th century most written works were in Latin. It was assumed that a learned person must express his thoughts in that language. However, there began to emerge a determination that vernacular English was valuable in writing, and it began to be defended. Elizabeth's tutor, Roger Ascham, for example, wrote in English.

Luther's thesis in 1517, which brought on the Reformation—an attempt to return to pure Christianity—brought on the breakup of Western Christendom and eventually the secularization of society and the establishment of the king or queen as the head of this new/old church. This also brought about a new feeling that being religious was also being patriotic; it promoted nationalism.
The ascension of Elizabeth to the throne also followed a very turbulent period regarding succession, and she ruled for 45 peaceful years, which allowed arts and literature to flourish. Although she, herself, was headstrong and difficult, she happened to have very shrewd political instincts and entrusted power to solid, talented men, most particularly Cecil, her Secretary and Walsingham, whom she put in charge of foreign policy. She identified with her country as no previous ruler had, and that, in itself, brought on a period of intense nationalism. She was a symbol of Englishness. The defeat of the Spanish Armada in 1588 was the direct result of the strong support she had from her own nation.

Drama was the principal form of literature in this age. Religious plays had been a part of the life of England for a long time, particularly the courtly life. But in the Elizabethan age, they became more and more secular and were created primarily for courtly entertainment. By the '60s, Latin drama, particularly the tragedies of Seneca and the comedies of Plautus and Terence began to wield an influence in England. Courtyards of inns became favorite places for the presentation of plays; but in 1576, the Earl of Leicester's Men constructed their own building outside the city and called it The Theatre. Other theatres followed. Each had its own repertory company, and performances were for profit, but also for the queen and her court. It is said that Shakespeare wrote *The Merry Wives of Windsor* at the specific command of the queen, who liked Falstaff and wanted to see him in love. It was also for the courtly audience that poetry was introduced into drama.

Shakespeare and Marlowe dominated the '80s and '90s; and at the turn of the century, only a few years before Elizabeth's death, Ben Jonson began writing his series of satirical comedies.

Court favor was notoriously precarious and depended on the whims of the queen and others. Much of the satire of the period reflects the disappointment of writers like Edmund Spenser and John Lyly and the superficiality and treachery of the court atmosphere. "A thousand hopes, but all nothing," wrote Lyly, "a hundred promises, but yet nothing."

Not all literature was dictated by the court. The middle classes were developing and had their own style. Thomas Heywood and Thomas Deloney catered to bourgeois tastes.

The two universities were also sources for the production of literature. The primary aim of the colleges was to develop ministers since there was a shortage brought on by the break with the Catholic Church. However, most university men couldn't make livings as ministers or academics, so they wrote as a way of earning income. Nashe, Marlowe, Robert Greene, and George Peele all reveal in their writings how difficult this path was. Remuneration came mostly from patrons.

Greene had sixteen different patrons, whereas Shakespeare had a satisfactory relationship with the Earl of Southampton and didn't need to seek other support. Publishers would also sometimes pay for a manuscript, which they would then own. Unfortunately, if the manuscript did not pass muster with all who could condemn it—the court, the religious leaders, prominent citizens—it was the author who was on the hot seat. Very few became as comfortable as Shakespeare did. His success was not only in writing, however, but also from his business acumen.

Writing was seen more as a craft than as an art in this period. There was not great conflict between art and nature; and little distinction between literature, sports of the field, or the arts of the kitchen.

Balance and control were important in the England of this day, and this is reflected in the writing, the poetry in particular. The sestina, a form in which the last words of each line in the first stanza are repeated in a different order in each of the following stanzas, became very popular. Verse forms ranged from the extremely simple four-line ballad stanza through the rather complicated form of the sonnet to the elaborate and beautiful eighteen-line stanza of Spenser's *Epithalamion*. Sonnets were called "quatorzains." The term "sonnet" was used loosely for any short poem. "Quatorzains" are fourteen-line poems in iambic pentameter with elaborate rhyme schemes. However, Chaucer's seven-line, rhymed royal stanza also survived in the 16th century. Shakespeare used it in *The Rape of Lucrece*, for example. An innovation was Spenser's nine-line stanza, called the Spenserian stanza, as used in *The Faerie Queene*.

As to themes, some of the darkness of the previous period can still be seen in some Elizabethan literature, for example, Shakespeare's Richard II (III.ii152-70). At the same time, a spirit of joy, gaiety, innocence, and lightheartedness can be seen in much of the most popular literature; and pastoral themes became popular. The theme of the burning desire for conquest and achievement was also significant in Elizabethan thought.

Some important writers of the Elizabethan age:

Sir Thomas More (1478-1535)
Sir Thomas Wyatt the Elder (1503-1542)
Sir Philip Sidney (1554-1586)
Edmund Spenser (1552-1599)
Sir Walter Raleigh (1552-1618)
John Lyly (1554-1606)
George Peele (1556-1596)
Christopher Marlowe (1564-1593)
William Shakespeare (1564-1616)

The Industrial Revolution in England began with the development of the steam engine.

However, the steam engine was only one component of the major technological, socioeconomic, and cultural innovations of the early 19th century that began in Britain and spread throughout the world. An economy based on manual labor was replaced by one dominated by industry and the manufacture of machinery. The textile industries also underwent very rapid growth and change. Canals were being built, roads were improving, and railways were being constructed.

Steam power (fueled primarily by coal) and powered machinery (primarily in the manufacture of textiles) drove the remarkable amplification of production capacity. All-metal machine tools had entered the picture by 1820, making it possible to produce more machines.

The date of the Industrial Revolution varies according to how it is viewed. Some say that it broke out in the 1780s and wasn't fully perceived until the 1830s or 1840s. Others maintain that the beginning was earlier, about 1760, and began to manifest visible changes by 1830. The effects spread through western Europe and North America throughout the 19th century, eventually affecting all major countries of the world. The impact on society has been compared to the period when agriculture began to develop and the nomadic lifestyle was abandoned.

The first Industrial Revolution was followed immediately by the Second Industrial Revolution around 1850 when the progress in technology and world economy gained momentum with the introduction of steam-powered ships, railways, the internal combustion engine, and electrical power generation.

In terms of what was going on socially, the most noticeable effect was the development of a middle class of industrialists and businessmen and a decline in the landed class of nobility and gentry. While working people had more opportunities for employment in the new mills and factories, working conditions were often less than desirable. Exploiting children for labor wasn't new—it had always existed—but it was more apparent and perhaps more egregious as the need for cheap labor increased. In England, laws regarding employment of children began to be developed in 1833. Other effects of industrialization were the enormous shift from hand-produced goods to machine-produced ones and the loss of jobs among weavers and others, which resulted in violence against the factories and machinery beginning in about 1811.

Eventually, the British government took measures to protect industry. Another effect was the organization of labor. Because laborers were now working together in factories, mines, and mills; they were better able to organize to gain advantages they felt they deserved. Conditions were bad enough in these workplaces that the energy to bring about change was significant; and, eventually, trade unions emerged. Laborers learned quickly to use the weapon of the strike to get what they wanted. The strikes were often violent; and, while the managers usually gave in to most of the demands made by strikers, the animosity between management and labor was endemic.

The mass migration of rural families into urban areas also resulted in poor living conditions, long work hours, extensive use of children for labor, and a polluted atmosphere.

Another effect of industrialization of society was the separation of husband and wife. One person stayed at home and looked after the home and family, and the other went off to work--a very different configuration from an agriculture-based economy where the entire family was usually involved in making a living. Eventually, gender roles began to be defined by the new configuration of labor in this new world order.

The application of industrial processes to printing brought about a great expansion in newspaper and popular book publishing. This, in turn, was followed by rapid increases in literacy and, eventually, in demands for mass political participation.

Romanticism (the literary, intellectual, and artistic movement that occurred along with the Industrial Movement) was actually a response to the increasing mechanization of society--an artistic hostility to what was taking over the world. Romanticism stressed the importance of nature in art and language in contrast to the monstrous machines and factories. Blake called them the "dark, satanic mills" in his poem, "And Did Those Feet in Ancient Time."

This movement followed on the heels of the Enlightenment period and was, at least in part, a reaction to the aristocratic and political norms of the previous period. Romanticism is sometimes called the Counter-Enlightenment. It stressed strong emotion, made individual imagination the critical authority, and overturned previous social conventions. Nature was important to the Romanticists, and it elevated the achievements of misunderstood heroic individuals and artists who participated in altering society.

Some Romantic Writers:

Johann Wolfgang von Goethe
Walter Scott
Ludwig Tieck
E. T. A. Hoffman
William Wordsworth
Samuel Taylor Coleridge
William Blake
Victor Hugo
Alexander Pushkin
Lord Byron
Washington Irving
James Fenimore Cooper
Henry Wadsworth Longfellow
Edgar Allen Poe
Emily Dickinson
John Keats
Percy Bysshe Shelley

World War I (also known as The First World War, the Great War, and The War to End All Wars) raged from July 1914 to the final Armistice on November 11, 1918. It was a world conflict between the Allied Powers led by Great Britain, France, Russia, and the United States (after 1917) and The Central Powers, led by the German Empire, the Austro-Hungarian Empire, and the Ottoman Empire. It brought down four great empires: The Austo-Hungarian, German, Ottoman, and Russian. It reconfigured European and Middle Eastern maps.
More than nine million soldiers died on the various battlefields and nearly that many more in the participating countries' home fronts thanks to food shortages and genocide committed under the cover of various civil wars and internal conflicts. However, more people died of the worldwide influenza outbreak at the end of the war and shortly after than died in the hostilities. The unsanitary conditions engendered by the war, severe overcrowding in barracks, wartime propaganda interfering with public health warnings, and migration of so many soldiers around the world contributed to causing the outbreak to become a pandemic.

The precipitating event of World War I was the June 28, 1914 assassination in Sarajevo of Archduke Franz Ferdinand, heir to the Austrian throne. Gavrilo Princip, a member of a group called Young Bosnia, whose aims included the unification of the South Slavs and independence from Austria, was the assassin. However, the real reasons for the war are still being debated. In the late '20s and early '30s, people felt that the war was an accident that precipitated events that simply got out of control. This was used as a major argument for the organization of the League of Nations to prevent such a thing from happening in the future.

At the same time, Germany, France, and Russia were involved in war plans that created an atmosphere where generals and planning staffs were anxious the take the initiatives and make their careers. Once mobilization orders were issued, there was no turning back. Communications problems in 1914 also played a role. Telegraphy and ambassadors were the primary forms of communication, which accounted for disastrous delays from hours to even days.

President Wilson blamed the war on militarism. He felt that aristocrats and military elites had too much control in Germany, Russia, and Austria, and that the war was a consequence of their desire for military power and disdain for democracy. Lenin famously asserted that the worldwide system of imperialism was responsible for the war This argument proved persuasive in the immediate wake of the war and was a precipitating factor in the rise of Marxism and Communism.

A proposal to Mexico to join the war against the Allies was exposed in February, 1917, bringing war closer to America.

Further U-boat (German submarines) attacks on American merchant ships led to Wilson's request that Congress declare war on Germany, which it did on April 6, 1917. Following the U.S. declaration of war, countries in the Western Hemisphere (Cuba, Panama, Haiti, Brazil, Guatemala, Nicaragua, Costa Rica, and Honduras) declared war on Germany. The Dominican Republic, Peru, Uruguay, and Ecuador contented themselves with the severance of relations. The entry of the United States into the war was the turning point. It's doubtful that the Allies would have won without the infusion of money, supplies, armament, and troops from the Western Hemisphere, primarily from the United States. The experiences of the war led to a sort of collective national trauma afterwards for all the participating countries. The optimism of the 1900s was entirely gone, and those who fought in the war became what is known as "the Lost Generation" because they never fully recovered from their experiences. For the next few years, memorials continued to be erected in thousands of European villages and towns.

Certainly a sense of disillusionment and cynicism became pronounced, and nihilism became popular. The world had never before witnessed such devastation, and the depiction in newspapers and on movie screens made the horrors more personal. War has always spawned creative bursts, and this one was no exception. Poetry, stories, and movies proliferated. In fact, it's still a fertile subject for art of all kinds, particularly literature and movies. In 2006, a young director by the name of Paul Gross created, directed, and starred in *Passchendaele* based on the stories told him by his grandfather, who was haunted all his life by his killing of a young German soldier in this War to End All Wars.

Some literature based on World War I:

"The Soldier," poem by Rupert Brooke
Goodbye to All That, autobiography by Robert Graves
"Anthem for Doomed Youth" and "Strange Meeting," poems by Wilfred Owen, published posthumously by Siegfried Sassoon in 1918
"In Flanders Fields," poem by John McCrae
Three Soldiers, novel by John Dos Passos
Journey's End, play by R. C. Sherriff
All Quiet on the Western Front, novel by Erich Maria Remarque
Death of a Hero, novel by Richard Aldington
A Farewell to Arms, novel by Ernest Hemingway
Memoirs of an Infantry Officer, novel by Siegfried Sassoon
Sergeant York, movie directed by Howard Hawks

The dissolution of the British empire, the most extensive empire in world history and for a time the foremost global power, began in 1867 with its transformation into the modern Commonwealth.

Dominion status was granted to the self-governing colonies of Canada in 1867, to Australia in 1902, to New Zealand in 1907, to Newfoundland in 1907, and to the newly-created Union of South Africa in 1910. Leaders of the new states joined with British statesmen in periodic Colonial Conferences, the first of which was held in London in 1887.

The foreign relations of the Dominions were conducted through the Foreign Office of the United Kingdom. Although Canada created a Department of External Affairs in 1909, diplomatic relations with other governments continued to be channeled through the Governors-General, Dominion High Commissioners in London, and British legations abroad. Britain's declaration of war in World War I applied to all of the Dominions, for instance. Even so, the Dominions had substantial freedom in their adoption of foreign policy where this did not explicitly conflict with British interests. The original arrangement of a single imperial military and naval structure became unsustainable as Britain faced new commitments in Europe and the challenge of an emerging German High Seas fleet after 1900. In 1919, it was decided that the Dominions should have their own navies, reversing a previous agreement that the then Australasian colonies should contribute to the Royal Navy in return for the permanent stationing of a squadron in the region.

The settlement at the end of World War I gave Britain control of Palestine and Iraq after the collapse of the Ottoman Empire in the Middle East. It also ceded control of the former German colonies of Tanganyika, Southwest Africa (now Namibia), and New Guinea. British zones of occupation in Germany after the war were not considered part of the Empire

Although the Allies won the war and Britain's rule expanded into new areas, the heavy costs of the war made it less and less feasible to maintain the vast empire. Economic losses as well as human losses put increasing pressure on the Empire to give up its far-flung imperial posts in Asia and the African colonies. At the same time, nationalist sentiment was growing in both old and new Imperial territories, fueled partly by their troops' contributions to the war and the anger of many non-white ex-servicemen at the racial discrimination they had encountered during their service.

Enthusiasm for the Empire coupled with an increase in nationalism in many of the Dominions created resistance to Britain's intention to take military action against Turkey in 1922.

Full Dominion independence was formalized in the 1926 Balfour Declaration and the 1931 State of Westminster. Each Dominion was henceforth to be equal in status to Britain herself, free of British legislative interference, and autonomous in international relations. The Dominions section created with the Colonial Office in 1907 was upgraded in 1925 to a separate Dominions Office and given its own Secretary of State in 1930.

Canada led the way, becoming the first Dominion to conclude an international treaty entirely independently (1923) and obtaining the appointment (1928) of a British High Commissioner in Ottawa, thereby separating the administrative and diplomatic functions of the Governor-General and ending the latter's anomalous role as the representative of the head of state and of the British Government. Canada's first permanent diplomatic mission to a foreign country opened in Washington, D.C. in 1927. Australia followed in 1940.

Egypt, formally independent by 1922 (but bound to Britain by treaty until 1936 and under partial occupation until 1956), similarly severed all constitutional links with Britain. Iraq, which became a British Protectorate in 1922, also gained complete independence in 1932.

In 1948, Ireland became a republic, fully independent from the United Kingdom, and withdrew from the Commonwealth. Ireland's constitution claimed the six counties of Northern Ireland as a part of the Republic of Ireland until 1998. The issue over whether Northern Ireland should remain in the United Kingdom or join the Republic of Ireland has divided Northern Ireland's people and led to a long and bloody conflict known as the Troubles. However, the Good Friday Agreement of 1998 brought about a ceasefire between most of the major organizations on both sides, creating hope for a peaceful resolution.

The rise of anti-colonial nationalist movements in the subject territories and the changing economic situation of the world in the first half of the 20th century challenged an imperial power now increasingly preoccupied with issues nearer home. The Empire's end began with the onset of the Second World War when a deal was reached between the British government and the Indian independence movement whereby India would cooperate and remain loyal during the war, but after which they would be granted independence. Following India's lead, nearly all of the other colonies would become independent over the next two decades.

In the Caribbean, Africa, Asia, and the Pacific, post-war decolonization was achieved with almost unseemly haste in the face of increasingly powerful nationalist movements, and Britain rarely fought to retain any territory.

Some Representative Literature:
Heart of Darkness, novel by Joseph Conrad
Passage to India novel by E. M. Forster
"Gunga Din," poem by Rudyard Kipling

COMPETENCY 22.0 UNDERSTAND THE LITERATURES OF ASIA, AFRICA, CONTINENTAL EUROPE, LATIN AMERICA, AND THE CARIBBEAN, INCLUDING MAJOR THEMES, CHARACTERISTICS, TRENDS, WRITERS, AND WORKS.

Skill 22.1 Distinguish major literary forms, works, and writers of ancient civilizations and their characteristics.

The epic is one of the major forms of narrative literature, which retells chronologically the life of a mythological person or group of persons. This genre has become uncommon since the early 20th century although the term has been used to define certain extraordinarily long prose works and films. Usually a large number of characters, multiple settings, and a long span of time are features that lead to its designation as an epic. This change in the use of this term might indicate that some prose works of the past might be called epics although they were not composed or originally understood as such.

The epic was a natural manifestation of oral poetic tradition in preliterate societies where the poetry was transmitted to the audience and from performer to performer by purely oral means. It was composed of short episodes, each of equal status, interest, and importance; which facilitated memorization. The poet recalls each episode and uses it to recreate the entire epic.

Some Ancient Epics:

The *Iliad* and the *Odyssey*, both ascribed to Homer

Lost Greek epics ascribed to the Cyclic poets:

Trojan War cycle
Theban Cycle
Argonautica by Apollonius of Rhodes
Mahabharata and *Ramayana*, Hindu mythologies
Aeneid by Virgil
Metamorphoses by Ovid
Argonautica by Gaius Valerius Flaccus

Some Medieval Epics (500-1500)

Beowulf (Anglo-Saxon mythology)
Bhagavata Purana (Sanskrit "Stories of the Lord")
Divina Commedia (The Divine Comedy) by Dante Alighieri
The Canterbury Tales by Geoffrey Chaucer
Alliterative *Morte Arthure*

Some Modern Epics (from 1500)

The Faerie Queene by Edmund Spenser (1596)
Paradise Lost by John Milton (1667)
Paradise Regained by John Milton (1671)
Prince Arthur by Richard Blackmore (1695)
King Arthur by Richard Blackmore (1697)
The Works of Ossian by James MacPherson (1765)
Hyperion by John Keats (1818)
Don Juan by George Gordon Byron, 6th Baron Byron (1824)

An Ode is generally a long lyric poem and as a form or poetry or song has an extensive history. Though odes vary in topic and occasionally structure, three forms have risen to the foreground in literature. These three forms are identifiable by their different features, and all odes carry characteristics that line up somewhere among the three. They may contain parts from one form and pieces from another, but this is generally true. The two best-known and best-established ode forms are the Pindaric and the Horatian odes of the Greek and Roman traditions, respectively.

Named after a 5th century B.C. Greek poet, the Pindaric ode consists of a triadic structure, which emulates the musical movement of the early Greek chorus. Though infrequently attempted in English, some examples do exist. The Horatian ode is also named after a poet. The Roman poet Horace is given credit for this form, which typically has equal-length stanzas with the same rhyme scheme and meter. The Horatian ode, unlike the Pindaric ode, also has a tendency to be personal rather than formal.

Pastoral odes differ from others mostly in subject matter. "Pastoral" designates a literary work that has to do with the lives of shepherds or rural life and usually draws a contrast between the innocence and serenity of the simple life and the discomforts and corruptions of the city and especially of court life. The poet's moral, social, and literary views are usually expressed.

In John Keats' short career, his writing shifted from the popular sonnet form to the older form of the ode toward the end of his life. His "Ode on a Grecian Urn," which is about a piece of pottery, is a twist on the pastoral theme. He focuses on the natural scene that is pictured on the urn. Instead of a concern with the disturbing forces of the world as with most pastoral works, he uses the sculptured panel on the urn as a sort of "frozen pastoral" and makes his statement about what is valuable and real.

Some Pastoral Odes:

"Intimations of Immortality" by William Wordsworth
"Ode to a Nightingale" by John Keats
"Ode to Psyche" by John Keats
"Ode to the West Wind" by Percy Bysshe Shelley

The Upanishads are Hindu treatises that deal with broad philosophic problems. The term means "to sit down near" and implies sitting at the feet of a teacher. There are approximately 108 that record views of many teachers over a number of years. Read chronologically, they exhibit a development toward the concept of a single supreme being and suggest ultimate reunion with it. Of special philosophical concern is the nature of reality.

Their appearance in Europe in the early 19th century captured the interest of philosophers, particularly in Germany. The work of Arthur Schopenhauer is reflective of the Upanishads.

Virgil (Publius Vergilius Maro, later called Virgilius and known in English as Virgil or Vergil, October 15, 70BC/September 21, 19BC) was a Latin poet, author of the *Eclogues,* the *Georgics,* and the *Aeneid.* The Aeneid is a poem of twelve books that became the Roman Empire's national epic.

Virgil has had a strong influence on English literature. Edmund Spenser's *The Faerie Queene* reflects that influence. It was also the model for John Milton's *Paradise Lost*, not only in structure, but also in style and diction. The Augustan poets considered Virgil's poetry the ultimate perfection of form and ethical content. He was not so popular during the Romantic period, but Victorians such as Matthew Arnold and Alfred, Lord Tennyson rediscovered Virgil and were influenced by the sensitivity and pathos that had not been so appealing to the Romantics.

Skill 22.2 Recognize major literary forms, works, writers, and characteristics of world literature written before the modern period in languages other than English.

Germany

German poet and playwright, Friedrich von Schiller, is best known for his history plays, *William Tell* and *The Maid of Orleans*. He is a leading literary figure in Germany's Golden Age of Literature. Also from Germany, Rainer Maria Rilke, the great lyric poet, is one of the poets of the unconscious, or stream of consciousness. Germany also has given the world Herman Hesse, (*Siddartha*), Gunter Grass (*The Tin Drum*), and the greatest of all German writers, Goethe.

Scandinavia

Scandinavia has encouraged the work of Hans Christian Andersen in Denmark, who advanced the fairy tale genre with such wistful tales as "The Little Mermaid" and "Thumbelina."

The social commentary of Henrik Ibsen in Norway startled the world of drama with such issues as feminism (*The Doll's House* and *Hedda Gabler*) and the effects of sexually-transmitted diseases (*The Wild Duck* and *Ghosts)*. Sweden's Selma Lagerlof is the first woman to ever win the Nobel Prize for literature. Her novels include *Gosta Berling's Saga* and the world-renowned *The Wonderful Adventures of Nils*, a children's work.

Russia

Russian literature is vast and monumental. Who has not heard of Fyodor Dostoyevski's *Crime and Punishment* or *The Brothers Karamazov*, or of Count Leo Tolstoy's *War and Peace*? These are examples of psychological realism. Dostoyevski's influence on modern writers cannot be overly stressed. Tolstoy's *War and Peace* is the sweeping account of the invasion of Russia and Napoleon's taking of Moscow, abandoned by the Russians. This novel is called the national novel of Russia. Further advancing Tolstoy's greatness is his ability to create believable, unforgettable female characters, especially Natasha in *War and Peace* and the heroine of *Anna Karenina*. Pushkin is famous for great short stories; Anton Chekhov for drama, (*Uncle Vanya, The Three Sisters, The Cherry Orchard*); Yvteshenko for poetry (*Babi Yar*).

France

France has a multifaceted canon of great literature that is universal in scope, almost always championing some social cause: the poignant short stories of Guy de Maupassant; the fantastic poetry of Charles Baudelaire (*Fleurs du Mal*); and the groundbreaking lyrical poetry of Rimbaud and Verlaine. Drama in France is best represented by Rostand's *Cyrano de Bergerac*, and the neo-classical dramas of Racine and Corneille (*El Cid*). The great French novelists include Andre Gide, Honore de Balzac (*Cousin Bette*), Stendel (*The Red and the Black*), the father/son duo of Alexandre Dumas (*The Three Musketeers* and *The Man in the Iron Mask*. Victor Hugo is the Charles Dickens of French literature, having penned the masterpieces, *The Hunchback of Notre Dame* and the French national novel, *Les Miserables*. The stream of consciousness of Proust's *Remembrance of Things Past*, and the Absurdist theatre of Samuel Beckett and Eugene Ionesco (*The Rhinoceros*) attest to the groundbreaking genius of the French writers.

Spain

Spain's great writers include Miguel de Cervantes (*Don Quixote*) and Juan Ramon Jimenez. The anonymous national epic, *El Cid*, has been translated into many languages.

Italy

Italy's greatest writers include Virgil, who wrote the great epic, *The Aeneid*; Giovanni Boccaccio (*The Decameron*); and Dante Alighieri (*The Divine Comedy*).

Ancient Greece

Greece will always be foremost in literary assessments due to Homer's epics, *The Iliad* and *The Odyssey*. No one, except Shakespeare, is more often cited. Add to these the works of Plato and Aristotle for philosophy; the dramatists Aeschylus, Euripides, and Sophocles for tragedy, and Aristophanes for comedy. Greece is the cradle not only of democracy, but of literature as well.

Far East

The classical Age of Japanese literary achievement includes the father Kiyotsugu Kanami and the son Motokkiyo Zeami who developed the theatrical experience known as No drama to its highest aesthetic degree. The son is said to have authored over 200 plays, of which 100 still are extant.

Katai Tayama (*The Quilt*) is touted as the father of the genre known as the Japanese confessional novel. He also wrote in the "ism" of naturalism. His works are definitely not for the squeamish.

The "slice of life" psychological writings of Ryunosuke Akutagawa gained him acclaim in the Western World. His short stories, especially "Rashamon" and "In a Grove," are greatly praised for style as well as content.

China, too, has given to the literary world. Li Po, the T'ang dynasty poet from the Chinese Golden Age, revealed his interest in folklore by preserving the folk songs and mythology of China. Po further allows his reader to enter into the Chinese philosophy of Taoism and to know this feeling against expansionism during the T'ang dynastic rule. Back to the T'ang dynasty, which was one of great diversity in the arts, the Chinese version of a short story was created with the help of Jiang Fang. His themes often express love between a man and a woman.

Skill 22.3 **Recognize major forms, works, writers, and characteristics of modern and contemporary literature written in English outside Great Britain and the United States.**

North American Literature

North American literature is divided between the United States, Canada, and Mexico.

The American writers have been amply discussed in 22.1. Canadian writers of note include feminist Margaret Atwood, (*The Hand Maiden's Tale*); Alice Munro, a remarkable short story writer; and W. P. Kinsella, another short story writer whose two major subjects are North American Indians and baseball. Mexican writers include 1990 Nobel Prize winning poet, Octavio Paz, (The Labyrinth of Solitude) and feminist Rosarian Castillanos (The Nine Guardians).

Africa

African literary greats include South Africans Nadine Gordimer (Nobel Prize for literature) and Peter Abrahams (*Tell Freedom: Memories of Africa*), an autobiography of life in Johannesburg. Chinua Achebe (*Things Fall Apart*) and the poet, Wole Soyinka, hail from Nigeria. Mark Mathabane wrote an autobiography *Kaffir Boy* about growing up in South Africa. Egyptian writer, Naguib Mahfouz, and Doris Lessing from Rhodesia, now Zimbabwe, write about race relations in their respective countries. Because of her radical politics, Lessing was banned from her homeland and The Union of South Africa, as was Alan Paton whose seemingly simple story, *Cry, the Beloved Country*, brought the plight of blacks and the whites' fear of blacks under apartheid to the rest of the world.

Skill 22.4 Recognize major forms, writers, works, and characteristics of modern and contemporary world literature in languages other than English.

Central American/Caribbean Literature

The Caribbean and Central America encompass a vast area and cultures that reflect oppression and colonialism by England, Spain, Portugal, France, and The Netherlands. The Caribbean writers include Samuel Selvon from Trinidad and Armado Valladres of Cuba. Central American authors include dramatist Carlos Solorzano, from Guatemala, whose plays include *Dona Beatriz, The Hapless, The Magician,* and *The Hands of God.*

South American Literature

Chilean Gabriela Mistral was the first Latin American writer to win the Nobel Prize for literature. She is best known for her collections of poetry, *Desolation and Feeling.* Chile was also home to Pablo Neruda, who, in 1971, also won the Nobel Prize for literature for his poetry. His 29 volumes of poetry have been translated into more than 60 languages, attesting to his universal appeal. *Twenty Love Poems* and *Song of Despair* are justly famous. Isabel Allende is carrying on the Chilean literary standards with her acclaimed novel, *House of Spirits.* Argentine Jorge Luis Borges is considered by many literary critics to be the most important writer of his century from South America. His collections of short stories, *Ficciones,* brought him universal recognition.

Also from Argentina, Silvina Ocampo, a collaborator with Borges on a collection of poetry, is famed for her poetry and short story collections, which include *The Fury* and *The Days of the Night.*

Noncontinental European Literature

Horacio Quiroga represents Uruguay, and Brazil has Joao Guimaraes Rosa, whose novel, *The Devil to Pay,* is considered first-rank world literature.

Russian Literature

Boris Pasternak won the Nobel Prize (*Dr. Zhivago*). Aleksandr Solzhenitsyn (*The Gulag Archipelago*) is only recently back in Russia after years of expatriation in Vermont. Ilya Varshavsky, who creates fictional societies that are dystopias, or the opposite of utopias, represents the genre of science fiction.

French Literature

French literature is defined by the existentialism of Jean-Paul Sartre (*No Exit, The Flies, Nausea*), Andre Malraux, (*The Fall*), and Albert Camus (*The Stranger, The Plague*), the recipient of the 1957 Nobel Prize for literature. Feminist writings include those of Sidonie-Gabrielle Colette, known for her short stories and novels, as well as Simone de Beauvoir.

Slavic nations

Austrian writer Franz Kafka (*The Metamorphosis, The Trial,* and *The Castle*) is considered by many to be the literary voice of the first-half of the twentieth century. Representing the Czech Republic is the poet Vaclav Havel. Slovakia has dramatist Karel Capek (*R.U.R.*) Romania is represented by Elie Weisel (*Night*), a Nobel Prize winner.

Far East Literature

Asia has many modern writers who are being translated for the western reading public. India's Krishan Chandar has authored more than 300 stories. Rabindranath Tagore won the Nobel Prize for literature in 1913 (*Song Offerings*). Narayan, India's most famous writer (*The Guide*), is highly interested in mythology and legends of India. Santha Rama Rau's work, *Gifts of Passage*, is her true story of life in a British school where she tries to preserve her Indian culture and traditional home.

Revered as Japan's most famous female author, Fumiko Hayashi (*Drifting Clouds*) by the time of her death had written more than 270 literary works.

In 1968 the Nobel Prize for literature was awarded to Yasunari Kawabata (*The Sound of the Mountain, The Snow Country*) considered to be his masterpieces. His Palm-of-the-Hand Stories take the essentials of Haiku poetry and transform them into the short story genre.

Modern feminist and political concerns are written eloquently by Ting Ling, who used the pseudonym Chiang Ping-Chih. Her stories reflect her concerns about social injustice and her commitment to the women's movement.

Resources

1. Abrams, M. H. ed. *The Norton Anthology of English Literature.* 6th ed. 2 vols. New York: Norton, 1979.

   A comprehensive reference for English literature, containing selected works from *Beowulf* through the twentieth century and information about literary criticism.

2. Beach, Richard. "Strategic Teaching in Literature." *Strategic Teaching and Learning: Cognitive Instruction in the Content Areas.* Edited by Beau Fly Jones and others. ASCD Publications, 1987: 135-159.

   A chapter dealing with a definition of and strategic teaching strategies for literature studies.

3. Brown, A. C. and others. *Grammar and Composition 3rd Course.* Boston: Houghton Mifflin, 1984.

   A standard ninth-grade grammar text covering spelling, vocabulary, and reading, listening, and writing skills.

4. Burmeister, L. E. *Reading Strategies for Middle and Secondary School Teachers.* Reading, MA: Addison-Wesley, 1978.

   A resource for developing classrooms strategies for reading and content area classes, using library references, and adapting reading materials to all levels of students.

5. Carrier, W. and B. Neumann, eds. *Literature from the World.* New York: Scribner, 1981.

   A comprehensive world literature text for high school students, with a section on mythology and folklore.

6. Cline, R. K. J. and W. G. McBride. *A Guide to Literature for Young Adults: Background, Selection, and Use.* Glenview, IL: Scott Foresman, 1983.

   A literature reference containing sample readings and an overview of adolescent literature and the developmental changes that affect reading.

7. Coater, Jr. R. B., ed. *Reading Research and Instruction*. Journal of the College Research Association. Pittsburgh, PA : 1995.

   A reference tool for reading and language arts teachers, covering the latest research and instructional techniques.

8. Corcoran, B. and E. Evans, eds. *Readers, Texts, Teachers*. Upper Montclair, NJ: Boynton/Cook, 1987.

   A collection of essays concerning reader response theory, including activities that help students interpret literature and help the teacher integrate literature into the course study.

9. Cutting, Brian. *Moving on in Whole Language: the Complete Guide for Every Teacher*. Bothell, WA: Wright Group, 1992.

   A resource of practical knowledge in whole language instruction.

10. Damrosch, L. and others. *Adventures in English Literature*. Orlando, FL: Harcourt, Brace, Jovanovich, 1985.

    One of many standard high school English literature textbooks with a solid section on the development of the English language.

11. Davidson, A. *Literacy 2000 Teacher's Resource. Emergent Stages 1&2.* 1990.

12. Devine, T. G. *Teaching Study Skills: A Guide for Teachers*. Boston: Allyn and Bacon, 1981.

13. Duffy, G. G. and others. *Comprehension Instruction: Perspectives and Suggestions*. New York: Longman, 1984.

    Written by researchers at the Institute of Research on Teaching and the Center for the Study of Reading, this reference includes a variety of instructional techniques for different levels.

14. Fleming, M. ed. *Teaching the Epic*. Urbana, IL: NCTE, 1974.

    Methods, materials, and projects for the teaching of epics with examples of Greek, religious, national, and American epics.

15. Flood, J. ed. *Understanding Reading Comprehension: Cognition, Language, and the Structure of Prose.* Newark, DE: IRA, 1984.

    Essays by preeminent scholars dealing with comprehension for learners of all levels and abilities.

16. Fry, E. B. and others. *The Reading Teacher's Book of Lists.* Edgewood Cliffs, NJ: Prentice-Hall, 1984.

    A comprehensive list of book lists for students of various reading levels.

17. Garnica, Olga K. and Martha L. King. *Language, Children, and Society.* New York: Pergamon Press, 1981.

18. Gere, A. R. and E. Smith. *Attitude, Language and Change.* Urbana, IL: NCTE, 1979.

    A discussion of the relationship between standard English and grammar and the vernacular usage, including various approaches to language instruction.

19. Hayakawa, S. I. *Language in Thought and Action*. 4th ed. Orlando, Fl: Harcourt, Brace, Jovanovich, 1979.

20. Hook, J. N. and others. *What Every English Teacher Should Know.* Champaign, IL: NCTE, 1970.

    Research based text that summarizes methodologies and specific application for us with students.

21. Johnson, D. D. and P. D. Pearson. *Teaching Reading Vocabulary.* 2nd ed. New York: Holt, Rinehart, and Winston, 1984.

    A student text that stresses using vocabulary study in improving reading comprehension, with chapters on instruction components in the reading and content areas.

22. Kaywell, I. F. ed. *Adolescent Literature as a Complement to the Classics.* Norwood, MA: Christopher-Gordon Pub., 1993.

    A correlation of modern adolescent literature to classics of similar themes.

23. Mack, M. ed. *World Masterpieces*. 3rd ed. 2 vols. New York: Norton, 1973.

    A standard world literature survey, with good introductory material on a critical approach to literature study.

24. McLuhan, M. *Understanding Media: The Extensions of Man*. New York: Signet, 1964.

    The most classic work on the effect media has on the public and the power of the media to influence thinking.

25. McMichael, G. ed. *Concise Anthology of American Literature*. New York: Macmillan, 1974.

    A standard survey of American literature text.

26. Moffett, J. *Teaching the Universe of Discourse*. Boston: Houghton Mifflin, 1983.

    A significant reference text that proposes the outline for a total language arts program, emphasizing the reinforcement of each element of the language arts curriculum to the other elements.

27. Moffett, James and Betty Jane Wagner. *Student - Centered Language Arts K-12*. 4th ed. Boston: Houghton Mifflin, 1992.

28. Nelms, B. F. ed. *Literature in the Classroom: Readers, Texts, and Contexts*. Urbana, IL: NCTE, 1988.

    Essays on adolescent and multicultural literature, social aspects of literature, and approaches to literature interpretation.

29. Nilsen, A. P. and K. L. Donelson. *Literature for Today's Young Adults*. 2nd ed. Glenview, IL: Scott, Foresman, and Co., 1985.

    An excellent overview of young adult literature - its history, terminologies, bibliographies, and book reviews.

30. Perrine, L. *Literature: Structure, Sound, and Sense*. 5th ed. Orlando, FL: Harcourt, Brace, Jovanovich, 1988.

    A much revised text for teaching literature elements, genres, and interpretation.

31. Piercey, Dorothy. *Reading Activities in Content Areas: An Ideabook for Middle and Secondary Schools.* 2nd ed. Boston: Allyn and Bacon, 1982.

32. Pooley, R. C. *The Teaching of English Usage.* Urbana, IL: NCTE, 1974.

    A revision of the important 1946 text which discusses the attitudes toward English usage through history and recommends specific techniques for usage instruction.

33. Probst, R. E. *Response and Analysis: Teaching Literature in Junior and Senior High School.* Upper Montclair, NJ: Boynton/Cook, 1988.

    A resource that explores reader response theory and discusses student-centered methods for interpreting literature. Contains a section on the progress of adolescent literature.

34. Pyles, T. and J. Alges. *The Origin and Development of the English Language.* 3rd ed. Orlando, FL: Harcourt, Brace, Jovanovich, 1982.

    A history of the English language; sections social, personal, historical, and geographical influences on language usage.

35. Readence, J. E. and others. *Content Area Reading: an integrated approach.* 2nd ed. Dubuque, IA: Kendall/Hunt, 1985.

    A practical instruction guide for teaching reading in the content areas.

36. Robinson, H. Alan. *Teaching Reading and Study Strategies: The Content Areas.* Boston: Allyn and Bacon, 1978.

37. Roe, B. D. and others. *Secondary School Reading Instruction: The Content Areas.* 3rd ed. Boston: Houghton Mifflin, 1987.

    A resource of strategies for the teaching of reading for language arts teachers with little reading instruction background.

38. Rosenberg, D. *World Mythology: An Anthology of the Great Myths and Epics.* Lincolnwood, IL: National Textbook, 1986.

    Presents selections of main myths from which literary allusions are drawn. Thorough literary analysis of each selection.

39. Rosenblatt, L. M. *The Reader, the Text, the Poem. The Transactional Theory of the Literary work.* Southern Illinois University Press, 1978.

    A discussion of reader response theory and reader-centered methods for analyzing literature.

40. Santeusanio, Richard P. *A Practical Approach to Content Area Reading.* Reading, MA.: Addison-Wesley Publishing Co., 1983.

41. Shepherd, David L. *Comprehensive High School Reading Methods.* 2nd ed. Columbus, OH: Charles F. Merrill Publishing, 1978.

42. Strickland, D. S. and others. *Using Computers in the Teaching of Reading.* New York: Teachers College Press, 1987.

    Resource for strategies for teaching and learning language and reading with computers and recommendations for software for all grades.

43. Sutherland, Zena and others. *Children and Books.* 6th ed. Glenview, IL: Scott, Foresman, and Co., 1981.

    Thorough study of children's literature, with sections on language development theory and chapters on specific genres with synopses of specific classic works for child/adolescent readers.

44. Tchudi, S. and D. Mitchell. *Explorations in the Teaching of English.* 3rd ed. New York: Harper Row, 1989.

    A thorough source of strategies for creating a more student-centered involvement in learning.

45. Tompkins, Gail E. *Teaching Writing: Balancing Process and Product.* 2nd ed. New York: Macmillan, 1994.

    A tool to aid teachers in integrating recent research and theory about the writing process, writing reading connections, collaborative learning, and across the curriculum writing with practices in the fourth through eighth grade classrooms.

46. Warriners, J. E. *English Composition and Grammar.* Benchmark ed. Orlando, FL: Harcourt, Brace, Jovanovich, 1988.

    Standard grammar and composition textbook, with a six book series for seventh through twelfth grades; includes vocabulary study, language history, and diverse approaches to writing process.

TEACHER CERTIFICATION STUDY GUIDE

Sample Test

Section I: Essay Test

You will respond to several prompts intended to gauge your competence in a variety of writing skills. In most testing situations, you will have 30 minutes to respond to these prompts. Some tests may allow 60 minutes for the essay in order to incorporate more than one question or to allow for greater preparation and editing time. Read the directions carefully and organize your time wisely.

Section II: Multiple - choice Test

This section contains 125 questions. In most testing situations, you would be expected to answer 35 - 40 questions in about 30 minutes. If you time yourself on the entire battery, try to finish it in about 90 minutes.

Section III: Answer Key

Section I: Essay Prompts

Prompt A

Write an expository essay discussing effective teaching strategies for helping a heterogeneous class of ninth graders to appreciate literature. Select any appropriate piece(s) of world literature to use as examples in the discussion.

Prompt B

After reading the following passage from Aldous Huxley's *Brave New World,* discuss the types of reader responses possible with a group of eight graders.

> "He hated them all - all the men who came to visit Linda. One afternoon, when he had been playing with the other children - it was cold, he remembered, and there was snow on the mountains - he came back to the house and heard angry voices in the bedroom. They were women's voices, and they were words he didn't understand; but he knew they were dreadful words. Then suddenly, crash! something was upset; he heard people moving about quickly, and there was another crash and then a noise like hitting a mule, only not so bony; then Linda screamed. 'Oh, don't, don't, don't!' she said. He ran in. There were three women in dark blankets. Linda was on the bed. One of the women was holding her wrists. Another was lying across her legs, so she couldn't kick. The third was hitting her with a whip. Once, twice, three times; and each time Linda screamed."

Prompt C

Write a persuasive letter to the editor on any contemporary topic of special interest. Employ whatever forms of discourse, stylistic devices, and audience-appeal techniques that seem appropriate to the topic.

Section II: Writing and Language Skills

Part A

Directions: Sentences 1 – 15 each contain four underlined words or phrases. If you determine that any underlined word or phrase has an error in grammar, usage, or mechanics, circle the letter underneath that underlined word or phrase. If there are no errors, circle the letter E at the end of the sentence. There is no more than one error in any sentence.

1. The volcanic eruption in Montserrat displaced residents of Plymouth <u>which</u>
                                                                                                   A
   felt that the <u>English government</u> <u>was</u> responsible for <u>their</u> evacuation. E
                   B   C   D

2. When the <u>school district</u> privatized the school cafeteria, <u>us</u> students <u>were</u>
                   A   B   C
   thrilled to purchase more than soggy <u>French fries</u>. E
                                         D

3. The homecoming <u>Queen and King</u> <u>were chosen</u> by the <u>student body</u> for
                           A   B   C
   <u>their</u> popularity. E
   D

4. If the practical joke <u>was</u> <u>Cullen's</u> idea, then he <u>must</u> suffer the
                       A   B   C
   <u>consequences</u>. E
   D

5. She, not her sister, <u>is</u> the one <u>who</u> the librarian <u>has questioned</u> about the
                     A   B   C
   missing books, <u>Butterfly's</u> Ball and the Bears' House. E
                         D

6. Jack told a <u>credulous</u> story about his trip <u>up the beanstalk</u> because each
                 A   B
   child in the room <u>was convinced</u> <u>by his reasoning</u>. E
                 C   D

7. There <u>are</u> <u>fewer</u> students in school this year despite the <u>principal's</u>
        A   B   C
   prediction of <u>increasing</u> enrollment. E
                      D

8. My mother is a <u>Methodist</u>. She married a <u>Southern Baptist</u> and took <u>us</u>
                       A   B   C
   children to the <u>First Baptist church</u> in Stuart. E
                             D

9. When we moved from Jacksonville, Florid<u>a,</u> to Little Roc<u>k,</u> Arkansas, my
                                           A   B
   <u>Dad</u> <u>was promoted</u> to store manager. E
    C   D

10. "One of the <u>burglar's</u> had been <u>already</u> <u>apprehended</u> before his colleagues
                    A   B   C
    left the buildin<u>g,"</u> bragged the officer. E
                     D

11. Walter said <u>that</u> his calculator <u>has been missing</u> <u>since</u> last Monday
                  A   B   C
    <u>responding to my question</u>. E
              D

12. Why was the girl <u>that</u> had plenty of money <u>arrested</u> for <u>shoplifting</u> some
                      A   B   C
    trinkets of <u>two dollar's worth</u>? E
                       D

13. The future <u>will be</u> <u>because of</u> the past; <u>by changing the past</u> <u>would alter</u>
                  A   B   C   D
    the future. E

14. <u>Mr. Thomas'</u> daughter-in-law encouraged her <u>husband's</u> boss to host a
         A   B
    fund-raiser for <u>the United Way</u>, a charity that Mr. Thomas <u>supports</u>. E
                          B   D

15. Miriam decided to remain <u>stationary</u> <u>since</u> <u>to move</u> would startle the horses,
                                  A   B   C
    one of <u>which</u> might bolt. E
              D

Part B

Directions: Each underlined portion of sentences 16 - 25 contains one or more errors in grammar, usage, mechanics, or sentence structure. Circle the choice which best corrects the error without changing the meaning of the original sentence. If you find no errors in the underlined portion, select the answer choice that repeats the underlined portion.

16. Joe **didn't hardly know his cousin Fred**, who'd had a rhinoplasty.

    A. hardly did know his cousin Fred

    B. didn't know his cousin Fred hardly

    C. hardly knew his cousin Fred

    D. didn't know his cousin Fred

    E. didn't hardly know his cousin Fred

17. **Mixing the batter for cookies**, the cat licked the Crisco from the cookie sheet.

    A. While mixing the batter for cookies

    B. While the batter for cookies was mixing

    C. While I mixed the batter for cookies

    D. While I mixed the cookies

    E. Mixing the batter for cookies

18. Mr. Brown is a school volunteer **with a reputation and twenty years service**.

    A. with a reputation for twenty years' service

    B. with a reputation for twenty year's service

    C. who has served twenty years

    D. with a service reputation of twenty years

    E. with a reputation and twenty years service

19. Walt Whitman was famous for **his composition, *Leaves of Grass*, serving as a nurse during the Civil War, and a devoted son**.

    A. *Leaves of Grass*, his service as a nurse during the Civil War, and a devoted son

    B. composing *Leaves of Grass*, serving as a nurse during the Civil War, and being a \ devoted son

    C. his composition, *Leaves of Grass*, his nursing during the Civil War, and his devotion as a son

    D. having authored *Leaves of Grass*, served as a nurse during the Civil War, and as a devoted son

    E. his composition, *Leaves of Grass*, serving as a nurse during the Civil War, and a devoted son.

20. A teacher <u>must know not only her subject matter but also the strategies of</u> content teaching.

    A. must not only know her subject matter but also the strategies of content teaching

    B. not only must know her subject matter but also the strategies of content teaching

    C. must not know only her subject matter but also the strategies of content teaching

    D. must know not only her subject matter but also the strategies of content teaching

21. My English teacher, Mrs. Hunt, <u>is nicer than any teacher at school and is</u> the most helpful.

    A. is as nice as any teacher at school and is

    B. is nicer than any other teacher at school and is

    C. is as nice as any other teacher at school and is

    D. is nicer than any teacher at school and is

22. The teacher <u>implied</u> from our angry words that there was conflict <u>between</u> you and me.

    A. implied ... between you and I

    B. inferred... between you and I

    C. inferred...between you and me

    D. implied ... between you and me

23. There were <u>fewer pieces</u> of evidence presented during the second trial.

    A. fewer peaces

    B. less peaces

    C. less pieces

    D. fewer pieces

24. Mr. Smith <u>respectfully submitted his resignation and had</u> a new job.

    A. respectively submitted his resignation and has

    B. respectively submitted his resignation before accepting

    C. respectfully submitted his resignation because of

    D. respectfully submitted his resignation and had

25. Wally groaned, "Why do I have to do an oral interpretation of "The Raven."

    A. groaned, "Why ... of 'The Raven' ?"

    B. groaned "Why ... of "The Raven" ?

    C. groaned ",Why ... of "The Raven?"

    D. groaned, "Why ... of "The Raven."

Part C

Directions: Select the best answer in each group of multiple choices.

26. The synonyms "gyro," "hero," and "submarine" reflect which influence on language usage?

   A. social

   B. geographical

   C. historical

   D. personal

27. The following passage is written from which point of view?

   As she mused the pitiful vision of her mother's life laid its spell on the very quick of her being - that life of commonplace sacrifices closing in final craziness. She trembled as she heard again her mother's voice saying constantly with foolish insistence: Derevaun Seraun! Derevaun Seraun !*
   * "The end of pleasure is pain!" (Gaelic)

   A. First person, narrator

   B. Second person, direct address

   C. Third person, omniscient

   D. First person, omniscient

28. The literary device of personification is used in which example below?

   A. "Beg me no beggary by soul or parents, whining dog!"

   B. "Happiness sped through the halls cajoling as it went."

   C. "O wind thy horn, thou proud fellow."

   D. "And that one talent which is death to hide."

29. Which of the writers below is a renowned Black poet?

   A. Maya Angelou

   B. Sandra Cisneros

   C. Richard Wilbur

   D. Richard Wright

30. Which of the following is not one of the four forms of discourse?

   A. exposition

   B. description

   C. rhetoric

   D. persuasion

31. **Among junior-high school students of low-to-average readability levels which work would most likely stir reading interest?**

    A. *Elmer Gantry*, Sinclair Lewis

    B. *Smiley's People*, John LeCarre

    C. *The Outsiders*, S. E. Hinton

    D. *And Then There Were None*, Agatha Christie

32. **"Every one must pass through Vanity Fair to get to the celestial city" is an allusion from a**

    A. Chinese folk tale.

    B. Norse saga.

    C. British allegory.

    D. German fairy tale.

33. **Which teaching method would best engage underachievers in the required senior English class?**

    A. Assign use of glossary work and extensively footnoted excerpts of great works.

    B. Have students take turns reading aloud the anthology selection.

    C. Let students choose which readings they'll study and write about.

    D. Use a chronologically arranged, traditional text, but assigning group work, panel presentations, and portfolio management.

34. **Which poem is typified as a villanelle?**

    A. "Do not Go Gentle into That Good Night"

    B. "Dover Beach"

    C. *Sir Gawain and the Green Knight*

    D. *Pilgrim's Progress*

35. Which term best describes the form of the following poetic excerpts?

And more to lulle him in his slumber soft,
A trickling streame from high rock tumbling downe,
And ever-drizzling raine upon the loft.
Mixt with a murmuring winde, much like a swowne
No other noyse, nor peoples troubles cryes.
As still we wont t'annoy the walle'd towne,
Might there be heard: but careless Quiet lyes,
Wrapt in eternall silence farre from enemyes.

A. Ballad

B. Elegy

C. Spenserian stanza

D. Octava rima

36. Which poet was a major figure in the Harlem Renaissance?

A. E. E. Cummings

B. Rita Dove

C. Margaret Atwood

D. Langston Hughes

37. To understand the origins of a word, one must study the

A. synonyms.

B. inflections.

C. phonetics.

D. etymology.

38. **Which sonnet form describes the following?**

   My galley charg'ed with forgetfulness
   Through sharp seas, in winter night doth pass
   'Tween rock and rock; and eke mine enemy, alas,
   That is my lord steereth with cruelness.
   And every oar a thought in readiness,
   As though that death were light in such a case.
   An endless wind doth tear the sail apace
   Or forc'ed sighs and trusty fearfulness.
   A rain of tears, a cloud of dark disdain,
   Hath done the wearied cords great hinderance,
   Wreathed with error and eke with ignorance.
   The stars be hid that led me to this pain
   Drowned is reason that should me consort,
   And I remain despairing of the poet.

   A. Petrarchan or Italian sonnet

   B. Shakespearean or Elizabethan sonnet

   C. Romantic sonnet

   D. Spenserian sonnet

39. **What is the salient literary feature of this excerpt from an epic?**

   Hither the heroes and the nymphs resort,
   To taste awhile the pleasures of a court;
   In various talk th'instructive hours they passed,
   Who gave the ball, or paid the visit last;
   One speaks the glory of the English Queen,
   And another describes a charming Indian screen;
   A third interprets motion, looks and eyes;
   At every word a reputation dies.

   A. Sprung rhythm

   B. Onomatopoeia

   C. Heroic couplets

   D. Motif

40. **What were two major characteristics of the first American literature?**

   A. Vengefulness and arrogance

   B. Bellicosity and derision

   C. Oral delivery and reverence for the land

   D. Maudlin and self-pitying egocentricism

41. Arthur Miller wrote *The Crucible* as a parallel to what twentieth century event?

    A. Sen. McCarthy's House un-American Activities Committee Hearing

    B. The Cold War

    C. The fall of the Berlin Wall

    D. The Persian Gulf War

42. Latin words that entered the English language during the Elizabethan Age include

    A. allusion, education, and esteem.

    B. vogue and mustache.

    C. canoe and cannibal.

    D. alligator, cocoa, and armadillo.

43. Which of the following is not a characteristic of a fable?

    A. animals that feel and talk like humans.

    B. happy solutions to human dilemmas.

    C. teaches a moral or standard for behavior.

    D. illustrates specific people or groups without directly naming them.

44. Which of the following is not an example of the subject of a tall-tale?

    A. John Henry.

    B. Paul Bunyan.

    C. George Washington.

    D. Rip Van Winkle.

45. If a student has a poor vocabulary, the teacher should recommend first that

    A. the student read newspapers, magazines and books on a regular basis.

    B. the student enroll in a Latin class.

    C. the student write the words repetitively after looking them up in the dictionary.

    D. the student use a thesaurus to locate synonyms and incorporate them into his/her vocabulary.

46. Which author did not write satire?

    A. Joseph Addison

    B. Richard Steele

    C. Alexander Pope

    D. John Bunyan

47. **Which of the following was not written by Jonathan Swift?**

   A. "A Voyage to Lilliput"

   B. "A Modest Proposal"

   C. "Samson Agonistes"

   D. "A Tale of a Tub"

48. **Which is not a Biblical allusion?**

   A. The patience of Job

   B. Thirty pieces of silver

   C. "Man proposes; God disposes"

   D. "Suffer not yourself to be betrayed by a kiss"

49. **Which definition below is the best for defining diction?**

   A. The specific word choices of an author to create a particular mood or feeling in the reader.

   B. Writing which explains something thoroughly.

   C. The background, or exposition, for a short story or drama.

   D. Word choices which help teach a truth or moral.

50. **Which is the best definition of free verse, or *vers libre*?**

   A. Poetry which consists of an unaccented syllable followed by an unaccented sound.

   B. Short lyrical poetry written to entertain but with an instructive purpose.

   C. Poetry which does not have a uniform pattern of rhythm.

   D. A poem which tells a story and has a plot.

51. **Which is not an accepted point of view in literary works?**

   A. First person, omniscient

   B. Third person, limited

   C. First person, limited

   D. Third person, omniscient

52. Which is an untrue statement about a theme in literature?

    A. The theme is always stated directly somewhere in the text.

    B. The theme is the central idea in a literary work.

    C. All parts of the work (plot, setting, mood) should contribute to the theme in some way.

    D. By analyzing the various elements of the work, the reader should be able to arrive at an indirectly stated theme.

53. Which is the least true statement concerning an author's literary tone?

    A. Tone is partly revealed through the selection of details.

    B. Tone is the expression of the author's attitude toward his/her subject.

    C. Tone in literature is usually satiric or angry.

    D. Tone in literature corresponds to the tone of voice a speaker uses.

54. Regarding the study of poetry, select the answer which is least applicable to all types of poetry.

    A. Setting and audience

    B. Theme and tone

    C. Pattern and diction

    D. Diction and rhyme scheme

55. Which of the following definitions best describes a parable?

    A. A short entertaining account of some happening, usually using talking animals as characters.

    B. A slow, sad song or poem, or prose work expressing lamentation.

    C. An extended narrative work expressing universal truths concerning domestic life.

    D. A short, simple story of an occurrence of a familiar kind, from which a moral or religious lesson may be drawn.

TEACHER CERTIFICATION STUDY GUIDE

56. **Which of the following is the best definition of existentialism?**

    A. The philosophical doctrine that matter is the only reality and that everything in the world (including thought, will and feeling) is rightly explained exclusively in terms of matter.

    B. Philosophy which views things as they should be or as one would wish them to be.

    C. A philosophical and literary movement, variously religious and atheistic, stemming from Kierkegaard and represented by Sartre.

    D. The belief that all events are determined by fate and are, hence, inevitable.

57. **Which of the following is the best definition of imagism?**

    A. A doctrine teaching that comfort is the only goal of value in life.

    B. A movement in modern poetry (c 1910-1918) characterized by precise, concrete images, free verse, and suggestion rather than complete statement.

    C. The belief that people are motivated entirely by self-centeredness.

    D. The doctrine that the human mind cannot know whether or not there is a God, an ultimate cause, or anything beyond material phenomenon.

58. Which choice below best fits defines naturalism?

   A. Belief that the writer or artist should apply scientific objectivity in his/her observation and treatment of life without imposing value of judgments.

   B. The doctrine that teaches that the existing world is the best to be hoped for.

   C. The doctrine teaching that God is not a personality, but that all laws, forces and manifestations of the universe are God-related.

   D. A philosophical doctrine professing that the truth of all knowledge must constantly be re-examined.

59. The tendency to emphasize and value the qualities and peculiarities of life in a particular geographic area exemplifies

   A. pragmatism.

   B. regionalism.

   C. pantheism.

   D. abstractionism.

60. A traditional, anonymous story, ostensibly having a historical basis, usually explaining some phenomenon of nature or aspect of creation, defines a

   A. proverb.

   B. idyll.

   C. myth.

   D. epic.

61. The arrangement and relationship of words in sentences or sentence structures best describes

   A. style.

   B. discourse.

   C. thesis.

   D. syntax.

62 Explanatory or informative discourse is

   A. exposition

   B. narration.

   C. persuasion.

   D. description.

63. The substitution of "went to his rest" for "died" is an example of a/an

   A. bowdlerism.
   B. jargon.
   C. euphemism.
   D. malapropism

64. A conversation between two or more people is called a

   A. parody.
   B. dialogue.
   C. monologue.
   D. analogy.

65. "Clean as a whistle" or "Easy as falling off a log" are examples of

   A. semantics.
   B. parody.
   C. irony.
   D. clichés.

66. Which of the following is most true of expository writing?

   A. It is mutually exclusive of other forms of discourse.
   B. It can incorporate other forms of discourse in the process of providing supporting details.
   C. It should never employ informal expression.
   D. It should be scored only with a summative evaluation.

67. The appearance of a Yankee from Connecticut in the Court of King Arthur is an example of a/an

   A. rhetoric.
   B. parody.
   C. paradox.
   D. anachronism

68. In literature, evoking feelings of pity or compassion is to create

   A. colloquy.
   B. irony.
   C. pathos.
   D. paradox.

69. "I'll die if I don't pass this course" is an example of

   A. barbarism.

   B. oxymoron.

   C. hyperbole.

   D. antithesis.

70. An extended metaphor comparing two very dissimilar things (one lofty, one lowly) is a definition of a/an

   A. antithesis.

   B. aphorism.

   C. apostrophe.

   D. conceit.

71. Addressing someone absent or something inhuman as though present and able to respond describes a figure of speech known as

   A. personification.

   B. synecdoche.

   C. metonymy.

   D. apostrophe.

72. Slang or jargon expressions associated with a particular ethnic, age, economic, or professional group are called

   A. aphorisms.

   B. allusions.

   C. idioms.

   D. euphemisms.

73. Which of the following is a complex sentence?

   A. Anna and Margaret read a total of fifty-four books during summer vacation.

   B. The youngest boy on the team had the best earned run average, which mystifies the coaching staff.

   C. Earl decided to attend Princeton; his twin brother Roy, who aced the ASVAB test, will be going to Annapolis.

   D. "Easy come, easy go," Marcia moaned.

74. **Piaget's learning theory asserts that adolescents in the formal operations period**

   A. behave properly from fear of punishment rather than from a conscious decision to take a certain action.

   B. see the past more realistically and can relate to people from the past more than preadolescents.

   C. are less self-conscious and thus more willing to project their own identities into those of fictional characters.

   D. have not yet developed a symbolic imagination.

75. **Which of the following is a formal reading-level assessment?**

   A. a standardized reading test

   B. a teacher-made reading test

   C. an interview

   D. a reading diary.

76. **Middle and high school students are more receptive to studying grammar and syntax**

   A. through worksheets and end-of-lesson practices in textbooks.

   B. through independent, homework assignments.

   C. through analytical examination of the writings of famous authors.

   D. though application to their own writing.

77. Which statement below best describes an author and his/her work?

    A. Zora Neale Hurston's *Their Eyes Were Watching God* dealt autobiographically with the strong faith that helped her through the years of her poor upbringing in rural Florida.

    B. Willa Cather's works, such as *My Antonia*, depict the regionalism of the Deep South.

    C. Emily Dickinson gained national recognition during her lifetime for the publication of over 300 poems.

    D. Upton Sinclair's writings, such as *The Jungle*, represent the optimism and trust of the American citizenry for its government.

78. Which of the following is the least preferable strategy for teaching literature?

    A. teacher-guided total class discussion

    B. small group discussion

    C. teacher lecture

    D. dramatization of literature selections

79. Which event triggered the beginning of Modern English?

    A. Conquest of England by the Normans in 1066

    B. Introduction of the printing press to the British Isles

    C. Publication of Samuel Johnson's lexicon

    D. American Revolution

80. Which of the following is not true about the English language?

    A. English is the easiest language to learn.

    B. English is the least inflected language.

    C. English has the most extensive vocabulary of any language.

    D. English originated as a Germanic tongue.

81. Which of the following is not a technique of prewriting?

    A. Clustering

    B. Listing

    C. Brainstorming

    D. Proofreading

82. Which of the following is the least effective procedure for promoting consciousness of audience?

   A. Pairing students during the writing process

   B. Reading all rough drafts before the students write the final copies

   C. Having students compose stories or articles for publication in school literary magazines or newspapers

   D. Writing letters to friends or relatives

83. The Elizabethans wrote in

   A. Celtic.

   B. Old English.

   C. Middle English.

   D. Modern English.

84. Which of the following writers did not win a Nobel Prize for literature?

   A. Gabriel Garcia-Marquez of Colombia

   B. Nadine Gordimer of South Africa

   C. Pablo Neruda of Chile

   D. Alice Walker of the United States

85. Children's literature became established in the

   A. seventeenth century.

   B. eighteenth century.

   C. nineteenth century.

   D. twentieth century.

86. Recognizing empathy in literature is mostly a/an

   A. emotional response.

   B. interpretive response.

   C. critical response.

   D. evaluative response.

87. Which of the following should not be included in the opening paragraph of an informative essay?

   A. Thesis sentence

   B. Details and examples supporting the main idea

   C. A broad general introduction to the topic

   D. A style and tone that grabs the reader's attention

88. In the following quotation, addressing the dead body of Caesar as though he were still a living being is to employ an

   "O, pardon me, thou bleeding piece of earth,
   That I am meek and gentle with these butchers."
   (Marc Antony in Julius *Caesar*)

   A. Apostrophe

   B. Allusion

   C. Antithesis

   D. Anachronism

89. What is the main form of discourse in this passage?

   "It would have been hard to find a passer-by more wretched in appearance.
   He was a man of middle height, stout and hardy, in the strength of maturity; he might have been forty-six or seven. A slouched leather cap hid half his face, bronzed by the sun and wind, and dripping with sweat."

   A. Description

   B. Narration

   C. Exposition

   D. Persuasion

90. In general, the most serious drawback of using a computer in writing is that

   A. the copy looks so good that students tend to overlook major mistakes.

   B. the spell check and grammar programs discourage students from learning proper spelling and mechanics.

   C. the speed with which corrections can be made detracts from the exploration and contemplation of composing.

   D. the writer loses focus by concentrating on the final product rather than the details.

91. After watching a movie of a train derailment, a child exclaims, "Wow, look how many cars fell off the tracks. There's junk everywhere. The engineer must have really been asleep." Using the facts that the child is impressed by the wreckage and assigns blame to the engineer, a follower of Piaget's theories would estimate the child to be about

   A. ten years old.

   B. twelve years old.

   C. fourteen years old.

   D. sixteen years old.

92. Oral debate is most closely associated with which form of discourse?

   A. Description

   B. Exposition

   C. Narration

   D. Persuasion

93. Written on the sixth grade reading level, most of S. E. Hinton's novels (for instance, *The Outsiders*) have the greatest reader appeal with

   A. sixth graders.

   B. ninth graders.

   C. twelfth graders.

   D. adults.

94. Which aspect of language is innate?

   A. Biological capability to articulate sounds understood by other humans

   B. Cognitive ability to create syntactical structures

   C. Capacity for using semantics to convey meaning in a social environment

   D. Ability to vary inflections and accents

95. Which of the following titles is known for its scathingly condemning tone?

   A. Boris Pasternak's *Dr. Zhivago*

   B. Albert Camus' *The Stranger*

   C. Henry David Thoreau's "On the Duty of Civil Disobedience"

   D. Benjamin Franklin's "Rules by Which A Great Empire May be Reduced to a Small One"

96. Which of the following is not a theme of Native American writing?

   A. Emphasis on the hardiness of the human body and soul

   B. The strength of multi-cultural assimilation

   C. Indignation about the genocide of native peoples

   D. Remorse for the loss of the Indian way of life

97. If a student uses slang and expletives, what is the best course of action to take in order to improve the student's formal communication skills?

A. ask the student to rephrase their writing; that is, translate it into language appropriate for the school principal to read.

B. refuse to read the student's papers until he conforms to a more literate style.

C. ask the student to read his work aloud to the class for peer evaluation.

D. rewrite the flagrant passages to show the student the right form of expression.

98. Which of the following contains an error in possessive punctuation?

A. Doris's shawl

B. mother's-in-law frown

C. children's lunches

D. ambassador's briefcase

99. Which of the following would be the most significant factor in teaching Homer's *Iliad* and *Odyssey* to any particular group of students?

A. Identifying a translation on the appropriate reading level

B. Determining the students' interest level

C. Selecting an appropriate evaluative technique

D. Determining the scope and delivery methods of background study

100. A punctuation mark indicating omission, interrupted thought, or an incomplete statement is a/an

A. ellipsis.

B. anachronism

C. colloquy.

D. idiom.

101. In the phrase "the Cabinet conferred with the president," Cabinet is an example of a/an

   A. metonym

   B. synecdoche

   C. metaphor

   D. allusion

102. The technique of starting a narrative at a significant point in the action and then developing the story through flashbacks is called

   A. in medias res

   B. octava rima

   C. irony

   D. suspension of willing disbelief

103. In 'inverted triangle' introductory paragraphs, the thesis sentence occurs

   A. at the beginning of the paragraph.

   B. in the middle of the paragraph.

   C. at the end of the paragraph.

   D. in the second paragraph.

104. A student informative composition should consist of a minimum of how many paragraphs?

   A. three

   B. four

   C. five

   D. six

105. In a timed essay test of an hour's duration, how much time should be devoted to prewriting.

   A. five

   B. ten

   C. fifteen

   D. twenty

106. Which of the following sentences is properly punctuated?

   A. The more you eat; the more you want.

   B. The authors - John Steinbeck, Ernest Hemingway, and William Faulkner - are staples of modern writing in American literature textbooks.

   C. Handling a wild horse, takes a great deal of skill and patience.

   D. The man, who replaced our teacher, is a comedian.

107. The students in Mrs. Cline's seventh grade language arts class were invited to attend a performance of *Romeo and Juliet* presented by the drama class at the high school. To best prepare, they should

   A. read the play as a homework exercise.

   B. read a synopsis of the plot and a biographical sketch of the author.

   C. examine a few main selections from the play to become familiar with the language and style of the author.

   D. read a condensed version of the story and practice attentive listening skills.

108. "The *U.S.S. Constitution* is the old man of the sea" is an example of

   A. hyperbole.

   B. simile.

   C. allegory.

   D. metaphor.

109. Which of the following sentences contains a capitalization error?

   A. The commander of the English navy was Admiral Nelson.

   B. Napoleon was the president of the French First Republic.

   C. Queen Elizabeth II is the Monarch of the entire British Empire.

   D. William the Conqueror led the Normans to victory over the British.

110. Which of the following sentences contains a subject-verb agreement error?

   A. Both mother and her two sisters were married in a triple ceremony.

   B. Neither the hens nor the rooster is likely to be served for dinner.

   C. My boss, as well as the company's two personnel directors, have been to Spain.

   D. Amanda and the twins are late again.

111. Writing ideas quickly without interruption of the flow of thoughts or attention to conventions is called

   A. brainstorming.

   B. mapping.

   C. listing.

   D. free writing.

12. A formative evaluation of student writing

   A. requires a thorough marking of mechanical errors with a pencil or pen.

   B. makes comments on the appropriateness of the student's interpretation of the prompt and the degree to which the objective was met.

   C. requires the student to hand in all the materials produced during the process of writing.

   D. involves several careful readings of the text for content, mechanics, spelling, and usage.

113. Reading a piece of student writing to assess the overall impression of the product is

   A. holistic evaluation.

   B. portfolio assessment.

   C. analytical evaluation.

   D. using a performance system.

114. Modeling is a practice that requires students to

   A. create a style unique to their own language capabilities.

   B. emulate the writing of professionals.

   C. paraphrase passages from good literature.

   D. peer evaluate the writings of other students.

115. The writing of Russian naturalists is

   A. optimistic

   B. pessimistic.

   C. satirical.

   D. whimsical.

116. Most children's literature prior to the development of popular literature was intended to be didactic. Which of the following would not be considered didactic?

   A. "A Visit from St. Nicholas" by Clement Moore

   B. *McGuffey's Reader*

   C. any version of *Cinderella*

   D. parables from the *Bible*

117. Words like *twanging* and *tintinnabulation* in Poe's "The Bells" are examples of

   A. onomatopoeia.

   B. consonance.

   C. figurative language.

   D. free verse.

118. Which of the following is a characteristic of blank verse?

   A. Meter in iambic pentameter

   B. Clearly specified rhyme scheme

   C. Lack of figurative language

   D. Unspecified rhythm

119. American colonial writers were primarily

   A. Romanticists.

   B. Naturalists.

   C. Realists.

   D. Neo-classicists.

120. Charles Dickens, Robert Browning, and Robert Louis Stevenson were

   A. Victorians.

   B. Medievalists.

   C. Elizabethans.

   D. Absurdists.

121. The most significant drawback to applying learning theory research to classroom practice is that

   A. today's students do not acquire reading skills with the same alacrity as when greater emphasis was placed on reading classical literature.

   B. development rates are complicated by geographical and cultural differences that are difficult to overcome.

   C. homogeneous grouping has contributed to faster development of some age groups.

   D. social and environmental conditions have contributed to an escalated maturity level than research done twenty or more years ago would seem to indicate.

122. Overcrowded classes prevent the individual attention needed to facilitate language development. This drawback can be best overcome by

   A. dividing the class into independent study groups.

   B. assigning more study time at home.

   C. using more drill practice in class.

   D. team teaching.

123. Which of the following responses to literature typically give middle school students the most problems?

   A. Interpretive

   B. Evaluative

   C. Critical

   D. Emotional

124. In the hierarchy of needs for adolescents who are becoming more team-oriented in their approach to learning, which need do they exhibit most?

   A. Need for competence

   B. Need for love/acceptance

   C. Need to know

   D. Need to belong

125. What is the best course of action when a child refuses to complete an assignment on the grounds that is morally objectionable?

   A. Speak with the parents and explain the necessity of studying this work.

   B. Encourage the child to sample some of the text before making a judgment.

   C. Place the child in another teacher's class where students are studying an acceptable work.

   D. Provide the student with alternative material that serves the same curricular purpose.

Answer Key

1. A	26. B	51. A	76. D	101. B
2. B	27. C	52. A	77. A	102. A
3. A	28. B	53. C	78. C	103. C
4. A	29. A	54. A	79. B	104. C
5. B	30. C	55. D	80. A	105. B
6. A	31. C	56. C	81. D	106. B
7. E	32. C	57. B	82. B	107. D
8. D	33. C	58. A	83. D	108. D
9. C	34. A	59. B	84. D	109. C
10. A	35. D	60. C	85. A	110. C
11. D	36. D	61. D	86. C	111. D
12. D	37. D	62. A	87. B	112. B
13. C	38. A	63. C	88. A	113. A
14. E	39. C	64. B	89. A	114. B
15. A	40. D	65. D	90. C	115. B
16. C	41. A	66. B	91. A	116. A
17. C	42. A	67. D	92. D	117. A
18. A	43. D	68. C	93. B	118. A
19. B	44. C	69. C	94. A	119. D
20. D	45. A	70. D	95. D	120. A
21. C	46. D	71. D	96. B	121. D
22. C	47. C	72. C	97. A	122. A
23. D	48. C	73. B	98. B	123. B
24. C	49. A	74. B	99. A	124. B
25. A	50. C	75. A	100. A	125. D

Rationales with Sample Questions

Directions: In sentences 1-15, four words or phrases have been underlined. If you determine that any underlined word or phrase has an error in grammar, usage, or mechanics, circle the letter underneath the underlining. If there are no errors, circle the letter E at the end of the sentence. There is no more than one error in any sentence.

1. The volcanic eruption in Montserrat displaced residents of Plymouth <u>which</u>
                                                                                                    A

   felt that the <u>English government</u> <u>was</u> responsible for <u>their</u> evacuation   E
                   B   C   D

   The error is A. "Which" is a relative pronoun whose antecedent is "residents of Plymouth". This antecedent represents persons, not things. If the antecedent were a thing or things, then "which" would be correct. "Who" is the correct pronoun.

2. When the <u>school district</u> privatized the school cafeteria, <u>us</u> students <u>were</u>
               A   B   C

   thrilled to purchase more than soggy <u>French fries</u>   E
                                             D

   The error is B. "Us" is an object pronoun, not the needed subject pronoun. "We" is the right pronoun.

3. The homecoming <u>Queen and King</u> <u>were chosen</u> by the <u>student body</u> for <u>their</u>
                           A   B   C   D

   popularity   E

   The error is A. "Queen and King" are used as common nouns here, and not as proper nouns naming a real sovereign such as Queen Elizabeth. Since the words "king and queen" are common nouns, they are not capitalized.

4. If the practical joke <u>was</u> <u>Cullen's</u> idea, then he <u>must</u> suffer the <u>consequences</u>
   E
                   A   B   C   D

   The error is A. In a sentence beginning with "If" and expressing a condition, it is necessary to use the correct subjunctive forms: "If I were, if you were, if he/she/it were, if we were, if you were, if they were". The sentence here should read: "If the practical joke were Cullen's idea..."

5. She, not her sister, <u>is</u> the one <u>who</u> the librarian <u>has questioned</u> about the
                    A   B   C
   missing books, <u>Butterfly's</u> Ball and the Bear's House   E
                          D

   The error is B. The relative pronoun "who" is a subject pronoun, but the sentence requires the object form at this point, "whom."

6. Jack told a <u>credulous</u> story about his trip <u>up the beanstalk</u> because each
               A   B
   child in the room <u>was convinced</u> <u>by his reasoning</u>   E
                         C   D

   The error is A: Only a person can be credulous, not a thing. It should read: "Jack told an incredible story about his trip..."

7. There <u>are</u> <u>fewer</u> students in school this year despite the <u>principal's</u> prediction
         A   B   C
   of <u>increasing</u> enrollment   E
      D

   The answer is E: There are no grammatical or syntactical errors in this sentence.

8. My mother is a <u>Methodist</u>. She married a <u>Southern Baptist</u> and took <u>us</u>
                  A   B   C
   children to the <u>First Baptist church</u> in Stuart   E
                     D

   The error is D: The name of the church should be completely capitalized. It should read: "... the First Baptist Church."

9. When we moved from Jacksonville, Florid<u>a</u> to Little Ro<u>ck,</u> Arkansas, my
                                               A   B

 <u>Dad</u> <u>was promoted</u> to store manager.   E
  C   D

 The error is C: "dad" is a common noun, which is indicated by the possessive "my". "Dad" used as an actual name gets capitalized.

10. "One of the <u>burglar's</u> was <u>already</u> <u>apprehended</u> before his colleagues left
                     A   B   C

 the buildi<u>ng,</u>" bragged the officer.   E
        D

 The error is A: "burglar" should be in the plural: "burglars". In this sentence, it is written as a possessive.

11. Walter said <u>that</u> his calculator <u>has been missing</u> <u>since</u> last Monday
                A   B   C

 <u>responding to my question</u>   E
      D

 The error is D: the participle phrase ("responding to my question") modifies Walter, not "Monday." The sentence should read: "Walter, responding to my question, said that his calculator has been missing since last Monday."

12. Why was the girl <u>that</u> had plenty of money <u>arrested</u> for <u>shoplifting</u> some
                    A   B   C

 trinkets of <u>two dollar's worth</u>?   E
         D

 The error is D. The sentence should read: "… trinkets of two dollars' worth". As it is, "two dollar's worth" is in the singular possessive.

13. The future <u>will be</u> <u>because of</u> the past: <u>by changing the past</u> <u>would alter</u> the
              A   B   C   D

 future.   E

 The answer is C: including "by" is incorrect here. The sentence should read: "… because of the past: changing the past would alter the future."

TEACHER CERTIFICATION STUDY GUIDE

14. <u>Mr Thomas</u>' daughter-in-law encouraged her <u>husband's</u> boss to host a
       A   B
    fund-raiser for <u>the United Way</u>, a charity that Mr Thomas <u>supports</u>. E
                    C   D

    The answer is E. There are no errors in this sentence.

15. Miriam decided to remain <u>stationary</u> <u>since</u> <u>to move</u> would startle the
                                    A   B C
    horses, one of <u>which</u> might bolt.   E
                 D

    The error is A: "stationary" is not an adjective used for persons. "Motionless" would be a viable correction.

ENGLISH HIGH SCHOOL

Part B

Each underlined portion of sentences 16-25 contains one or more errors in grammar, usage, mechanics, or sentence structure. Circle the choice which best corrects the error without changing the meaning of the original sentence. Choice D or E repeats the underlined portion. Select the identical phrase if you find no error.

16. Joe <u>didn't hardly know his cousin Fred</u> who'd had a rhinoplasty.

   A. hardly did know his cousin Fred

   B. didn't know his cousin Fred hardly

   C. hardly knew his cousin Fred

   D. didn't know his cousin Fred

   E. didn't hardly know his cousin Fred

The answer is C: using the adverb "hardly" to modify the verb creates a negative, and adding "not" creates the dreaded double-negative.

TEACHER CERTIFICATION STUDY GUIDE

17. <u>Mixing the batter for cookies</u>, the cat licked the crisco from the cookie sheet.

    A. While mixing the batter for cookies

    B. While the batter for cookies was Mixing

    C. While I mixed the batter for cookies

    D. While I mixed the cookies

    E. Mixing the batter for cookies

The answer is C. A and E give the impression that the cat was mixing the batter (it is a "dangling modifier"), B that the batter was mixing itself, and D lacks precision: it is the batter that was being mixed, not the cookies themselves.

18. Mr. Brown is a school volunteer with a reputation and twenty years service

    A. with a reputation for twenty years' service

    B. with a reputation for twenty year's service

    C. who has served twenty years

    D. with a reputation and twenty years service

    E. with a reputation and twenty years service

The answer is A. B is a singular genitive ('s), C lacks the reputation part, and D and E lack the genitive plural (s') that is necessary here.

19. Walt Whitman was famous for his composition, *Leaves of Grass*, serving as a nurse during the Civil War, and a devoted son

A. *Leaves of Grass*, his service as a nurse during the Civil War, and a devoted son

B. composing *Leaves of Grass*, serving as a nurse during the Civil War, and being a devoted son

C. his composition, *Leaves of Grass*, his nursing during the Civil War, and his devotion as a son

D. his composition, *Leaves of Grass*, serving as a nurse during the Civil War, and a devoted son

E. his composition, *Leaves of Grass*, serving as a nurse during the Civil War, and a devoted son

The answer is B: in order to be parallel, the sentence needs three gerunds. The other sentences use both gerunds and nouns, which is a lack of parallelism.

20. A teacher must know not only her subject matter but also the strategies of content teaching

A. must not only know her subject matter but also the strategies of content teaching

B. not only must know her subject matter but also the strategies of content teaching

C. must not know only her subject matter but also the strategies of content teaching

D. must know not only her subject matter but also the strategies of content teaching

The answer is D: "not only" must come directly after "know" because the intent is to create the clearest meaning link with the "but also" predicate section later in the sentence.

21. My English teacher, Mrs. Hunt, is nicer than any teacher at school and is the most helpful

   A. is as nice as any teacher at school and is

   B. is nicer than any other teacher at school and is

   C. is as nice as any other teacher at school and is

   D. is nicer than any teacher at school and is

The answer is C. When comparing one thing to others in a group, you need to exclude the thing under comparison from the rest of the group. Thus, you need the word "other" in the sentence.

22. The teacher implied from our angry words that there was conflict between you and me

   A. Implied… between you and I

   B. Inferred… between you and I

   C. Inferred… between you and me

   D. Implied… between you and me

The answer is C: the difference between the verb "to imply" and the verb "to infer" is that implying is directing an interpretation toward other people; to infer is to deduce an interpretation from someone else's discourse. Moreover, "between you and I" is grammatically incorrect: after the preposition "between," the object (or 'disjunctive' with this particular preposition) pronoun form, "me," is needed.

23. There were <u>fewer pieces</u> of evidence presented during the second trial

　　A. fewer peaces

　　B. less peaces

　　C. less pieces

　　D. fewer pieces

The answer is D. "less" is impossible is the plural, and "peace" is the opposite of war, not a "piece" of evidence.

24. Mr. Smith <u>respectfully submitted his resignation and had</u> a new job.

　　A. respectfully submitted his resignation and has

　　B. respectfully submitted his resignation before accepting

　　C. respectfully submitted his resignation because of

　　D. respectfully submitted his resignation and had

The answer is C. A eliminates any relationship of causality between submitting the resignation and having the new job. B just changes the sentence and does not indicate the fact that Mr. Smith had a new job before submitting his resignation. D means that Mr. Smith first submitted his resignation, then got a new job.

25. Wally groaned, "Why do I have to do an oral interpretation of "The Raven.""

    A. groaned "Why… of 'The Raven'?"

    B. groaned "Why… of "The Raven"?

    C. groaned ", Why… of "The Raven?"

    D. groaned, "Why… of "The Raven."

The answer is A. The question mark in a quotation that is an interrogation should be within the quotation marks. Also, when quoting a work of literature within another quotation, one should use single quotation marks ('…') for the title of this work, and they should close before the final quotation mark.

26. The synonyms "gyro," "hero," and "submarine" reflect which influence on language usage?

    A. social

    B. geographical

    C. historical

    D. personal

The answer is B. They are interchangeable but their use depends on the region of the United States, not on the social class of the speaker. Nor is there any historical context around any of them. The usage can be personal, but will most often vary with the region.

TEACHER CERTIFICATION STUDY GUIDE

27. The following passage is written from which point of view?

As she mused the pitiful vision of her mother's life laid its spell on the very quick of her being –that life of commonplace sacrifices closing in final craziness. She trembled as she heard again her mother's voice saying constantly with foolish insistence: Dearevaun Seraun! Dearevaun Seraun!*

* "The end of pleasure is pain!"

(Gaelic)

    A. First person, narrator

    B. Second person, direct address

    C. Third person, omniscient

    D. First person, omniscient

The answer is C. The passage is clearly in the third person (the subject is "she"), and it is omniscient since it gives the characters' inner thoughts.

28. The literary device of personification is used in which example below?

    A. "Beg me no beggary by soul or parents, whining dog!"

    B. "Happiness sped through the halls cajoling as it went."

    C. "O wind thy horn, thou proud fellow."

    D. "And that one talent which is death to hide."

The answer is B. "Happiness," an abstract concept, is described as if it were a person.

29. Which of the writers below is a renowned Black poet?

    A. Maya Angelou

    B. Sandra Cisneros

    C. Richard Wilbur

    D. Richard Wright

The answer is A. Among her most famous work are *I Know Why the Caged Bird Sings* (1970), *And Still I Rise* (1978), and *All God's Children Need Traveling Shoes* (1986). Richard Wilbur is a poet and a translator of French dramatists Racine et Moliere, but he is not African American. Richard Wright is a very important African American author of novels such as *Native Son* and *Black Boy* or *The Outsider*. However, he was not a poet. Sandra Cisneros is a Latina author who is very important in developing Latina Women's literature,

30. Which of the following is not one of the four forms of discourse?

    A. exposition

    B. description

    C. rhetoric

    D. persuasion

The answer is C. Rhetoric is an umbrella term for techniques of expressive and effective speech. Rhetorical figures are ornaments of speech such as anaphora, antithesis, metaphor, etc. The other three choices are specific forms of discourse.

31. Among junior-high school students of low-to-average readability levels, which work would most likely stir reading interest?

    A. *Elmer Gantry*, Sinclair Lewis

    B. *Smiley's People*, John Le Carre

    C. *The Outsiders*, S.E. Hinton

    D. *And Then There Were None*, Agatha Christie.

The answer is C. The students can easily identify with the characters and the gangs in the book. S.E. Hinton has actually said about this book: "*The Outsiders* is definitely my best-selling book; but what I like most about it is how it has taught a lot of kids to enjoy reading."

32. "Every one must pass through Vanity Fair to get to the celestial city" is an allusion from a

    A. Chinese folk tale.

    B. Norse saga.

    C. British allegory.

    D. German fairy tale.

The answer is C. This is a reference to John Bunyan's *Pilgrim's Progress from this World to That Which Is to Come* (Part I, 1678; Part II, 1684), in which the hero, Christian, flees the City of Destruction and must undergo different trials and tests to get to the Celestial City.

33. **Which teaching method would best engage underachievers in the required senior English class?**

   A. Assign use of glossary work and extensively footnoted excerpts of great works.

   B. Have students take turns reading aloud the anthology selection

   C. Let students choose which readings they'll study and write about.

   D. Use a chronologically arranged, traditional text, but assigning group work, panel presentations, and portfolio management

The answer is C. It will encourage students to react honestly to literature. Students should take notes on what they're reading so they will be able to discuss the material. They should not only react to literature, but also experience it. Small-group work is a good way to encourage them. The other answers are not fit for junior-high or high school students. They should be encouraged, however, to read critics of works in order to understand criteria work.

34. **Which poem is typified as a villanelle?**

   A. "Do not go gentle into that Good Night"

   B. "Dover Beach"

   C. *Sir Gawain and the Green Knight*

   D. *Pilgrim's Progress*

The answer is A. This poem by Dylan Thomas typifies the villanelle because it was written as such. A villanelle is a form which was invented in France in the XVIth century, and used mostly for pastoral songs. It has an uneven number (usually five) of tercets rhyming *aba*, with a final quatrain rhyming *abaa*. This poem is the most famous villanelle written in English. "Dover Beach" by Matthew Arnold is not a villanelle, while *Sir Gawain and The Green Knight* was written in alliterative verse by an unknown author usually referred to as The Pearl Poet around 1370. The *Pilgrim's Progress* is a prose allegory by John Bunyan.

35. Which term best describes the form of the following poetic excerpt?

> And more to lulle him in his slumber soft,
> A trickling streake from high rock tumbling downe,
> And ever-drizzling raine upon the loft.
> Mixt with a murmuring winde, much like a swowne
> No other noyse, nor peoples troubles cryes.
> As still we wont t'annoy the walle'd towne,
> Might there be heard: but careless Quiet lyes,
> Wrapt in eternall silence farre from enemyes.

A. Ballad

B. Elegy

C. Spenserian stanza

D. Octava rima

The answer is D. The Octava Rima is a specific eight-line stanza whose rhyme scheme is abababcc.

36. Which poet was a major figure in the Harlem Renaissance?

    A. E.E. Cummings

    B. Rita Dove

    C. Margaret Atwood

    D. Langston Hughes

The answer is D. Hughes' collection of verse includes *The Weary Blues* (1926), *Shakespeare in Harlem* (1942), and *The Panther and the Lash* (1967). E. E. Cummings referred the lower case in the spelling of his name until the 1930's. He is also a celebrated poet, but is not a part of the Harlem Renaissance. Rita Dove is a very famous African American poet, but she was born in 1952 and therefore is not a part of the Harlem Renaissance. Margaret Atwood is a Canadian novelist.

37. To understand the origins of a word, one must study the

    A. synonyms

    B. inflections

    C. phonetics

    D. etymology

The answer is D. Etymology is the study of word origins. A synonym is an equivalent of another word and can substitute for it in certain contexts. Inflection is a modification of words according to their grammatical functions, usually by employing variant word-endings to indicate such qualities as tense, gender, case, and number. Phonetics are the science devoted to the physical analysis of the sounds of human speech, including their production, transmission, and perception.

38. Which sonnet form describes the following?

My galley charg'd with
  forgetfulness,
Through sharp seas, in
  winter night doth pass
'Tween rock and rock; and
  eke mine enemy, alas,
That is my lord steereth with
  cruelness.
And every oar a thought with
  readiness,
As though that death were
  light in such a case.
An endless wind doth tear
  the sail apace
Or forc'ed sighs and trusty
  fearfulness.
A rain of tears, a cloud of dark
  disdain,
Hath done the wearied
  cords great hinderance,
Wreathed with error and eke
  with ignorance.
The stars be hid that led me
  to this pain
Drowned is reason that
  should me consort,
And I remain despairing
  of the poet

A. Petrarchan or Italian sonnet

B. Shakespearian or Elizabethan sonnet

C. Romantic sonnet

E. Spenserian sonnet

The answer is A. The Petrarchan Sonnet, also known as Italian sonnet, is named after the Italian poet Petrarch (1304-74). It is divided into an octave rhyming *abbaabba* and a sestet normally rhyming *cdecde*.

39. What is the salient literary feature of this excerpt from an epic?

Hither the heroes and the nymphs resorts,
To taste awhile the pleasures of a court;
In various talk th'instructive hours they passed,
Who gave the ball, or paid the visit last;
One speaks the glory of the English Queen,
And another describes a charming Indian screen;
A third interprets motion, looks and eyes;
At every word a reputation dies.

A. Sprung rhythm

B. Onomatopoeia

C. Heroic couplets

D. Motif

The answer is C. A couplet is a pair of rhyming verse lines, usually of the same length. It is one of the most widely used verse-forms in European poetry. Chaucer established the use of couplets in English, notably in the *Canterbury Tales*, using rhymed iambic pentameters (a metrical unit of verse having one unstressed syllable followed by one stressed syllable) later known as heroic couplets. Other authors who used heroic couplets include Ben Jonson, Dryden, and especially Alexander Pope, who became the master of them.

40. What were two major characteristics of the first American literature?

A. Vengefulness and arrogance

B. Bellicosity and derision

C. Oral delivery and reverence for the land

D. Maudlin and self-pitying egocentricism

The answer is D. This characteristic can be seen in Captain John Smith's work, as well as William Bradford's, and Michael Wigglesworth's works.

41. Arthur Miller wrote *The Crucible* as a parallel to what twentieth century event?

A. Sen. McCarthy's House un-American Activities Committee Hearing?

B. The Cold War

C. The fall of the Berlin wall

D. The Persian Gulf War

The answer is A. The episode of the seventeenth century witch hunt in Salem, Mass., gave Miller a storyline that was very comparable to what was happening to persons suspected of communist beliefs in the 1950's.

TEACHER CERTIFICATION STUDY GUIDE

42. Latin words that entered the English language during the Elizabethan age include

   A. allusion, education, and esteem

   B. vogue and mustache

   C. canoe and cannibal

   D. alligator, cocoa, and armadillo

   The answer is A. self explanatory

43. Which of the following is not a characteristic of a fable?

   A. animals that feel and talk like humans.

   B. happy solutions to human dilemmas.

   C. teaches a moral or standard for behavior.

   D. illustrates specific people or groups without directly naming them.

The answer is D. A fable is a short tale with animals, humans, gods, or even inanimate objects as characters. Fables often conclude with a moral, delivered in the form of an epigram (a short, witty, and ingenious statement in verse). Fables are among the oldest forms of writing in human history: it appears in Egyptian papyri of c1,500 BC. The most famous fables are those of Aesop, a Greek slave living in about 600 BC. In India, the Pantchatantra appeared in the third century. The most famous modern fables are those of seventeenth century French poet Jean de La Fontaine.

44. Which of the following is not an example of the subject of a tall-tale?

    A. John Henry

    B. Paul Bunyan

    C. George Washington

    D. Rip Van Winkle

The answer is C. George Washington really existed.

45. If a student has a poor vocabulary, the teacher should recommend first that

    A. the student read newspapers, magazines and books on a regular basis.

    B. the student enroll in a Latin class.

    C. the student write the words repetitively after looking them up in the dictionary.

    D. the student use a thesaurus to locate synonyms and incorporate them into his/her vocabulary

The answer is A. It is up to the teacher to help the student choose reading material, but the student must be able to choose where to search for the reading pleasure indispensable for enriching vocabulary.

46. Which author did not write satire?

    A. Joseph Addison

    B. Richard Steele

    C. Alexander Pope

    D. John Bunyan

The answer is D. John Bunyan was a religious writer, known for his autobiography, *Grace Abounding To The Chief of Sinners*, as well as other books, all religious in their inspiration, such as *The Holy City, or the New Jerusalem* (1665), *A Confession of my Faith, and a Reason of my Practice* (1672), or *The Holy War* (1682).

47. Which of the following was not written by Jonathan Swift?

    A. "A Voyage to Lilliput"

    B. "A Modest proposal"

    C. Samson Agonistes"

    D. "A Tale of a Tub"

The answer is C. *Samson Agonistes* is a poem by John Milton. It was published in 1671 in the same volume as *Paradise regain'd*.

48. Which is not a Biblical allusion?

A. The patience of Job

B. Thirty pieces of silver

C. "Man proposes; God disposes"

D. "Suffer not yourself to be betrayed by a kiss"

C is the answer. This saying is attributed to Thomas à Kempis (1379-1471) in his *Imitation of Christ,* Book 1, chapter 19.

49. Which definition is the best for defining diction?

A. The specific word choices of an author to create a particular mood or feeling in the reader.

B. Writing which explains something thoroughly.

C. The background, or exposition, for a short story or drama.

D. Word choices which help teach a truth or moral.

The answer is A. Diction refers to an author's choice of words, expressions and style to convey his/her meaning.

TEACHER CERTIFICATION STUDY GUIDE

50. Which is the best definition of free verse, or *vers libre*?

   A. Poetry which consists of an unaccented syllable followed by an unaccented sound.

   B. Short lyrical poetry written to entertain but with an instructive purpose.

   C. Poetry which does not have a uniform pattern of rhythm.

   D. A poem which tells the story and has a plot

C is the answer. Free verse has lines of irregular length (but it does not run on like prose).

51. Which is not an accepted point of view in literary works?

   A. First person, omniscient.

   B. Third person, limited.

   C. First person, limited.

   D. Third person, omniscient.

The answer is A. If a story is narrated in the first person, the point of view cannot be omniscient; it is limited to the view of the first person narrator.

ENGLISH HIGH SCHOOL

52. Which is an untrue statement about a theme in literature?

A. The theme is always stated directly somewhere in the text.

B. The theme is the central idea in a literary work.

C. All parts of the work (plot, setting, mood) should contribute to the theme in some way.

D. By analyzing the various elements of the work, the reader should be able to arrive at an indirectly stated theme.

The answer is A. The theme may be stated directly, but it can also be implicit in various aspects of the work, such as the interaction between characters, symbolism, or description.

53. Which is the least true statement concerning an author's literary tone?

A. Tone is partly revealed through the selection of details.

B. Tone is the expression of the author's attitude towards his/her subject.

C. Tone in literature is usually satiric or angry.

D. Tone in literature corresponds to the tone of voice a speaker uses.

The answer is C. Tone in literature conveys a mood and can be as varied as the tone of voice of a speaker (see D), e.g. sad, nostalgic, whimsical, angry, formal, intimate, satirical, sentimental, etc.

54. Regarding the study of poetry, select the answer which is least applicable to all types of poetry.

  A. Setting and audience

  B. Theme and tone

  C. Pattern and diction

  D. Diction and rhyme scheme

The answer is A. Setting and audience are important elements of narrative but there are many poems where the setting and audience are unimportant.

55. Which of the following definitions best describes a parable?

  A. A short entertaining account of some happening, usually using talking animals as characters.

  B. A slow, sad song or poem, or prose work expressing lamentation.

  C. An extensive narrative work expressing universal truths concerning domestic life.

  D. A short, simple story of an occurrence of a familiar kind, from which a moral or religious lesson may be drawn.

The answer is D. A parable is usually brief, and should be interpreted as an allegory teaching a moral lesson. Jesus's forty parables are the model of the genre, but modern, secular examples exist: such as Wilfred Owen's *The Parable of The Young Man and The Young* (1920), or John Steinbeck's prose work *The Pearl* (1948).

56. Which of the following is the best definition of existentialism?

A. The philosophical doctrine that matter is the only reality and that everything in the world, including thought, will and feeling, can be explained only in terms of matter.

B. Philosophy which views things as they should be or as one would wish them to be.

C. A philosophical and literary movement, variously religious and atheistic, stemming from Kierkegaard and represented by Sartre.

D. The belief that all events are determined by fate and are hence inevitable.

The answer is C. Even though there are other very important thinkers in the movement known as Existentialism, such as Camus and Merleau-Ponty, Sartre remains the main figure in this movement.

57. Which is the best definition of Imagism?

A. A doctrine which teaches that comfort is the only goal of value in life.

B. A movement in modern poetry (c. 1910-1918) characterized by precise, concrete images, free verse, and suggestion rather than complete statement.

C. The belief that people are motivated in all their [sic] only by self-centeredness.

D. The doctrine that the human mind cannot know where there is a God or an ultimate cause, or anything beyond material phenomenon.

The answer is B. The group was led by Ezra Pound at first, but he left for Vorticism and was replaced by Amy Lowell. They rejected 19th century poetry and were looking for clarity and exactness. Their poems were usually short and built around a single image. Other writers representative of the movement are Richard Addington, "H.D." (Hilda Doolittle), F.S. Flint, D.H. Lawrence, Ford Madox Ford, and William Carlos Williams.

58. Which choice below best defines naturalism?

A. A belief that the writer or artist should apply scientific objectivity in his/her observation and treatment of life without imposing value judgments.

B. The doctrine that teaches that the existing world is the best to be hoped for.

C. The doctrine which teaches that God is not a personality, but that all laws, forces and manifestations of the universe are God-related.

D. A philosophical doctrine which professes that the truth of all knowledge must always be in question.

The answer is A. Naturalism is a movement that was started by French writers Jules and Edmond de Goncourt with their novel *Germinie Lacerteux* (1865), but its real leader is Emile Zola, who wanted to bring "a slice of life" to his readers. His saga, *Les Rougon Macquart*, consists in twenty-two novels depicting various aspects of social life. English writing authors representative of this movement include George Moore and George Gissing in England, but the most important naturalist novel in English is Theodore Dreiser's *Sister Carrie.*

59. The tendency to emphasize and value the qualities and peculiarities of life in a particular geographic area exemplifies

A. pragmatism.

B. regionalism.

C. pantheism.

D. abstractionism.

The answer is B. Pragmatism is a philosophical doctrine according to which there is no absolute truth. All truths change their trueness as their practical utility increases or decreases. The main representative of this movement is William James who in 1907 published *Pragmatism: A New Way for Some Old Ways of Thinking*. Pantheism is a philosophy according to which God is omnipresent in the world, everything is God and God is everything. The great representative of this sensibility is Spinoza. Also, the works of writers such as Wordsworth, Shelly and Emerson illustrate this doctrine. Abstract Expressionism is one of the most important movements in American art. It began in the 1940's with artists such as Willem de Kooning, Mark Rothko and Arshile Gorky. The paintings are usually large and non representational.

60. A traditional, anonymous story, ostensibly having a historical basis, usually explaining some phenomenon of nature or aspect of creation, defines a

   A. proverb.

   B. idyll.

   C. myth.

   D. epic.

The answer is C. A myth is usually traditional and anonymous and explains natural and supernatural phenomena. Myths are usually about creation, divinity, the significance of life and death, and natural phenomena.

61. The arrangement and relationship of words in sentences or sentence structures best describes

   A. style.

   B. discourse.

   C. thesis.

   D. syntax.

The answer is D. Syntax is the grammatical structure of sentences.

62. Explanatory or informative discourse is

    A. exposition.

    B. narration.

    C. persuasion.

    D. description.

The answer is A. Exposition sets forth a systematic explanation of any subject. It can also introduce the characters of a literary work, and their situations in the story

63. The substitution of "went to his rest" for "died" is an example of a/an

    A. bowdlerism.

    B. jargon.

    C. euphemism.

    D. malapropism.

The answer is C. A euphemism replaces an unpleasant or offensive word or expression by a more agreeable one. It also alludes to distasteful things in a pleasant manner, and it can even paraphrase offensive texts.

64. A conversation between two or more people is called a

    A. parody.

    B. dialogue.

    C. monologue.

    D. analogy.

The answer is B. Dialogues are indispensable to dramatic work, and they often appear in narrative and poetry. A parody is a work that adopts the subject and structure of another work in order to ridicule it. A monologue is a work or part of a work written in the first person. An analogy illustrates an idea by means of a more familiar one that is similar or parallel to it.

65. "Clean as a whistle or "Easy as falling of a log" are examples of

    A. semantics.

    B. parody.

    C. irony.

    D. clichés.

The answer is D. A cliché is a phrase or expression that has become dull due to overuse.

66. Which of the following is most true of expository writing?

A. It is mutually exclusive of other forms of discourse.

B. It can incorporate other forms of discourse in the process of providing supporting details.

C. It should never employ informal expression.

D. It should only be scored with a summative evaluation.

The answer is B. Expository writing sets forth an explanation or an argument about any subject.

67. The appearance of A Yankee from Connecticut in the Court of King Arthur is an example of a/an

A. rhetoric.

B. parody.

C. paradox.

D. anachronism.

The answer is D. Anachronism is the placing of characters, persons, events or things out of their time. Very famous examples of anachronism are Shakespeare's clock in *Julius Caesar*, and billiards in *Antony and Cleopatra*.

68. In literature, evoking feelings of pity or compassion is to create

    A. colloquy.

    B. irony.

    C. pathos.

    D. paradox

The answer is C. A very well known example of pathos is Desdemona's death in Othello, but there are many other examples of pathos.

69. "I'll die if I don't pass this course" is an example of

    A. barbarism.

    B. oxymoron.

    C. hyperbole.

    D. antithesis.

The answer is C. A hyperbole is an exaggeration for the sake of emphasis. It is a figure of speech that should not be understood literally. Hyperboles appear in everyday vernacular as well as in literature.

70. **An extended metaphor comparing two very dissimilar things (one lofty one lowly) is a definition of a/an**

    A. antithesis.

    B. aphorism.

    C. apostrophe.

    D. Conceit.

The answer is D. A conceit is an unusually far-fetched metaphor in which an object, person or situation is presented in a parallel and simpler analogue between two apparently very different things or feelings, one very sophisticated and one very ordinary, usually taken either from nature or a well known every day concept, familiar to both reader and author alike. The conceit was first developed by Petrarch and spread to England in the sixteenth century.

71. **Addressing someone absent or something inhuman as though present and able to respond describes a figure of speech known as**

    A. personification.

    B. synechdoche.

    C. metonymy

    D. apostrophe.

The answer is D. An apostrophe does address and absent person or something inhuman as though that person or thing were present and able to respond.

TEACHER CERTIFICATION STUDY GUIDE

72. Slang or jargon expressions associated with a particular ethnic, age, economic, or professional group are called

    A. aphorisms.

    B. allusions.

    C. idioms.

    D. euphemisms.

The answer is C. An idiom is a word or expression that cannot be translated word for word in another language, such as "I am running low on gas". By extension, it is used for a way of speaking and writing typical of a group of people.

73. Which of the following is a complex sentence?

    A. Anna and Margaret read a total of fifty-four books during summer vacation.

    B. The youngest boy on the team had the best earned run average, which mystifies the coaching staff.

    C. Earl decided to attend Princeton; his twin brother Roy, who aced the ASVAB test, will be going to Annapolis.

    D. "Easy come, easy go," Marcia moaned.

The answer is B. Here, the relative pronoun "which" introduces a clause that comments on and is dependent on the independent clause, "The youngest boy on the team had the best run average."

74. **Piaget's learning theory asserts that adolescents in the formal operations period**

   A. behave properly from fear of punishment rather than from a conscious decision to take a certain action.

   B. see the past more realistically and can relate to people from the past more than preadolescents.

   C. are less self-conscious and thus more willing to project their own identities into those of fictional characters.

   D. have not yet developed a symbolic imagination.

The answer is B, since according to Piaget, adolescents 12-15 years old begin thinking beyond the immediate and obvious, and theorize. Their assessment of events shifts from considering an action as "right" or "wrong" to considering the intent and behavior in which the action was performed. Fairy tale or other kinds of unreal characters have ceased to satisfy them and they are able to recognize the difference between pure history and historical fiction.

75. **Which of the following is a formal reading-level assessment?**

   A. a standardized reading test

   B. a teacher-made reading test

   C. an interview

   D. a reading diary

The answer is A. If assessment is standardized, it has to be objective, whereas B, C and D are all subjective assessments.

76. Middle and high school students are more receptive to studying grammar and syntax

A. through worksheets and end of lessons practices in textbooks.

B. through independent, homework assignment.

C. through analytical examination of the writings of famous authors.

D. through application to their own writing.

The answer is D. At this age, students learn grammatical concepts best through practical application in their own writing.

77. Which statement below best describes an author and his/her work?

A. Zora Neale Hurston's *Their Eyes Were Watching God* dealt autobiographically with the strong faith that helped her through the years of her poor upbringing in rural Florida.

B. Willa Cather's works, such as *My Antonia,* depicts the regionalism of the Deep South.

C. Emily Dickinson gained national recognition for the publication of over 300 poems.

D. Upton Sinclair's writings, such as *The Jungle*, represent the optimism and trust of the American citizenry for its government.

The answer is A. Zora Neale Hurston's autobiographical novel tells of her experience with poverty and racism in the South. She was also very influential in gender studies.

78. Which of the following is the least preferable strategy for teaching literature?

A. teacher-guided total class discussion

B. small group discussion

C. teacher lecture

D. dramatization of literature selections

The answer is C. In order to engage students' interest, it is necessary that they be involved whether through discussion or dramatization. A lecture is a much too passive technique to involve students of this age.

79. Which event triggered the beginning of Modern English?

A. Conquest of England by the Normans in 1066

B. Introduction of the printing press to the British Isles

C. Publication of Samuel Johnson's lexicon.

D. American Revolution

The answer is B. With the arrival of the written word, reading matter became mass produced, so the public tended to adopt the speech and writing habits printed in books and the language became more stable.

80. Which of the following is not true about the English language?

    A. English is the easiest language to learn.

    B. English is the least inflected language.

    C. English has the most extensive vocabulary of any language.

    D. English originated as a Germanic tongue.

The answer is A. Just like any other language, English has inherent difficulties which make it difficult to learn, even though English has no declensions such as those found in Latin, Greek, or contemporary Russian, or a tonal system such Chinese.

81. Which of the following is not a technique of prewriting?

    A. Clustering

    B. Listing

    C. Brainstorming

    D. Proofreading

The answer is D. Proofreading cannot be a method of prewriting, since it is done on already written texts only.

82. Which of the following is the least effective procedure for promoting consciousness of audience?

A. Pairing students during the writing process

B. Reading all rough drafts before the students write the final copies

C. Having students compose stories or articles for publication in school literary magazines or newspapers

D. Writing letters to friends or relatives

The answer is B. Reading all rough drafts will not encourage the students to take control of their text and might even inhibit their creativity. On the contrary, pairing students will foster their sense of responsibility, and having them compose stories for literary magazines will boost their self esteem as well as their organization skills.

83. The Elizabethans wrote in

A. Celtic

B. Old English

C. Middle English

D. Modern English

The answer is D. There is no document written in Celtic in England, and a work such as *Beowulf* is representative of Old English in the eighth century. It is also the earliest Teutonic written document. Before the fourteenth century, little literature is known to have appeared in Middle English, which had absorbed many words from the Norman French spoken by the ruling class, but at the and of the fourteenth century there appeared the works of Chaucer, John Gower, and the novel *Sir Gawain and The Green King*. The Elizabethans wrote in modern English and their legacy is very important: they imported the Petrarchan, or Italian, sonnet, which Sir Thomas Wyatt and Sir Philip Sydney illustrated in their works. Sir Edmund Spencer invented his own version of the Italian sonnet and wrote *The Faerie Queene.* Other literature of the time includes the hugely important works of Shakespeare and Marlowe.

84. Which of the following writers did not win a Nobel Prize for literature?

A. Gabriel Garcia-Marquez of Colombia

B. Nadine Gordimer of South Africa

C. Pablo Neruda of Chile

D. Alice Walker of the United States

The answer is D. Even though Alice Walker received the Pulitzer Price and the American Book Award for her best known novel, *The Color Purple*, and is the author of six novels and three collections of short stories that have received wide critical acclaim, she has not yet received the Nobel Prize.

85. Children's literature became established in the

A. seventeenth century

B. eighteenth century

C. nineteenth century

D. twentieth century

The answer is A. In the seventeenth Century, authors such as Jean de La Fontaine and his *Fables*, Pierre Perreault's *Tales*, Mme d'Aulnoye's Novels based on old folktales and Mme de Beaumont's *Beauty and the Beast* all created a children's literature genre. In England, Perreault was translated and a work allegedly written by Oliver Smith, *The renowned History of Little Goody Two Shoes*, also helped to establish children's literature in England.

86. Recognizing empathy in literature is mostly a/an

A. emotional response.

B. interpretive response.

C. critical response.

D. evaluative response.

The answer is C. In critical responses students make value judgments about the quality and atmosphere of a text. Through class discussion and written assignments, students react to and assimilate a writer's style and language.

87. Which of the following should not be included in the opening paragraph of an informative essay?

    A. Thesis sentence

    B. Details and examples supporting the main idea

    C. broad general introduction to the topic

    D. A style and tone that grabs the reader's attention

The answer is B. The introductory paragraph should introduce the topic, capture the reader's interest, state the thesis and prepare the reader for the main points in the essay. Details and examples, however, should be given in the second part of the essay, so as to help develop the thesis presented at the end of the introductory paragraph, following the inverted triangle method consisting of a broad general statement followed by some information, and then the thesis at the end of the paragraph.

88. **In the following quotation, addressing the dead body of Caesar as though he were still a living being is to employ an**

O, pardon me, though

Bleeding piece of earth

That I am meek and gentle with

These butchers.

    -Marc Antony from *Julius Caesar*

    A. Apostrophe

    B. Allusion

    C. Antithesis

    D. Anachronism

The answer is A. This rhetorical figure addresses personified things, absent people or gods. An allusion, on the other hand, is a quick reference to a character or event known to the public. An antithesis is a contrast between two opposing viewpoints, ideas, or presentation of characters. An anachronism is the placing of an object or person out of its time with the time of the text. The best known example is the clock in Shakespeare's *Julius Caesar*.

89. What is the main form of discourse in this passage?

"It would have been hard to find a passer-by more wretched in appearance. He was a man of middle height, stout and hardy, in the strength of maturity; he might have been forty-six or seven. A slouched leather cap hid half his face, bronzed by the sun and wind, and dripping with sweat.

- A. Description
- B. Narration
- C. Exposition
- D. Persuasion

The answer is A. A description presents a thing or a person in detail, and tells the reader about the appearance of whatever it is presenting. Narration relates a sequence of events (the story) told through a process of narration (discourse), in which events are recounted in a certain order (the plot). Exposition is an explanation or an argument within the narration. It can also be the introduction to a play or a story. Persuasion strives to convince either a character in the story or the reader.

90. **In general, the most serious drawback of using a computer in writing is that**

    A. the copy looks so good that students tend to overlook major mistakes.

    B. the spell check and grammar programs discourage students from learning proper spelling and mechanics.

    C. the speed with which corrections can be made detracts from the exploration and contemplation of composing.

    D. the writer loses focus by concentrating on the final product rather than the details.

The answer is C. Because the process of revising is very quick with the computer, it can discourage contemplation, exploring, and examination, which are very important in the process of writing.

91. **After watching a movie of a train derailment, a child exclaims, "Wow, look how many cars fell off the tracks. There's junk everywhere. The engineer must have really been asleep." Using the facts that the child is impressed by the wreckage and assigns blame to the engineer, a follower of Piaget's theories would estimate the child to be about**

    A. ten years old.

    B. twelve years old.

    C. fourteen years old.

    D. sixteen years old.

The answer is A. According to Piaget's theory, children seven-to-eleven years old begin to apply logic to concrete things and experiences. They can combine performance and reasoning to solve problems. They have internalized moral values and are willing to confront rules and adult authority.

92. Oral debate is most closely associated with which form of discourse?

    A. Description

    B. Exposition

    C. Narration

    D. Persuasion

The answer is D. It is extremely important to be convincing while having an oral debate. This is why persuasion is so important, because this is the way that you can influence your audience.

93. Written on the sixth grade reading level, most of S. E. Hinton's novels (for instance, *The Outsiders*) have the greatest reader appeal with

    A. sixth graders.

    B. ninth graders.

    C. twelfth graders.

    D. adults.

The answer is B. Adolescents are concerned with their changing bodies, their relationships with each other and adults, and their place in society. Reading *The Outsiders* makes them confront different problems that they are only now beginning to experience as teenagers, such as gangs and social identity. The book is universal in its appeal to adolescents.

94. Which aspect of language is innate?

A. Biological capability to articulate sounds understood by other humans

B. Cognitive ability to create syntactical structures

C. Capacity for using semantics to convey meaning in a social environment

D. Ability to vary inflections and accents

A is the answer. Language ability is innate and the biological capability to produce sounds lets children learn semantics and syntactical structures through trial and error. Linguists agree that language is first a vocal system of word symbols that enable a human to communicate his/her feelings, thoughts, and desires to other human beings.

95. Which of the following titles is known for its scathingly condemning tone?

A. Boris Pasternak's *Dr Zhivago*

B. Albert Camus' *The Stranger*

C. Henry David Thoreau's "On the Duty of Civil Disobedience"

D. Benjamin Franklin's "Rules by Which a Great Empire May Be Reduced to a Small One"

The answer is D. In this work, Benjamin Franklin adopts a scathingly ironic tone to warn the British about the probable outcome in their colonies if they persist with their policies. These are discussed one by one in the text, and the absurdity of each is condemned.

TEACHER CERTIFICATION STUDY GUIDE

96. Which of the following is not a theme of Native American writing?

    A. Emphasis on the hardiness of the human body and soul

    B. The strength of multi-cultural assimilation

    C. Contrition for the genocide of native peoples

    D. Remorse for the love of the Indian way of life

The answer is B. Native American literature was first a vast body of oral traditions from as early as before the fifteenth century. The characteristics include reverence for and awe of nature and the interconnectedness of the elements in the life cycle. The themes often reflect the hardiness of body and soul, remorse for the destruction of the Native American way of life, and the genocide of many tribes by the encroaching settlements of European Americans. These themes are still present in today's contemporary Native American literature, such as in the works of Duane Niatum, Gunn Allen, Louise Erdrich and N. Scott Momaday.

97. If a student uses slang and expletives, what is the best course of action to take in order to improve the student's formal communication skills?

A. ask the student to paraphrase their writing, that is, translate it into language appropriate for the school principal to read.

B. refuse to read the student's papers until he conforms to a more literate style.

C. ask the student to read his work aloud to the class for peer evaluation.

D. rewrite the flagrant passages to show the student the right form of expression.

The answer is A. Asking the student to write for a specific audience will help him become more involved in his writing. If he continues writing to the same audience—the teacher—he will continue seeing writing as just another assignment and he will not apply grammar, vocabulary and syntax the way they should be. By rephrasing his own writing, the student will learn to write for a different public.

98. Which of the following contains an error in possessive punctuation?

　　A. Doris's shawl

　　B. mother's-in-law frown

　　C. children's lunches

　　D. ambassador's briefcase

The answer is B. Mother-in-Law is a compound common noun and the inflection should be at the end of the word, by convention.

99. Which of the following would be the most significant factor in teaching Homer's *Iliad* and *Odyssey* to any particular group of students?

　　A. Identifying a translation on the appropriate reading level

　　B. Determining the students' interest level

　　C. Selecting an appropriate evaluative technique

　　D. Determining the scope and delivery methods of background study

The answer is A. Students will learn the importance of these two works if the translation reflects both the vocabulary that they know and their reading level. Greece will always be foremost in literary assessments due to Homer's works. Homer is the most often cited author, next to Shakespeare. Greece is the cradle of both democracy and literature. This is why it is so crucial that Homer be included in the works assigned.

100. **A punctuation mark indicating omission, interrupted thought, or an incomplete statement is a/an**

    A. ellipsis.

    B. anachronism.

    C. colloquy.

    D. idiom.

The answer is A. In an ellipsis, word or words that would clarify the sentence's message are missing, yet it is still possible to understand them from the context.

101. In the phrase "The Cabinet conferred with the President", Cabinet is an example of a/an

    A. metonym

    B. synecdoche

    C. metaphor

    D. allusion

The answer is B. In a synecdoche, a whole is referred to by naming a part of it. Also, a synecdoche can stand for a whole of which it is a part: for example, the Cabinet for the Government.

102. The technique of starting a narrative at a significant point in the action and then developing the story through flashbacks is called

    A. in medias res

    B. octava rima

    C. irony

    D. suspension of willing disbelief

The answer is A, as its Latin translation suggests: in the middle of things. An octava rima is a specific eight-line stanza of poetry whose rhyme scheme is abababcc. Lord Byron's *Don Juan* is written in octava rima. Irony is an unexpected disparity between what is stated and what is really implied by the author. Benjamin Franklin's "Rules by Which A Great Empire May be Reduced to a Small One" and Voltaire's tales are texts which are written using irony. Drama is what Coleridge calls "the willing suspension of disbelief for the moment, which constitutes poetic faith."

103. In 'inverted triangle' introductory paragraphs, the thesis sentence occurs

    A. at the beginning of the paragraph.

    B. in the middle of the paragraph.

    C. at the end of the paragraph.

    D. in the second paragraph.

The answer is C. The introduction to an essay should begin with a broad general statement, followed by one or more sentences adding interest and information to the topic. The thesis should be written at the end of the introduction.

104. **A student informative composition should consist of a minimum of how many paragraphs?**

    A. three

    B. four

    C. five

    D. six

The answer is C. The student should write an introduction, then three body paragraphs making three points with at least two supporting details each with a final sentence each time, followed by a conclusion.

105. **In a timed essay test of an hour's duration, how much time should be devoted to prewriting.**

    A. five

    B. ten

    C. fifteen

    D. twenty

The answer is B. In the hour the students have to write the essay, they should not take more than ten minutes prewriting. As the students pre-write, they should remember to have at least three main points and at least two to three details to support the main ideas.

106. Which of the following sentences is properly punctuated?

   A. The more you eat; the more you want.

   B. The authors—John Steinbeck, Ernest Hemingway, and William Faulkner—are staples of modern writing in American literature textbooks.

   C. Handling a wild horse, takes a great deal of skill and patience.

   D. The man, who replaced our teacher, is a comedian.

The answer is B. Dashes should be used instead of commas when commas are used elsewhere in the sentence for amplification or explanation –here within the dashes.

107. The students in Mrs. Cline's seventh grade language arts class were invited to attend a performance of *Romeo and Juliet* presented by the drama class at the high school. To best prepare, they should

   A. read the play as a homework exercise.

   B. read a synopsis of the plot and a biographical sketch of the author.

   C. examine a few main selections from the play to become familiar with the language and style of the author.

   D. read a condensed version of the story and practice attentive listening skills.

The answer is D. By reading a condensed version of the story, students will know the plot and therefore be able to follow the play on stage. It is also important for them to practice listening techniques such as one one-to-one tutoring and peer-assisted reading.

108. "The *U.S.S.* Constitution is the old man of the sea" is an example of

    A. allusion.

    B. simile.

    C. allegory.

    D. metaphor.

The answer is D. The metaphor is the most common rhetorical figure. It refers to something through the use of another word or expression, and by this introduces a comparison between what is being compared and what it is compared to: the metaphor equates the two things being compared. An allusion is a reference to someone, something, or a work of art, and it relies on the reader's familiarity with what is mentioned. A simile is different from a metaphor because the comparison it makes between two unlike things is introduced by "as" or "like". An allegory is a representation of something abstract through mostly personification, such as Liberty through the Statue of Liberty. John Bunyan's *Pilgrim's Progress* is also an example through its use of human qualities personified.

109. Which of the following sentences contains a capitalization error?

    A. The commander of the English navy was Admiral Nelson

    B. Napoleon was the president of the French First Republic

    C. Queen Elizabeth II is the Monarch of the British Empire

    D. William the Conqueror led the Normans to victory over the British

The answer is C. Words that represent titles and offices are not capitalized unless used with a proper name. This is not the case here.

110. Which of the following sentences contains a subject-verb agreement error?

A. Both mother and her two sisters were married in a triple ceremony.

B. Neither the hen nor the rooster is likely to be served for dinner.

C. My boss, as well as the company's two personnel directors, have been to Spain.

D. Amanda and the twins are late again.

The answer is C. The reason for this is because the true subject of the verb is "My boss", not "two personnel directors".

111. Writing ideas quickly without interruption of the flow of thoughts or attention to conventions is called

A. brainstorming.

B. mapping.

C. listing.

D. Free writing.

The answer is D. Free writing for ten or fifteen minutes allows students to write out their thoughts about a subject. This technique allows the students to develop ideas that they are conscious of, but it also helps them to develop ideas that are lurking in the subconscious. It is important to let the flow of ideas run through the hand. If the students get stuck, they can write the last sentence over again until inspiration returns.

TEACHER CERTIFICATION STUDY GUIDE

112. A formative evaluation of student writing

A. requires thorough markings of mechanical errors with a pencil or pen.

B. making comments on the appropriateness of the student's interpretation of the prompt and the degree to which the objective was met.

C. should require that the student hand in all the materials produced during the process of writing.

D. several careful readings of the text for content, mechanics, spelling, and usage.

The answer is B. It is important to give students numerous experiences with formative evaluation (evaluation as the student writes the piece). Formative evaluation will assign points to every step of the writing process, even though it is not graded. The criteria for the writing task should be very clear, and the teacher should read each step twice. Responses should be non critical and supportive, and the teacher should involve students in the process of defining criteria, and make it clear that formative and summative evaluations are two distinct processes.

113. Reading a piece of student writing to assess the overall impression of the product is

A. holistic evaluation.

B. portfolio assessment.

C. analytical evaluation.

D. using a performance system.

The answer is A. Holistic Scoring assesses a piece of writing as a whole. Usually a paper is read quickly through once to get a general impression. The writing is graded according to the impression of the whole work rather than the sum of its parts. Often holistic scoring uses a rubric that establishes the overall criteria for a certain score to evaluate each paper.

114. Modeling is a practice that requires students to

A. create a style unique to their own language capabilities.

B. emulate the writing of professionals.

C. paraphrase passages from good literature.

D. peer evaluate the writings of other students.

The answer is B. Modeling has students analyze the writing of a professional writer and try to reach the same level of syntactical, grammatical and stylistic mastery as the author whom they are studying.

115. The writing of Russian naturalists is

A. optimistic.

B. pessimistic.

C. satirical.

D. whimsical.

The answer is B. Although the movement, which originated with the critic Vissarion Belinsky, was particularly strong in the 1840's, it can be said that the works of Dostoevsky, Tolstoy, Chekov, Turgenev and Pushkin owe much to it. These authors' works are among the best in international literature, yet are shrouded in stark pessimism. Tolstoy's *Anna Karenina* or Dostoevsky's *Crime and Punishment* are good examples of this dark outlook.

116. Most children's literature prior to the development of popular literature was intended to be didactic. Which of the following would not be considered didactic?

    A. "A Visit from St. Nicholas" by Clement Moore

    B. *McGuffy's Reader*

    C. any version of *Cinderella*

    D. parables from the *Bible*

The answer is A. "A Visit from St. Nicholas" is a cheery, non-threatening child's view of "The Night before Christmas." Didactic means intended to teach some lesson.

117. Words like *twanging* and *tintinnabulation* in Poe's "The Bells" are examples of

    A. onomatopoeia.

    B. consonance.

    C. figurative language.

    D. free verse.

The answer is A. Onomatopoeia is using a word or a group of words that sound like what they mean. In this example, these three words evoke the different sounds made by the bells.

118. Which of the following is a characteristic of blank verse?

A. Meter in iambic pentameter

B. Clearly specified rhyme scheme

C. Lack of figurative language

D. Unspecified rhythm

The answer is A. An iamb is a metrical unit of verse having one unstressed syllable followed by one stressed syllable. This is the most commonly used metrical verse in English and American poetry. An iambic pentameter is a ten-syllable verse made of five of these metrical units, either rhymed as in sonnets, or unrhymed as in free –or blank-verse.

119. American colonial writers were primarily

A. Romanticists.

B. Naturalists.

C. Realists.

D. Neo-classicists.

The answer is D. The early colonists had been schooled in England, and even though their writing became quite American in content, their emphasis on clarity and balance in their language remains British. This literature reflects the lives of the early colonists, such as William Bradford's excerpts from *The Mayflower Compact*, Anne Bradstreet's poetry and William Byrd's journal, *A History of the Dividing Line*.

120. Charles Dickens, Robert Browning, and Robert Louis Stevenson were

A. Victorians.

B. Medievalists.

C. Elizabethans.

D. Absurdists.

The answer is A. The Victorian Period is remarkable for the diversity and quality of its literature. Robert Browning wrote chilling monologues such as "My Last Duchess", and long poetic narratives such as *The Pied Piper of Hamlin*. Robert Louis Stevenson wrote his works partly for young adults, whose imaginations were quite taken by his *Treasure Island* and *The Case of Dr Jekyll and Mr Hyde*. Charles Dickens tells of the misery of the time and the complexities of Victorian society in novels such as *Oliver Twist* or *Great Expectations*.

121. The most significant drawback to applying learning theory research to classroom practice is that

A. today's students do not acquire reading skills with the same alacrity as when greater emphasis was placed on reading classical literature.

B. development rates are complicated by geographical and cultural differences that are difficult to overcome.

C. homogeneous grouping has contributed to faster development of some age groups.

D. social and environmental conditions have contributed to an escalated maturity level than research done twenty of more years ago would seem to indicate.

The answer is D. Because of the rapid social changes, topics which did not use to interest younger readers are now topics of books for even younger readers. There are many books dealing with difficult topics, and it is difficult for the teacher to steer students toward books which they are ready for and to try to keep them away from books whose content, although well written, is not yet appropriate for their level of cognitive and social development. There is a fine line between this and censorship.

122. Overcrowded classes prevent the individual attention needed to facilitate language development. This drawback can be best overcome by

A. dividing the class into independent study groups.

B. assigning more study time at home.

C. using more drill practice in class.

D. Team teaching.

The answer is A. Dividing a class into small groups fosters peer enthusiasm and evaluation, and sets an atmosphere of warmth and enthusiasm. It is much preferable to divide up the class into smaller study groups than to lecture, which will bore students and therefore fail to facilitate curricular goals. Also, it is preferable to do this than to engage the whole class in a general teacher-led discussion because such discussion favors the loquacious and inhibits the shy.

123. Which of the following responses to literature typically give middle school students the most problems?

A. Interpretive

B. Evaluative

C. Critical

D. Emotional

The answer is B. Middle school readers will exhibit both emotional and interpretive responses. In Middle/Junior High School, organized study models make it possible for the student to identify main ideas and supporting details, to recognize sequential order, to distinguish fact from opinion, and to determine cause/effect relationships. Also, a child's being able to say why a particular book was boring or why a particular poem made him/her sad evidences critical reactions on a fundamental level. It is a bit early for evaluative responses, however. These depend on the reader's consideration of how the piece represents its genre, how well it reflects the social/ethical mores of a given society, and how well the author has approached the subject for freshness and slant. Evaluative responses are only made by a few advanced high school students.

124. In the hierarchy of needs for adolescents who are becoming more team-oriented in their approach to learning, which need do they exhibited most?

A. Need for competence

B. Need for love/acceptance

C. Need to know

D. Need to belong

The answer is B. In Abraham's Maslow's Theory of Humanistic Development, there is a hierarchy of needs, from basic physiological needs to the need for self-actualization. The need for love presupposes that every human being needs to love and be loved. With young children this reciprocal need is directed at and received from family members, pets, and friends. In older children and adolescents, this need does not disappear. On the contrary, it extends to new recipients such as peers and romantic partners.

125. What is the best course of action when a child refuses to complete a reading/ literature assignment on the grounds that it is morally objectionable?

A. Speak with the parents and explain the necessity of studying this work

B. Encourage the child to sample some of the text before making a judgment

C. Place the child in another teacher's class where they are studying an acceptable work

D. Provide the student with alternative selections that cover the same performance standards that the rest of the class is learning.

The answer is D. In the case of a student finding a reading offensive, it is the responsibility of the teacher to assign another title. As a general rule, it is always advisable to notify parents if a particularly sensitive piece is to be studied.

XAMonline, INC. 21 Orient Ave. Melrose, MA 02176

Toll Free number 800-509-4128

TO ORDER Fax 781-662-9268 OR www.XAMonline.com

CERTIFICATION EXAMINATION FOR OKLAHOMA EDUCATORS - CEOE - 2007

PO#   Store/School:

Address 1:

Address 2 (Ship to other):
City, State Zip

Credit card number ___-___-___-___   expiration _____
EMAIL _____
PHONE   FAX

13# ISBN 2007	TITLE	Qty	Retail	Total
978-1-58197-781-3	CEOE OSAT Advanced Mathematics Field 11			
978-1-58197-775-2	CEOE OSAT Art Sample Test Field 02			
978-1-58197-780-6	CEOE OSAT Biological Sciences Field 10			
978-1-58197-776-9	CEOE OSAT Chemistry Field 04			
978-1-58197-778-3	CEOE OSAT Earth Science Field 08			
978-1-58197-794-3	CEOE OSAT Elementary Education Fields 50-51			
978-1-58197-795-0	CEOE OSAT Elementary Education Fields 50-51 Sample Questions			
978-1-58197-777-6	CEOE OSAT English Field 07			
978-1-58197-779-0	CEOE OSAT Family and Consumer Sciences Field 09			
978-1-58197-786-8	CEOE OSAT French Sample Test Field 20			
978-1-58197-798-1	CEOE OGET Oklahoma General Education Test 074			
978-1-58197-792-9	CEOE OSAT Library-Media Specialist Field 38			
978-1-58197-787-5	CEOE OSAT Middle Level English Field 24			
978-1-58197-789-9	CEOE OSAT Middle Level Science Field 26			
978-1-58197-790-5	CEOE OSAT Middle Level Social Studies Field 27			
978-1-58197-788-2	CEOE OSAT Middle Level-Intermediate Mathematics Field 25			
978-1-58197-791-2	CEOE OSAT Mild Moderate Disabilities Field 29			
978-1-58197-782-0	CEOE OSAT Physical Education-Health-Safety Field 12			
978-1-58197-783-7	CEOE OSAT Physics Sample Test Field 14			
978-1-58197-793-6	CEOE OSAT Principal Common Core Field 44			
978-1-58197-796-7	CEOE OPTE Oklahoma Professional Teaching Examination Fields 75-76			
978-1-58197-784-4	CEOE OSAT Reading Specialist Field 15			
978-1-58197-785-1	CEOE OSAT Spanish Field 19			
978-1-58197-797-4	CEOE OSAT U.S. & World History Field 17			
FOR PRODUCT PRICES GO TO WWW.XAMONLINE.COM			SUBTOTAL	
			Ship	$8.25
			TOTAL	

www.ingramcontent.com/pod-product-compliance
Lightning Source LLC
Chambersburg PA
CBHW080536300426
44111CB00017B/2752